AMERICAN JOURNALISTS IN THE GREAT WAR

Studies in War, Society, and the Military

GENERAL EDITORS

Kara Dixon Vuic
Texas Christian University

Richard S. Fogarty
University at Albany, State University of New York

EDITORIAL BOARD

Peter Maslowski
University of Nebraska–Lincoln

David Graff
Kansas State University

Reina Pennington
Norwich University

American Journalists in the Great War

Rewriting the Rules of Reporting

CHRIS DUBBS

University of Nebraska Press
LINCOLN & LONDON

Library of Congress Cataloging-in-
Publication Data
Names: Dubbs, Chris (Military histo-
rian), author
Title: American journalists in the Great
War: rewriting the rules of reporting /
Chris Dubbs.
Description: Lincoln: University of
Nebraska Press, 2017. | Series: Stud-
ies in war, society, and the military |
Includes bibliographical references and
index.
Identifiers: LCCN 2016039771 |
ISBN 9780803285743 (cloth: alk. paper)
ISBN 9781496200174 (epub)
ISBN 9781496200181 (mobi)
ISBN 9781496200198 (pdf)
Subjects: LCSH: World War,
1914–1918—Press coverage—United
States. | Journalism—United States—
History—20th century. | Journalists—
United States—History—20th century.
Classification: LCC D632 .D83 2017 |
DDC 070.4/4994—dc23
LC record available at https://
lccn.loc.gov/2016039771

Set in Iowan Old Style by John Klopping.

Contents

Illustrations

Acknowledgments

No writing project gets far unless the writer has sympathetic friends or family members willing to lend an ear and provide guidance. Frank Holowach and John-Daniel Kelley helped me through the long gestation period of this book and provided much-needed editorial assistance. Karen McKenna was always ready to set aside real work to scan photographs. Tracy Simmons Bitonti cast a critical, professional eye over the finished product.

Nash Library at Gannon University became my second home during the writing of this book. I am especially indebted to Mary Beth Earll in its interlibrary loan department for scouring the world to find obscure volumes and vintage magazine articles.

For assistance in locating photographs and permission to use them, I want to thank the following: Special Collections, Raymond H. Folger Library, University of Maine; Dowagiac (Michigan) Area History Museum; James A. Cannavino Library, Archives & Special Collections, Marist College; Occidental College Special Collections and the Beatty family; Louise Bryant Papers, Manuscripts and Archives, Yale University Library. I am grateful to David Mould for permission to use a photograph from his private collection.

And I offer affection and gratitude to my wife, Patricia, for once again being patient and tolerant with a spouse pursuing an obsession.

Finally, I must salute the men and women who inspired me to write this book—the American journalists who covered the Great War. They lived a great adventure and shared it with the rest of us. This book is dedicated to their memory.

AMERICAN JOURNALISTS IN THE GREAT WAR

Introduction

In 1904, when American war correspondent Stanley Washburn traveled with the Japanese army, a telegraph wire extended from a mud hut at army headquarters, across hundreds of miles of barren Manchurian plain, and over the Korean mountains to Fusan, where it connected by cable to Nagasaki and from there to the outside world. It was through that link that Washburn's editor at the *Chicago Daily News* could reach him with the news that the Russo-Japanese War had ended. Washburn knew it before the Japanese army. The next morning he pounded out a story on what the army thought about peace and cabled it off. It ran in the *Daily News* that afternoon. Before Washburn could catch his breath, revolution stirred in Russia, and he was off to his next assignment.

Stanley Washburn was what was known in the trade as a "cable man." The job owed its existence to the vast network of telegraph lines and undersea cables that crisscrossed the world as the twentieth century began. The first transpacific cable had just been completed in 1903. Washburn chased down wars and political upheaval in any dark corner of the globe, tethered himself to a telegraph line, and filled it with stories that would interest newspaper readers in the American Midwest. His job was to inform readers about the war—even wars in which America did not participate—but also to maintain their interest. A good war sold newspapers. A good reporter found a hundred ways to squeeze the juice out of a conflict. When public interest in one conflict waned, Washburn's editor sent him to the next. Fortunately for American newspapers, the world never lacked for conflicts or adventurous individuals wanting to report on them.

If a war seemed substantial enough, an editor sent in another breed of war correspondent: the "feature man." These were the literary artists who had established their fame by writing novels, short stories, and plays. Beginning in the 1890s, writers such as Stephen Crane, Jack London, and Richard Harding Davis popularized a brand of war reporting that used fiction techniques and often placed them at the center of a war adventure. These men could make war entertaining and mold public opinion. Whereas cable men worked anonymously, the names of feature men ran beneath banner headlines and graced the covers of magazines.

The two decades that straddled the start of the twentieth century provided both types of war reporter with ample opportunity to practice their craft in multinational wars, civil wars, revolutions, colonial disputes, and Latin American incursions. So in August 1914, when the world found itself suddenly embroiled in the largest war in history, America enjoyed a surplus of veteran war correspondents. They hurried across the Atlantic confident that they would cover this new conflict in the same way they had covered so many others. They would attach themselves to one army or another and cable home captivating accounts of battles. They would write stirring stories of their own war-zone adventures. However, as it turned out, little about this new war was like any other. Its scale, brutality, duration, novelty, censorship, and social impact challenged news organizations to keep the public informed. It was the largest story any publication had ever covered.

The very long four years of the Great War brought one complete evolutionary cycle of war reporting. At the start journalists were totally banned from the war zone. Those few who ventured in were arrested, accused of spying, and sometimes threatened with execution. By the end of the war, every nation had learned to appreciate the power of publicity and understood that news, just like any other resource of war, had to be managed.

No group of journalists participated more fully in this evolution—indeed, helped to shape it—than those from the United States. Being from the largest neutral country gave them the advantage of being able to operate from both sides of the battle line. American publications, unlike their heavily censored counterparts in the warring nations, could provide fuller and more accurate war coverage. Once printed in American newspapers, those same articles were often then republished in the Allied press, giving their readers a level of candor unavailable from their own correspondents. When the United States joined the fight in the spring of 1917, American reporters took on a new role. They chronicled the transformation of raw American troops into effective soldiers and followed them into battle.

Throughout the war, American readers were better informed about the conflict than those in any other country. All reporters struggled against severe censorships, but the variety and depth of American reporting, from the battle lines and behind the scenes, by cable men and feature men (and women), helped to define for readers the exact nature of this modern, industrial war, its toll on individuals and nations, and its implications for the future.

American Journalists in the Great War examines the unique role played by these trailblazing reporters in World War I. It follows the evolution of news reporting during the war: the variety of writers, the types of stories, struggles against censorship, battlefield experiences, hair-raising adventures, the reporters' moments of fame or infamy, and the landmark eyewitness stories that helped to define how we view the Great War today.

CHAPTER ONE

Prelude to Armageddon

I have been under fire without fighting; known the comradeship of arms without bearing arms, and the hardships and the humors of the march with only an observer's incentive.

—War correspondent FREDERICK PALMER, *The Last Shot*, 1914

In early 1914 when anyone spoke of "the war," it referred to the conflict in Mexico, otherwise known as the Tampico Affair. In the midst of Mexico's civil war, a dizzying series of alleged atrocities and insults against U.S. citizens and U.S. pride prompted the United States to mass an army on its southern border and sail a fleet into the port of Veracruz. The moves set off alarm bells among that distinct brotherhood of journalists who specialized in war, who knew war more intimately than most of the soldiers and generals they wrote about: the war correspondents.

The major city newspapers and large-circulation magazines rushed their veteran war reporters to Veracruz, men who had covered the Spanish-American War, the Philippine Insurrection, the Russo-Japanese War, the Boer War, assorted Balkan wars, and dozens of other conflicts over the past few decades. The United States had never been so well supplied with experienced war correspondents. *Collier's Weekly* hired novelist Jack London and photographer Jimmy Hare. Reporter-illustrator John McCutcheon went down for the *Chicago Tribune*, Robert Dunn for the *New York Evening Post*, Frederick Palmer for *Everybody's Magazine*, and Chicago reporter Medill McCormick for the *Times* of London.

The legendary war reporter Richard Harding Davis sailed from Galveston with the commander of U.S. forces, General Frederick Funston. Davis became the first correspondent to be officially credentialed by the army for this campaign. The fifty-year-old Davis had been enticed into covering yet another war by a lucrative joint offer from the *New York Tribune* and the Wheeler Syndicate, guaranteeing that his unique brand of war reporting would reach a large audience.

Davis expected his stay to be brief. Mexico's presidential pretender Victoriano Huerta could barely hold off his revolutionary rivals, let alone withstand the United States Army. Funston would likely battle his way the 250 miles to Mexico City, making light work of the Mexican army, while Davis kept the telegraph cable hot with rousing, eyewitness reports. Other correspondents might record the "morbid realism" of war, but Davis's colorful prose focused on that brand of human drama that only war provided and on his own, often perilous, involvement in the fighting. Readers loved it.

General Funston had his own ideas about how any fighting would be covered by the press. He wanted to avoid the scandalous free-for-all that had occurred during the Spanish-American War, when reporters of every description swarmed over Cuba like maddened tourists pursuing adventure and souvenir experiences. They had operated virtually without censorship, and their newspapers exaggerated and sensationalized events. Despite the vows of secrecy to which correspondents swore, the invasion of Cuba was about "as well advertised as the arrival of a circus in town."

Things would be different in Mexico. The number of reporters would be limited and their role strictly defined. Only the press associations and a few dozen newspapers and magazines could send reporters, and for each they must post a substantial bond to cover their expenses and ensure their good behavior. Reporters could not just wander off on their own in search of a story. Instead, they would be given official accreditation, which would allow them to travel with the army, enjoying most of the privileges of officers or neutral military attachés. Their dispatches would have to pass the scrutiny of a military censor.

While he awaited the fighting, Davis took up residence at the finest hotel in town. Each evening, precisely at six, he donned his dinner jacket and dined on the hotel's open-air arcade, where he could observe the pageantry of the town plaza. Over the past twenty-five years, Davis had worked his way up from a beat reporter to a national celebrity, gaining fame as a journalist, fiction writer, and dramatist. At times in his illustrious career his reportage appeared in a major magazine, simultaneous with one of his novels being a bestseller and several of his plays running on Broadway. Middle age may have rounded his dashing good looks, but he still cut the figure of a gentleman, instantly recognizable to all who saw him.

In Veracruz Davis regularly hosted dinners for General Funston and his staff, along with select correspondents. The correspondents enjoyed a relaxed camaraderie with the officers, many of whom they knew from previous conflicts. Their dinner conversation might range over fighting in the Philippines or the United States' interventions in Panama, Nicaragua, Dominican Republic, or Honduras. Veracruz's other senior war correspondent, Frederick Palmer, fit well into those dinners. Hardly any world conflict in the past two decades had escaped the attention of either or both Davis and Palmer. They could regale the guests with tales of wars in Europe, Africa, or Asia. Although the two men shared so many experiences, in the summer of 1914 they stood as curious bookends on their profession.

At the age of forty-one, Frederick Palmer's reportorial résumé already included coverage of the Greco-Turkish War, the Philippine-American War, the Boxer Rebellion, the Boer War, the Russo-Japanese War, and the Balkan War of 1912. He missed the Spanish-American War while in the frozen north covering the Klondike gold rush. Over half a million readers followed his articles on war and adventure in *Everybody's Magazine*.

At that very moment, bookstore shelves held Palmer's just-released novel *The Last Shot*, about a modern European war of unparalleled scale. In Palmer's scenario two European nations put an astounding eight million men on the battlefield. With the deadliest cannons and rifles, supported by fleets of dirigibles and airplanes, they fight a nightmarishly modern, industrial, scientific war.

Their leaders are not generals in the traditional sense but rather professors of mathematics, able to compute the best formulas for death and destruction. There is no pageantry or noble cause in Palmer's fictional war. No heroes, no right or wrong. Just slaughter. The end comes when individual soldiers, reduced to dumb, obedient cogs in a modern war machine, regain their individuality and brush away "outworn militaristic traditions and make war forever impossible." For now it was seen as speculative fiction, in the vein of H. G. Wells. Within a few months it would be hailed as an extraordinarily prophetic piece of writing.

Although only nine years Palmer's senior, Richard Harding Davis had one foot more firmly rooted in the nineteenth century. His writing tapped into a mix of youthful idealism, noble causes, polished manners, and American exceptionalism that defined the Progressive Era. Davis had covered the same wars as Palmer but cemented his war correspondent reputation during the Spanish-American War, in the heyday of "yellow journalism," when newspapers sensationalized news—and sometimes *invented* news—to build circulation. Sent to Cuba two years before the United States went to war with Spain, Davis wrote dramatic stories of Spain's brutal treatment of Cubans rebelling against Spanish rule. The bodies of fallen rebels had been mutilated, he reported. To prevent the civilian population from aiding the rebels, Spain set up internment camps, where thousands of women and children died of disease and starvation. The concept of journalistic objectivity had not yet taken firm root in the profession, allowing Davis to make such observations as, "The cannibal, who has been supposed hitherto to be the lowest grade of man, is really of a higher caste than these Spanish murderers." Davis bluntly called for U.S. intervention.

Good and evil, right and wrong, heroes and villains existed in Davis's wars. When the United States eventually declared war on Spain, Davis lionized American fighters, in particular Theodore Roosevelt and his Rough Riders. Sitting around the campfire, Davis could chat with these warriors about books, opera, travel, and plays. In battle he could attest to their grit and bravery. These men were not mindless cogs in a military machine but rather perfect role models for the modern American gentleman forced into war to preserve the values of civilization. His reporting made a hero out of Roosevelt and smoothed his path to the presidency.

Only months before Davis arrived in Veracruz, America's fledgling movie industry produced one of its first-ever feature-length films based on Davis's novel *Soldiers of Fortune*. The plot involved an American engineer caught in a Latin American revolution who leads a ragtag group of fighters against the uprising. As advisor on the movie set in Cuba, Davis coached the actors on how an American hero dressed and behaved when suppressing a native revolt. The story was a paean to past wars rather than a vision of the future.

Soldiers and correspondents alike paid a curious deference to the mythical Richard Harding Davis—but they didn't know quite what to make of him. The best known and highest paid war correspondent, a cultural icon, and a caricature of manliness, Davis crafted war reporting that could be melodramatic, naive, jingoistic, or brilliantly evocative. Regardless, it ran in countless newspapers and the best magazines. On the movie set in Cuba, Davis joked that with one machine gun and two thousand soldier-actors borrowed from the movie, he could clean up the whole mess in Mexico. Correspondent Robert Dunn described Davis in Veracruz dressed like a cavalry colonel in khaki, with military-style campaign ribbons on his chest.

To the great disappointment of the waiting journalists, the United States chose not to invade Mexico but to submit the dispute to mediation by Argentina, Brazil, and Chile. Although the correspondents in Veracruz protested to editors that nothing was happening and they should come home, editors held out. The United States would not park an army on the border and thirty-five warships in the harbor unless it intended to do some fighting.

To satisfy editorial offices impatient for war news, correspondents wrote behind-the-scenes stories about the American crackdown on bullfights and brothels, the battle against city garbage and flies, the armament of U.S. battleships, and the first hydroplanes deployed by the navy. Reporters cruised on a destroyer, went on scouting missions with the cavalry, visited marines on sentry duty, and flew in the hydroplanes for a breathtaking view of the ships in the fleet. When Davis went aloft and flew inland, Mexican troops fired on his plane. Coming under fire from the enemy while soaring in the novel contraption of a seaplane made for a great story.

The Wheeler Syndicate made arrangements for Davis to interview the dictator Huerta in Mexico City. It would be a difficult, possibly dangerous, assignment that violated military restrictions on journalists. But if he brought it off, it would be the biggest scoop of that quiet summer. Along with Frederick Palmer and Medill McCormick, Davis set off by train on the unauthorized excursion.

At their first stop, the trio was promptly arrested and marched through a village by four barefoot boys armed with rifles and bayonets—an ignominious predicament for the seasoned war reporters. A local official deemed Palmer's U.S. passport insufficient for him to continue and sent him to walk back to Veracruz through the desert. Davis and McCormick, who had taken the precaution of acquiring letters from the Brazilian and British ambassadors in Mexico City, were allowed to continue. However, when they arrived in Mexico City, they were immediately rearrested and put on a train back to Veracruz. The hoped-for interview with Huerta never happened, but the adventure itself, the mere pursuit of news against obstacles and hardships—the more the better—always provided sufficient fodder for a colorful story.

Near the end of June, Davis finally despaired of seeing any fighting and sailed for home, just days before the correspondents read in the El Paso newspaper about the assassination of Austria's Archduke Franz Ferdinand in Sarajevo. Subsequent reports of building tension in that region failed to rouse much interest from the reporters. That fractious corner of Europe—the Balkan "powder keg"—had become a journalistic cliché. Scarcely a year turned on the calendar without a minor Balkan war erupting.

Even though European powers built armies and competed in

the development of warships and weaponry, peace had reigned on the continent for the past forty years. A system of national alliances helped to maintain a "balance of power" that kept each country and each headstrong monarch in check. In idle moments correspondents might speculate about a cataclysm unleashed in Europe, but none believed it would happen. It was simply too horrendously unthinkable. Even Frederick Palmer, whose novel *The Last Shot* actually foretold just such a scenario, thought "all the repeated talk about its possibilities had only the conjectural interest of a collision between two planets."

The correspondents were more likely to be interested in an article about Mexico's civil war that had just appeared in the large-circulation *Metropolitan Magazine*, written by a young upstart journalist named John Reed. The previous year Reed had ingratiated himself to one of Mexico's revolutionary leaders, Francisco "Pancho" Villa, a move that landed him in the thick of battles and allowed him to share life with Villa's fighters. His vivid accounts that began appearing in the *New York World* in February read more like fiction than the typical war report. "When Mr. Reed describes a battle, the reader sniffs powder," one commentator noted. Not content to merely summarize military events, Reed painted impressionistic word pictures of the people, the land, and the undercurrent of revolutionary violence in the country.

With Villa's army, Reed worked unfettered by military minders and stifling censorship. It was something more akin to the war correspondents of yesteryear who ranged freely over a war zone on horseback, immersed in the action, and cabling home exclusive stories. Reed had read Davis's swashbuckling accounts of the Spanish-American War, and now people compared their styles. "Reed has done for Mexico what Richard Harding Davis and Stephen Crane did for the Spanish-American War," one reviewer noted about Reed's book *Insurgent Mexico*. However, Reed's accounts tapped a deeper social and political vein that had never attracted Davis's attention. Readers met Mexican characters and came to understand their motivations and aspirations. In short Reed had taken ownership of the Mexico story. He was now back in New York, famous and feted as an expert on the conflict.

The bored correspondents languishing in Veracruz got the message. As the summer progressed, they turned their attention away from the idle U.S. Army and onto the country's bloody revolution. Reporters could avoid all entanglements with the U.S. military simply by entering Mexico via Texas. Frederick Palmer and John McCutcheon ventured into Mexico's northern provinces where competing revolutionary leaders seemed poised to attack each other or launch their own march on Mexico City.

Out from under the control of the military, Palmer gained a deep appreciation for the beleaguered Mexicans and a better understanding of the Mexican situation. He realized that the United States' rationale for intervention was merely a smokescreen for commercial interests and military glory. "All foreigners are in Mexico for money," he wrote, "and in the oil-fields the strife for control of oil-leases is more intense than that of other great enterprises in Mexico." It was a war story that Richard Harding Davis would never have written.

But at the tail end of America's "dud war" and Mexico's protracted revolution, a major conflict erupted in Europe. At the end of July urgent telegrams flew from editorial offices to the correspondents in Veracruz and the villages in northern Mexico—*Forget Mexico . . . War imminent in Europe . . . Hurry there*. Dozens of America's best war correspondents boarded trains and hurried home, eager to take on a war with greater potential for good stories. Mexico had served them as one final rehearsal for the Great War, but it in no way prepared them for what lay in store.

CHAPTER TWO

Learning to Report a World War

When I was a cub in Pittsburgh the dizzy pinnacle of fame presented itself as the opportunity of riding a tired horse through the Balkans after a smashing big battle and staggering into an obscure telegraph office with the scoop of the century. MacGahan and Forbes, the Russo-Turkish war correspondents, were my heroes; anyone could be president of the United States as far as I was concerned.

—Correspondent PERCIVAL PHILLIPS,
Saturday Evening Post, February 1, 1913

The outbreak of the war caught former U.S. Army captain Granville Fortescue and family vacationing at Ostend on the Belgian coast. Europe's overnight mobilization of its armies trapped some two hundred thousand American travelers inside countries that were suddenly at war. As hotels and businesses closed, the banking system froze, and armies commandeered transportation, travelers journeyed as best they could to the neutral countries of Italy, Switzerland, or Holland, or to the major urban gathering points of Brussels or Paris.

For several weeks at the start of the war, America's newspapers were obsessed with stranded travelers. Frightening stories came out of Europe of tourists abused, inconvenienced, arrested, or simply lost in the chaos. Travelers crowded at embassies, consulates, banks, and steamship offices, possessed with the single, overriding desire to find passage on one of the few remaining ships sailing for home. Groups of travelers chartered tramp steamers, and millionaires traveled in steerage simply to get away. The Atlantic filled with shiploads of Americans grateful to escape the madness.

1. A 1905 photo of U.S. army captain and former Rough Rider Granville Fortescue. Vacationing in Europe at the outbreak of war, he hurried to the Belgium city of Liège to report on the opening engagement of the war and then continued to work as a correspondent. Source: Lewis Randolph Hamersly, *Biographical Sketches of Distinguished Officers of the Army and Navy* (New York: L. R. Hamersly, 1905), Wikimedia Commons.

Granville Fortescue was not one to flee from war. He had fought as a Rough Rider with his cousin Teddy Roosevelt, served as a military attaché during the Russo-Japanese War and then as military advisor in the Roosevelt White House. When Germany and France mobilized, Fortescue spread out a railroad map of Europe and placed his finger on the point where he guessed the German army would launch its attack through neutral Belgium—the fortified city of Liège, opposite the Prussian rail center of Aachen

(Aix-la-Chapelle). It made perfect military sense, and as he knew, the first requirement for a warrior, or a war correspondent, was to be in the right place at the right time. If he couldn't fight in this war, he could at least take advantage of being in Europe and report on the fighting.

He hustled his family off to England and quickly arranged to serve as correspondent for the London *Daily Telegraph*. In Brussels he hired a grand touring car with chauffer and set out for Liège wearing a Savile Row golf suit with striking checks. He rather fancied himself in checks. His auto bucked the flood of refugees clogging the roads. At frequent intervals civil guard sentries halted his car to poke a bayonet at his chest and question his intentions. In the heat of the moment, how did a cautious sentry distinguish between a journalist and a spy? Fortescue was arrested four times that morning before ultimately being turned back to Brussels. There he made the happy discovery that trains still ran directly to Liège, and no one was asking questions.

Liège was a kettle beginning to boil. Units of soldiers streamed into town. Red Cross and Belgian army automobiles zipped madly through the streets on urgent missions, while anxious citizens crowded the town square. German army units had been spotted in the area, and an attack seemed imminent. It began in the middle of the night with the boom of cannons. Fortescue hurried to a vantage point on the bluff overlooking the Meuse River. "On the night of the fifth of August, 1914, that view was startling," he reported. A full moon illuminated one of the fortresses in Liège's defensive ring, the Fort of Fléron, as did artillery shells bursting like fireworks above its ramparts and its own guns flashing reply. The fort's searchlights sweeping the open ground silhouetted the approaching infantry. The ebb and flow of fighting transfixed Fortescue the entire night.

Soldier, tourist, war correspondent Granville Fortescue was witnessing the first engagement by the mammoth German army about to steamroller over neutral Belgium on its way to France. In the morning, after being arrested and released several more times as a German spy, Fortescue caught a refugee-packed train

2. Although he abandoned the sidearm, this was the typical outfit for famous war correspondent Richard Harding Davis early in the war. Note the campaign ribbons above the pocket, denoting other wars in which he had reported. The Germans thought he looked like a British officer, threw him in prison, and threatened to execute him. Source: Author's collection.

3. When he headed to Europe in August 1914, Frederick Palmer was one
of the most experienced war correspondents in the world, having covered
six previous wars. Source: George Grantham Bain Collection, Prints and
Photographs Division, Library of Congress, LC-DIG-ggbain-18737.

back to his Brussels hotel, eager to capture the emotions of the past twenty-four hours. He banged out his story and rushed it by courier to the *Daily Telegraph*.

Fortescue had overcome all obstacles and risked personal danger to witness the start of fighting on the western front and then scooped the competition to inform the world. It was about as perfect an experience as a war correspondent could hope for. In the opening weeks of the war, he managed to repeatedly place himself in those Belgian towns coming under German assault. He would soon be joined by a legion of professional war reporters.

The Rush to Europe

On the same day that Granville Fortescue watched the German assault on Liège, the *New York Times* announced Britain's declaration of war on Germany and the United States' intention to remain neutral. On that day, August 5, two of the most storied practitioners of the art of war corresponding—Frederick Palmer and Richard Harding Davis—sailed for Europe on the *Lusitania*. War and adventure had often taken them to the far corners of the globe. Now they embarked on the greatest adventure of them all. The nations of Europe, the heartland of the civilized world, were at each other's throats, promising a conflict of historic proportions and significance.

Because they were two well-respected war correspondents from a neutral country, they expected to be credentialed by either, or both, the British and the French, which would allow them to travel with the armies to see the fighting and file eyewitness accounts. Neither entertained any hope of seeing anything from the German side. But "credentialing" could operate in different ways. It might put them in the thick of the action or sequester them far to the rear, tightly managed by the military.

In 1904 Davis had traveled halfway around the world to report on the Russo-Japanese War. He wasted four months waiting in Tokyo as a credentialed correspondent, before being escorted on a ten-day voyage to the mainland, then another twelve-day march through mud and dust pursuing the army, then a twelve-day wait while battles raged nearby, before finally being conducted to a vantage point from which he was indulgently shown the smoke of a distant battle.

Canny politicians might appreciate the value of publicity in winning popular support for the war effort, but generals feared reporters would divulge information helpful to the enemy or embarrassing to the War Office. The pervasiveness of telegraph cables and the advent of wireless communication had only heightened their concern. Battlefield action viewed in the morning in some remote corner of the world could be cabled back to America in time for a newspaper's evening edition. Veteran war correspondents already bemoaned censorship restrictions as a threat to their profession. In future wars the public might learn of battles only what some War Office propagandist chose to reveal.

With Palmer and Davis on the high seas, an army of individuals flocked to New York, seeking passage to the war. Ships arriving from Europe disgorged stranded American tourists grateful for their safe return from the war and then filled with an odd assortment of characters eager to hurry off to the conflict. Three days after the *Lusitania* sailed, the first American-owned ship, the *St. Paul*, headed to the war zone with the "most mixed assortment of passengers that [had] traveled on a single ship since Noah sailed the Ark."

Correspondent Philip Gibbs characterized the contingent of aspiring war reporters as "men of sporting instincts and jaunty confidence, eager to be 'in the middle of things,' willing to go out on any terms, so long as they could see 'a bit of fun.'" In newsrooms across the United States, reporters yearned to be named their paper's war correspondent, since it provided the opportunity for great adventure and the chance to become a household name overnight. As Gibbs described it,

> Special correspondents, press photographers, the youngest reporters on the staff, sub-editors emerging from the little dark rooms with a new excitement in their eyes that had grown tired with

proof correcting, passed each other on the stairs and asked for their chance. It was a chance of seeing the greatest drama in life with real properties, real corpses, real blood, real horrors with a devilish thrill in them. It was not to be missed by any self-respecting journalist to whom all life is a stage play which he describes and criticizes from a free seat in the front of the house.

On the *St. Paul,* along with these eager reporters, traveled men off to rescue stranded relatives, businessmen hungry for war contracts, military observers, conscripts for the French army, American volunteers for the British army, and young women who wanted to be Red Cross nurses. Newspaper reports of English and German ships fighting off the U.S. coast, kept passengers on deck for hours, expecting at any minute to witness actual hostilities. One "tomboy sort of girl in a boyish sailor suit" keeping the vigil beside journalist Arthur Ruhl explained her motivation for going to war.

> "Listen here!" she would say, grabbing my arm. "I want to tell you something. I'm going to see this thing—d'you know what I mean?—for what it'll do to me—you know—for its effect on my mind! I didn't say anything about it to anybody—they'd only laugh at me—d'you know what I mean? They don't think I've got any serious side to me. Now, I don't mind things—I mean blood—you know—they don't affect me, and I've read about nursing—I've prepared for this! Now, I don't know how to go about it, but it seems to me that a woman who can—you know—go right with 'em—jolly 'em along—might be just what they'd want—d'you know what I mean?"

Ruhl scribbled notes on that encounter, realizing that this young lady herself was a war story. Something about the war possessed her, just as it possessed everyone else on the ship. Ruhl had given up a position as a newspaper drama critic to chase a disappointing war in Mexico. In Veracruz he heard the veteran correspondents spin their tales of war adventures in exotic locales. Now he too hoped to "see this thing," a real war and real battles, with the fate of nations hanging in the balance. Experts confidently predicted that the war would last for six months at most. Ruhl was glad that he would arrive in Europe before the whole thing wrapped up.

Collier's magazine writer Will Irwin also logged time on the *St. Paul's* deck, as did John T. McCutcheon and the well-known journalist-humorist Irvin S. Cobb. Stout, with a melancholy expression, rosy cheeks, prominent eyebrows, and a constant cigar, Cobb stood out in a crowd. He represented the *Saturday Evening Post*, one of America's largest circulation magazines. In recent years Cobb had turned his quirky satirical voice to travel writing, publishing a pair of books—*Roughing It De Luxe* (1913) and *Europe Revised* (1914)—that used McCutcheon's illustrations. Both books mined the humor of a traveler out of his element—an easterner in the American West and an American traveler observing the customs and idiosyncrasies of England, France, and Germany in prewar Europe.

Now he had been assigned to revisit those same European countries in a time of war to see how things had changed. He had never covered a war and didn't know what to expect. He carried with him a letter from Secretary of State William Jennings Bryan commending him to all U.S. diplomats, a letter of credit, a generous supply of traveler's checks, a forty-pound satchel containing $6,000 in gold sovereigns, and a revolver.

Finding the Fighting

The term "fog of war" had come into use by the end of the nineteenth century to describe the lack of situational awareness experienced by participants in military operations. It would be used so aptly and often throughout this war. When some two hundred American journalists gathered in London, the war fog enveloped them. Britain's hastily approved Defence of the Realm Act imposed stifling press censorship that made it a crime to "spread reports likely to cause disaffection or alarm among any of His Majesty's forces or among the civilian population."

To keep their readers abreast of developments in the war, London newspapers relied on official bulletins from the British and French War Offices that were masterpieces of brevity and vagueness. All the fighting was taking place in Belgium, but for all the anxious British public knew, the British Expeditionary Force (BEF), which had crossed into France to confront the German army, might just as well have dropped off the edge of the Earth. Newspapers filled out the picture by publishing any unsubstantiated news from any source. According to them, the German army systematically engaged in atrocities in Belgium, it met defeat at every turn, and Germany's home population was starving. The duration of the war was calculated in weeks.

The British, the French, and the Belgians all refused to accredit reporters with their armies. In fact they forbade reporters from entering the war zone. Should any journalists manage to do so, they would be little more than tourists engaged in the dangerous work of viewing and reporting military activities—actions that nervous sentries or suspicious officers might easily mistake for the work of a spy. Many of the journalists, especially those from the neutral United States, ignored these possible difficulties and dangers and headed for eastern France, Belgium, and Holland, near to where they thought the fighting to be.

When Richard Harding Davis and Frederick Palmer made their way to Brussels, they got a vastly different picture of the situation than that portrayed in the London papers. The secretary of the U.S. legation, Hugh Gibson, informed them that the massive German army had just captured the last fort at Liège, a mere sixty miles away, which opened the door to the rest of Belgium. Beleaguered Belgian forces could do little more than slow their advance. Rumors swirled in Brussels of German cavalry in the suburbs, spies disguised as nuns, sentries shooting at airplanes, and trainloads of wounded entering the city under cover of night so as not to alarm the civilian population. The following day the Belgian government moved to the better-defended city of Antwerp.

The two correspondents had landed themselves in the perfect location for covering the war, except for one complication: without credentials, and expressly forbidden from traveling in the battle zone, they were left with the single, dangerous option of acting on their own. Credentialed reporters traveled as part of an army, and if captured by the opposing side, they were treated as prisoners of war. Freebooting, news-gathering civilians, on the other hand, were shot as spies. The best they could do was to arm themselves with U.S passports, letters from their editors and local diplomats, and a travel pass from whatever civil or military officer could be cajoled into signing his name. And hope for the best.

The few correspondents in Brussels gathered like a war council each morning over their hotel breakfast, studying the Brussels newspapers for clues about where they might find the fighting. Every day the papers reported skirmishes at one location or another. One paper suggested that things were happening at Diest, while others favored Tirlemont or Louvain. Davis compared it to picking the winner in a horse race—bet on the right town and be rewarded with a good story.

In previous wars Davis had often worked in isolated locations, living in a tent, banging out stories every night with his typewriter perched on a cracker box. He was famous for his kit, the equipment and supplies that he took on military campaigns, which might include several pack animals and servants to manage the safari-like mountain of such luxury items as a folding bathtub and a hoard of food and fine wines. So much more civilized to be operating out of a delightful city such as Brussels, an "imitation Paris."

Each morning Davis hired a luxury auto, adorned it with "more English, Belgian, French, and Russian flags than [flew] from the roof of the New York Hippodrome" and ventured out to take up with whatever military unit he came upon. He might encounter some Belgian army units, find the scene of a skirmish, or draw a blank. Then he would return to Brussels to write his story and send it off by cable before settling down to a "perfectly served dinner and a luxurious bed."

Refugees appeared as the first stark evidence of war. They filled the roads that Davis took on his excursions, trudging wearily toward Brussels or sleeping beneath roadside hedges. On a drive to the city of Louvain, his car had to inch through a counterflow of taxicabs, racing cars, and limousines, all blaring their horns. Occupied by women and children of the rich, white-faced with dust from the road, those cars overflowed with trunks, suitcases, and packages. Thousands of forlorn and weary peasants surrounded them, maneuvering their carts or clutching bundles containing all their worldly possessions.

Davis used the plight of one such family to wring the pathos from the tragedy. He found them sitting on a bench outside his hotel: a woman, her three young children, and two maidservants. Her husband had been killed and her château destroyed. She was on her way to England. She wore around her neck several strings of pearls. The little boy clutched a small dog, and the two girls each held a birdcage, one with a canary and the other a parrot. It was all they had saved. In their own way, they were "just as homeless, friendless, just as much in need of food and sleep" as the throngs on the roadways. At this stage in the conflict, such images came to represent "poor little Belgium," the innocent victim of war.

Like many in the Allied countries and America too, Frederick Palmer had warm admiration for Belgium standing up to the German colossus rather than granting it free passage. But he gave the Belgians no chance of success. The Germans had pounced on Liège with a modern, trained army, pounding its forts to rubble with mammoth siege cannons. The Belgian soldiers Palmer saw looked like an ill-equipped, raw militia, wearing "uniforms taken from their grandfather's trunk," using wheeled machine guns pulled by dogs.

Newspapers in Brussels had reported a Belgian victory in the town of Haelen. When Palmer visited that battlefield, he found a few broken cavalry lances. He learned that a Belgian machine-gun squadron had ambushed a unit of German cavalry working as advance scouts. The "Battle of Haelen" had gained fame in British and French papers and those in America, when in fact it had been but a minor skirmish. With no official accounts of the fighting coming from the belligerents and no accrediting of correspondents, war news fell into the hands of a ragtag collection of travelers and make-believe reporters. British newspapers, from which American papers got much of their war news, published "any scrap of description, any glimmer of truth, any wild statement, rumour, fairy tale, or deliberate lie, which reached them from France and Belgium; and it must be admitted that the liars had a great time."

Before Palmer could further raise the level of objective war reporting, he was unexpectedly summoned to London, where the British War Office had undergone a change of heart regarding credentialing journalists. The War Office agreed to approve a small number of trusted British reporters and one American to travel with the BEF and, under strict censorship, report on activities. By special arrangement the American reporter would represent all three major U.S. news services: the Associated Press (AP), the United Press (UP), and the International News Service (INS). He would in essence be reporting to nearly every newspaper in the United States. To the chagrin of Richard Harding Davis, this honor fell to Frederick Palmer.

To serve three masters, Palmer would have to put three different slants on the news. The AP wanted only "colorless reports of facts"; the UP liked "lively" human interest articles; and the INS wanted its articles to be even livelier. However, the real challenge might be providing any war news at all. Strict rules governed what could and could not be included in a reporter's dispatches from the war zone. No mention could be made of troop movements, their location, strength, or composition; no mention of casualties or troop morale; and no criticism or praise of a personal nature. More to the point, it quickly became apparent that the British were in no hurry to implement their new strategy. Palmer returned to the continent to forage for news on his own.

No correspondent enjoyed greater success searching on his own for news than Granville Fortescue. He had been reporting from Belgium ever since his exclusive story of the attack on Liège, and his military intuition continued to place him in the right locations for a story. He predicted that the main invasion force would move from Liège along the Meuse River toward France. Before other correspondents even arrived in Belgium, Fortescue traveled by train to the southern end of the Meuse, to the town of Dinant, near the French border.

After examining the terrain and the town's defenses for several days, he concluded that the French were far too confident in their ability to hold off the approaching German force. A British military observer with several motorcycle scouts reported the Germans advancing toward town on every road. A French cavalry unit of one hundred men ventured out one morning, and only thirteen returned that night, half of them wounded. Fortescue seemed to be alone in worrying about what lay in store for the defenders, observing, "I had seen war; many of these men—perhaps all of them—had not; they had no disquieting visions of the morrow." He tried to get out a short dispatch to his newspaper, but the French censor robbed it of any substance.

The following day, watching from a good vantage point, Fortescue trained his binoculars on the action as the Germans captured the town and then French artillery successfully drove them out. More so than any other correspondent, Fortescue distilled "military impressions" from his experience. At Dinant, for instance, he noted how the French barricades were not high enough to protect against German snipers and how the red pants of the French uniforms made them too easily visible.

After the first day of fighting, Fortescue left to locate the main French force. Moving around in so active a military zone was fraught with danger, but from the start he had taken scrupulous care to comply with all regulations. He reported dutifully to every new commander and acquired a pass to move to the next location. Assuming he would eventually meet the French army, he had acquired a letter from the French minister in Brussels, imploring French officers to treat him with courtesy and a similar one from the Belgian minister of war. These credentials proved sufficient for the small French force in Dinant, but they carried no weight elsewhere.

The French had a reputation for having an exaggerated fear of reporters, springing from an incident in the Franco-German War of 1870. Fortescue heard the story from every French officer who arrested him. Supposedly a British reporter published a story that revealed a critical piece of information that led to a French defeat.

When the French returned him to Paris, Fortescue made his way back to London, where the ignorance or indifference of the English to the unfolding disaster alarmed him. The official policy of the British War Office prevented the publication of any unsettling news, but Fortescue sounded the alarm in the *Daily Telegraph* on August 24: "Solemnly, I warn the people of England that this is the beginning of a time of great trial." It took a military man to know the gravity of the situation. It took an American to ignore British restrictions. No one yet knew the size of the German force advancing through Belgium or exactly where it would fall upon the small British army, but England had to be ready. Fortescue warned, "Many lives must be sacrificed to dam the engulfing flood. A gigantic battle may open on the morrow." He was accused of exaggerating the threat, of being an alarmist.

It fell to Irvin Cobb and a few other reporters to get the first face-to-face encounter with the invading force. Cobb and reporter-illustrator John McCutcheon, along with Will Irwin (*Collier's*) and Arno Dosch-Fleurot (*New York World*), arrived in Brussels on August 17, the day the Belgian government left the city.

These war correspondent wannabes couldn't make sense of the chaos. They had little understanding of Belgian geography and little appreciation for the risks of being an unaccredited journalist. Only McCutcheon had any war reporting experience, and only Irwin spoke a rusty textbook French. They learned from the U.S. minister Brand Whitlock that a German column was heading straight for the Belgian capital by way of the town of Louvain, pushing ahead of it thousands of fleeing refugees. That seemed as good a place as any to see some action. They found a taxi driver willing to undertake the risky journey.

To smooth their passage through the front lines, they acquired from the U.S. consul a very official-looking document splashed with large red seals. In reality it merely indicated that they were American citizens. Without any clear rules on travel, correspondents armed themselves with as many passes and permits as possible. Local civil authorities, police, diplomats, or military officers might sign a pass to get them through the lines or to travel within a city or district. Using them to roam the war zone was a game of bluff that worked surprisingly well in this time of confusion. A wad of wrinkled passes with official-looking stamps usually satisfied guards on the road or at rail stations.

Cobb and his group left a city preparing for a siege, weaving their taxi through defensive breastworks, trenches, lines of barbed wire, and overturned streetcar barricades. At every blockade and crossroads, soldiers studied their documents, shrugged, and let them through. If these strangers were crazy enough to be rushing into the maelstrom, then so be it.

A trickle of refugees on the road became a flood: old people in their finest clothes, women and children struggling with heavy bundles, trudging wearily, silently away from the advancing enemy for the safety of Brussels. Will Irwin called them the "living exemplars of misery." They reminded Dosch-Fleurot of those left destitute by the great San Francisco earthquake, which he had covered.

Battered units of the Belgian army dotted the roadside, many wounded and all of them "so dirty, so utterly bedraggled and weary." In repeated skirmishes, they had been beaten back from their eastern frontier by a German tidal wave. "Where are the French and the British armies?" they repeatedly asked the correspondents.

A few miles from Louvain, two British motion-picture photographers racing their car in the opposite direction pulled to a stop. "Better keep out, gov'ner," they warned. "There's fighting just beyond. We filmed a Belgian troop of cavalry going into action an' filmed 'em twenty minutes later coming back with half the saddles empty." Rising smoke and the rattle of rifle fire put an exclamation point to the warning. When the driver refused to go any farther, the correspondents continued on foot.

Will Irwin chose that moment to point out that it was his understanding that correspondents caught by the German army would be shot. The men were all bravado about not wanting to miss the grand entry of the German army into Louvain, but Irwin would later admit to having deeper, more emotional reasons for discounting the obvious dangers. They felt "exalted" by these first brushes with war, even the horrors of it. Otherwise, nothing could have induced them to push beyond the frontline defenders.

The four journalists were enjoying cheese and coffee at an outdoor café in Louvain when the war found them. German scouts on bicycles appeared in town, followed by a troop of Uhlan lancers on impressive black horses. Cut off from escape, the reporters had no choice but to watch in sober fascination as the main army entered town. Will Irwin described the awe-inspiring spectacle for his *Collier's* readers in the article "Detained by the Germans."

> Round the corner swung the head of an infantry brigade giving full voice to "Die Wacht am Rhein." They were singing in absolute time; they were singing in parts, like a trained chorus! Never have I heard anything quite like the beat and ring of their marching. They wore heavy, knee-high cowhide boots, and those boots, propelled by heavy, stalwart German bodies, struck the road with a concerted shuffling thump which shook the earth. . . . Intent on their singing and marching, looking neither to right nor left, they shuffled and stamped onto conquest and death. It had become a horde by now—cavalry, infantry, artillery, cavalry, infantry, artillery, rolling, pouring toward Brussels and toward France.

With considerable trepidation, the group reported its presence to an English-speaking German officer. When the journalists explained to him that they had made their way through the battle lines in a taxicab, he roared with laughter. "Through gasps he translated to the others. Their laughter rattled the windows." With precise Prussian thoroughness, Germany had gone to war with an army of over three million men, while these blundering American correspondents had gone to war in a taxicab. "'You came right through a battle in a taxi cab!' he repeated and went off again into roars of laughter."

The correspondents waited in town unmolested while the military procession continued unbroken for three days. The sheer size of the invading force, its organization, and its discipline were on an unprecedented scale. And despite learning from off-duty soldiers about the "town wrecking" that had happened further back when the army exacted vengeance on inhabitants who had fired upon them, the correspondents were impressed by how civilly the Germans behaved in occupied Louvain. It was quite unlike the stories of atrocities that filled the Allied newspapers.

The dramatic entry of the German army into Louvain repeated itself in Brussels, where the stark realization of the true character of this European war struck Richard Harding Davis. He penned one of the most memorable pieces of writing to emerge from the war for *Scribner's Magazine*. For the first time someone put words to the unprecedented scale and character of the conflict unfolding on the continent and the extent of the threat to the Allies.

> All through the night, like the tumult of a river when it races between the cliffs of a canyon, in my sleep I could hear the steady roar of the passing army. And when early in the morning I went to the window the chain of steel was still unbroken. . . . As a correspondent I have seen all the great armies and the military processions at the coronations in Russia, England, and Spain, and our own inaugural parades down Pennsylvania Avenue, but those armies and processions were made up of men. This [the German army] was a machine, endless, tireless, with the delicate organization of a watch and the brute power of a steam roller. And for three days and three nights through Brussels it roared and rumbled, a cataract of molten lead . . . like a river of steel . . . a monstrous engine.

Davis was renowned for his colorful metaphors, and war provided many opportunities for their use. But this was transformative prose. Will Irwin described the German invasion force in Louvain as an army of well-disciplined men, singing like a trained chorus. But veteran war correspondent Davis saw something totally alien. This was not war as he knew it, full of pageantry, noble causes, and heroic figures. This was not even an army composed of men, but instead some nightmarish creation of the industrial age: machines, steel chains, steamrollers, and engines.

In the opening months of the conflict, both Davis and Cobb struggled to grasp the character of this new brand of warfare.

How did the German war machine function? What thinking animated it? How could gallant, little Belgium and its allies stop it? But their coverage would be markedly different in tone. Cobb and the other reporters covered war as they might have covered some natural disaster back home in the United States—the San Francisco earthquake or the Johnstown flood—immersing themselves in the scene, describing the graphic images and suffering, interviewing participants, exploring its many angles. Davis, on the other hand, fulminated about the wreck of Western civilization.

Chasing the German Army

The German occupation of Brussels interrupted the correspondents' ability to cable stories to London for transmission via the transatlantic cable to the United States. It therefore eliminated the need to remain tethered to that city. For Davis and the other frustrated reporters who had scoured the countryside in search of the fighting, their direction now became clear. Somewhere to the south of Brussels, in the general direction of Paris, great armies would soon collide in what might be the largest battle in history. Britain had landed its expeditionary force, and the French army lay in wait for the invaders. Perhaps, as many had predicted, that climactic battle would bring a rapid close to the war.

The correspondents had no credentials, but the German military governor of Brussels, General Thaddeus von Jarotsky, issued passes for correspondents to travel freely in the environs of Brussels. Unfortunately, the fighting that the correspondents so longed to see could not be found around that city. Disregarding German army policy forbidding such activity, Richard Harding Davis and Gerald Morgan, writing for *Metropolitan Magazine*, started in a taxi for the town of Hal, where fighting had occurred. They assumed their pass would carry them through German lines and they would then eventually link up with either the French or the British and try their luck with them. It was a risky strategy. Uncredentialed correspondents had no uniform or badge to distinguish them from civilians or spies.

Davis embarked on this excursion dressed in the customary

khaki military-style outfit he had worn on many previous campaigns when attached to an army. It proudly displayed a narrow bar of military-style silk campaign ribbons above his breast pocket, indicating that he had seen more of war than any of the German officers he was likely to meet. In fact he set off on this risky excursion looking so much like a British officer that he was arrested as a spy the instant he arrived at Hal.

Davis had inadvertently stumbled on the German army under forced march to ambush the British army. He had seen too much, a German officer informed him, and they were justified in executing him as a spy. After a long interrogation and repeated threats of execution, Davis arranged his release by offering to walk all the way back to Brussels, reporting to every German officer along the route, until he could establish his identity with the American consul. Davis had been through six wars and never been as frightened as he was in Hal. This war was already getting the best of him.

Back in Brussels after their adventure in Louvain, Irvin Cobb and his cohorts used a bit of trickery to alter the wording on their pass from the German governor to eliminate the clause restricting them to Brussels. Confident that this would give them greater freedom to travel in search of the fighting, they struck out on August 23 in hired carriages that deposited them a dozen miles to the south, where they continued on foot. Three wearying, footsore days later, they acquired an ancient horse, a dog cart, and two bicycles, allowing them to better keep pace with the supply trains and rear units of the German army as they moved relentlessly toward the French border. They found themselves in the unique position of being the first reporters to travel with the German army, even if it was in a most unofficial, illegitimate capacity. They hoped to be on hand for the climactic battle when the German juggernaut collided with the French and British forces. Cobb characterized their predicament:

> We knew that our credentials were, for German purposes, of most dubious and uncertain value. We knew that the Germans were permitting no correspondents—not even German correspondents—to

accompany them. We knew that any alien caught in the German front was liable to death on the spot. . . . We knew all these things; and the knowledge of them gave a fellow tingling sensations in the tips of his toes when he permitted himself to think about his situation. But, after the first few hours, we took heart unto ourselves; for everywhere we met only kindness and courtesy at the hands of the Kaiser's soldiers, men and officers alike.

Irvin Cobb had something of a déjà vu moment while marching past the towns along his route. He thought he might have passed these same villages a year ago while traveling for his book *Europe Revised*. Or if not these towns, then dozens just like them. Last year they had all looked very much the same—a line of gray houses strung like beads along a straight white road, with a small, ugly church, a wine shop, a priest, and a solitary policeman preposterously garbed with epaulets and a saber. In the aftermath of the fighting, the destruction they had suffered made them once again resemble one another.

The town of La Buissiere had been left a smoking ruin, policed now by German soldiers, inhabited by a few frightened villagers and wounded French prisoners. The French had made a stand here, digging entrenchments and bringing up supplies, and the Germans had run over them like a freight train. More of the same met the correspondents at the next village of Montignies-Saint-Christophe, just inside the French border. Cobb chose this village as the subject of his first article for the *Saturday Evening Post*, which appeared on October 10. The signs of a hasty departure by the French showed everywhere: abandoned uniforms and equipment, interrupted meals. Nearly every home and building had sustained damage. The only living creatures to be found were one old woman and three cats. Outside town Red Cross workers laid the bodies of fallen French soldiers in shallow graves.

These battered villages gave Cobb his first up-close view of war, and it caused in him an emotional numbness that came through in his reporting. Montignies-Saint-Christophe was a completely ordinary village of perhaps twenty houses, he observed, "but now

tragedy had given it distinction; had painted that straggling frontier hamlet over with such colors that the picture of it is going to
live in my memory as long as I do live." He knew that like himself,
his readers would recoil from the mindless destruction wrought
on innocent lives. This early in the war, the destruction of houses,
the artifacts of disrupted lives, and the casualness of death still
held the power to jar readers. In fact nearly everything that correspondents saw in August 1914 radiated wartime significance—the
face of a soldier, a broken toy in the road, dead animals, frightened
travelers. They lacked the words to describe their experience, so
they padded their dispatches with great handfuls of impressions
meant to convey to readers the wild disorder of the war.

Surprisingly, the vagabond reporters got on well with the back-
end units of the German army. Correspondents might be officially
verboten in the German army, but here in the field there existed a
more elemental camaraderie. Many German soldiers spoke some
English, had been to America, or had relatives there, and they
warmly accepted these neutral strangers in their midst. Common
soldiers often shared their sandwiches and beer with the correspondents. Officers showed their maps, explained their actions,
swapped gossip, loaned their binoculars, and gave advice on where
to locate the fighting. Cobb attributed this to the "inherent kind-
liness of the German gentleman's nature," and to the soldiers'
desire to counter the stories that the German army was commit-
ting atrocities as it fought its way through Belgium.

In these opening weeks of the war, with the German army steam-
rolling through neutral Belgium, little of the news coverage showed
Germany in a favorable light. Allied propaganda stirred poisonous hatred of the barbarian invaders. However, since the United
States was officially neutral in the conflict and since many American newspaper readers had strong German sympathies, publishers
urged reporters to give a balanced account of the conflict. Personal
glimpses of German soldiers made for more evenhanded coverage.

The war had now entered France, and based on what they had
seen so far, Cobb's group of correspondents believed they would
follow the invaders on a swift course all the way to Paris. How-

ever, their war adventure came to an abrupt end when they inadvertently slipped through a gap in the German rear guard into the village of Beaumont, then serving as temporary headquarters for the German Seventh Army. At the moment of their arrival, the town bustled with all the well-groomed trappings of a military ceremony. Prince August Wilhelm, the Kaiser's fourth son, held a regal posture on the steps of a château reviewing the troops and taking crisp salutes from bemedaled Prussian officers in dress uniforms. A military band played in the background.

Into this august ceremony, so colorful, crisp, and radiant with martial pride, strolled the bedraggled band of American correspondents. They had been gypsies for over a week and looked it. Cobb considered himself the most presentable of the group, which is saying much, given this self-description, rendered with his typical humor:

> That morning to save myself from the occasional showers, I had purchased from a wayside butcher his long canvas blouse, which I wore—and so coated over was this garment with suet and tallow and hog grease and other souvenirs of his calling, that had it caught fire I am sure it would have burned for at least half a day with a clear blue flame.
>
> Two day earlier than this I had walked the shoes off my feet and, with the shoes, some tender portions of the feet themselves. So, for this, the occasion of my advent into fashionable military society, I had on a pair of homemade carpet slippers which I had acquired by barter from an elderly Belgian lady. These slippers were gray in color, mottled with white, and of a curious swollen shape, so that they looked rather like a pair of Maltese cats which had died of dropsy and then been badly embalmed.

As Cobb's group marched boldly to the center of the ceremony, the band came to an abrupt stop, and incredulous officers gaped in astonishment. The reporters told a questioning officer that they were American correspondents looking for the fighting. The very notion that this bedraggled band of American hobos had blundered into the heart of the German invasion force once again struck a Teutonic funny bone and gave the officers a good laugh. For the second time, the Cobb group's naive pursuit of war news had shielded it from trouble.

But it did not change the fact that the journalists could not be tolerated at the front. In an age when automobiles whisked reporters from cities to battlefields within hours, and telegraphs, telephones, wireless, and transatlantic cables flashed news in an instant, it would hardly do for newsmen to be privy to the secrets of the German army.

CHAPTER THREE

What Is an Atrocity?

It is quite incredible what the American public will swallow in the way of lies if they are only repeated often enough and properly served up. It all turns on which side gets the news in first, for the first impression sticks.

—JOHANN HEINRICH VON BERNSTORFF, German ambassador to the United States, 1908–17, *My Three Years in America*

Less than a month into the war, unwelcomed journalists had become a problem for all the armies. The correspondent E. Alexander Powell referred to this period of the war for reporters as the "free-for-all." The majority of the news gathered in the field came from unattached freelancers, those who traveled at their own expense for the chance of "stumbling onto something." Powell encountered one freelancer whose only credentials consisted of a letter from the editor of a well-known magazine stating that he "would be pleased to consider any articles [the journalist] cared to submit," and also a clergyman from Boston gathering material for a series of sermons on the horrors of war.

Because public appetite for war news was insatiable, editors back home gratefully accepted any nugget of news sent their way, with little concern for its source or veracity. Ignoring restrictions on their travel, freelancers, correspondents, news photographers, war artists, and cinematographers popped up in every corner of the war zone, giving all the armies headaches. At best they were a nuisance; at worst, they inadvertently reported information useful to the enemy or were actually spies masquerading as newsmen.

In the last week of August 1914, two separate trains carried

American correspondents out of occupied Belgium. Under virtual arrest for being in the restricted war zone, Irvin Cobb and company were shipped to the German city of Aachen, along with prisoners of war and German wounded, to be detained until their true identities could be determined. Richard Harding Davis and the other correspondents in Brussels had worn out their welcome as well. Hearing rumors that they would soon be arrested and deported, they left on their own, heading to neutral Holland by way of Aachen. Along the route Davis had an experience that transformed his outlook on the war.

Correspondents of the Great War often commented on the conditions under which they worked and how it affected their reporting. They were too close or too removed from the fighting. They were harassed, manipulated, restricted, arrested, or mindlessly censored by the war offices. They strove to be meticulously objective and neutral in their reporting or betrayed a bias for one side. A reporter's sympathies could also be swayed by personal contact with soldiers. Robert McCormick and James O'Donnell Bennett, correspondents for the *Chicago Tribune*, conceded, "Soldiers in the field take so prodigious a hold on the imagination and the affections that even the neutral observer soon comes to believe in and to love the soldiers with whom his lot happens to be cast."

The two groups of correspondents traveling out of Belgium at the end of August dramatically illustrated that conundrum. How does the neutral eyewitness to the carnage maintain objectivity? Under what conditions should objectivity be abandoned? And what trade-off must journalists make to gain access to the news? These questions were brought into sharp focus by the issue of the alleged atrocities committed by the German army as it battled its way through Belgium.

The Night Louvain Burned

For Davis and his companions on the train to Aachen, the sight of burning houses and wasted villages began a few miles outside Brussels and continued to Liège. The once-beautiful countryside "looked as though a cyclone had uprooted its houses, gardens, and orchards and a prairie fire had followed." The tide of refugees crowding into Brussels had signaled the impact of fighting on the civilian population, but until now Davis had not witnessed the brutal tactics used by the Germans.

The worst of the destruction fell on the picturesque university city of Louvain. All the correspondents on the train had visited Louvain prior to German occupation or during it. They had wandered its narrow, twisting streets lined with attractive shops and cafés and been charmed by its white-walled houses with red roofs and gardens. Its church of Saint Pierre and its university dated from the fifteenth century. Its five-hundred-year-old town hall was the most famous in Belgium.

When the train stopped for a two-hour layover on August 27, Louvain was in flames. The correspondents—Davis, Arno Dosch-Fleurot (*New York World*), Gerald Morgan (*New York Tribune*), Will Irwin (*New York Sun* and *Collier's*), and Mary Boyle O'Reilly (Newspaper Enterprise Association)—were not permitted to leave the train. But crowding wide-eyed at the windows, they saw that the entire heart of the city lay in ruins. Flames rose from the university, including its library, which housed a collection of irreplaceable medieval manuscripts. Davis had heard in Brussels that some citizens in Louvain had killed German soldiers and therefore the town had been marked for retribution, even though the Hague Convention of 1899 expressly forbade such collective punishment.

Amid explosions and gunshots, German soldiers moved street to street, house to house, burning. The spreading flames worked their way toward the train station, sweeping before them a stream of terrified residents carrying children and bundles of their possessions. From the group soldiers selected a dozen men for reprisal execution. A firing squad led them away, and moments later came the shots. One soldier thrust his head through the open train window, yelling and drunk with the violence. To the sound of distant explosions, he pantomimed shooting, cutting, and thrusting with a bayonet.

4. A 1913 photo of Mary Boyle O'Reilly, who covered the early months of the war for the Newspaper Enterprise Association. Source: Harris & Ewing Collection, Prints and Photographs Division, Library of Congress, LC-DIG-hec-01937.

Davis was no stranger to atrocities. Those poisonous flowers bloomed in every war he ever covered. In Cuba he had seen the bodies of women and children dead from starvation in Spanish internment camps. Just as the evidence spoke then, his eyes now recorded the truth of events in Louvain. Except how could one instance of depravity be measured against another? In Cuba he had labeled Spanish behavior "an offense against humanity" that justified war. But how did one describe the Germans engaged in the systematic murder of civilians, the burning of a library, and the destruction of cities? The world needed a new definition for "atrocities."

When the correspondents reached the safety of neutral Holland, only Mary O'Reilly turned around and returned to Louvain. She knew she had an important story and was willing to risk danger to get it. Since arriving in Belgium in mid-August, O'Reilly had been jolted by one shock of war after another. In destroyed villages she heard horror stories from residents. She saw the bodies of two old men hanging from roadside trees. With three other women, she appealed to a German officer in occupied Brussels to allow milk deliveries into the city for starving babies. Her article about that experience ended with the officer's reply: "You ask the absurd—the impossible. We Prussians recognize no distinction of persons. Men, women, children, ALL are enemies of the Fatherland when Germany makes war!" She closed with "today a hundred babies lie dead in Brussels." Her articles sounded the alarm about the appalling conduct of the German army, but Louvain was the worst.

Concealing her identity as a journalist, O'Reilly convinced a German official to grant her a travel pass. Back in Louvain she found the bodies of thirty civilians, eleven of them women. German soldiers continued to burn and bomb additional buildings. Residents disputed the German justification for the carnage that civilians had fired on them. O'Reilly described the horror: "For every soldier reported shot, 10 men and women suffered death. At sunset the mayor, police chief, the principal of the university, and two professors were publically executed." She did not hesitate to call it a war crime.

For four days O'Reilly sat in her hired car watching the continuing destruction and harsh occupation that followed: "I, an American woman, armed only with a German vice-consul's pass, innocently obtained in Holland, sat in a motor car WATCHING WAR AS 20TH CENTURY CIVILIZATION APPLIES IT!"

Davis already had his Louvain story, and being the first to report it meant more to him than gathering additional details. His account of Louvain reached American readers on August 31, two weeks ahead of O'Reilly's. For Davis what he saw in Louvain was unconscionable behavior for an army and validated the charges of atrocities that appeared in the Allied press. In his coverage of previous conflicts, Davis had always found something alluring and glamorous in war. He glorified commanders and saw nobility in the way soldiers faced death. But Germany had declared "war upon the defenseless, war upon churches, colleges, shops of milliners and lace-makers," he told his readers, "war brought to the bedside and the fireside; against women harvesting the fields, against children in wooden shoes at play in the street," and there was only villainy in such behavior.

To adequately convey the horrors of Louvain, Davis abandoned all pretext of journalistic objectivity and the pose of neutrality espoused by many American reporters. His vivid account of the destruction of Louvain, which ran in hundreds of U.S. newspapers, adopted a strident anti-German tone, casting the war as a battle between good and evil. "When a mad dog runs amuck in a village," he proposed to his readers, "it is the duty of every farmer to get his gun and destroy it, not to lock himself indoors and preserve toward the dog and those who face him a neutral mind."

The Wheeler Syndicate news service, for which Davis worked, sent its star correspondent a carefully worded telegram pointing out that its member newspapers wanted more-balanced coverage of the war and asking him to be more neutral in his reporting. Davis would have none of it. Along with his eyewitness stories on the German entry into Brussels and the later destruction of Rheims Cathedral, his reporting characterized the German army as a heartless, efficient machine of destruction, at war with civilians and civilization itself. Henceforth Davis became a passionate foe of German militarism and an advocate for ending American neutrality.

The No-Atrocities Letter

Few topics became linked to the fighting in Belgium so completely as that of German atrocities. From the first engagement at Liège, reports filtered to the Allied and neutral press about the execution of civilians and other outrageous violations of the rules of war. The conduct of German soldiers became such an incendiary issue in the opening months of the war and the public's appetite for such stories so keen, that exaggerations and manufactured stories began to mix liberally with real accounts, until the charge itself became suspect. British newspapers accused German soldiers of cutting the hands off boys, raping nuns, bayoneting babies, crucifying captured soldiers, and slaughtering civilians.

A counterthread of coverage emerged of reporters actually searching for atrocities. Reporters interviewed eyewitnesses and visited hospitals looking for solid evidence. Such explorations invariably drew a blank or concluded that incidents had resulted from accidents of war, isolated cases of overreaction by individual officers, or justifiable reprisals against illegitimate civilian snipers. Journalist Albert Rhys Williams traveled through Belgium at this time with war photographers desperate for one confirming image of an atrocity. Refugees asked, what proof did they want?

"Children with their hands cut off. Are there any around here?" Williams replied.

"Oh, yes! Hundreds of them," was the invariable assurance.

"Yes, but all we want is one—just one in flesh and bone. Where can we find that?"

"The answer was ever the same," Williams discovered. "In the hospital at the rear, or at the front. Back in such-and-such a village, etc. Always somewhere else; never where we were."

No objective observers were in a better position to substantiate such charges than Irvin Cobb and his group of American journalists. In their two-week trek behind the German invasion force, the group interacted with solders, visited destroyed towns, and interviewed villagers. Cobb found that every village he passed

5. Humorist/war reporter Irvin Cobb. In the opening weeks of the war, Cobb and other reporters ventured forth from Brussels in taxicabs searching for the fighting. Source: Prints and Photographs Division, Library of Congress, LC-USZ62-38207.

through had a tale to tell of German atrocities inflicted on noncombatants. But they never held up under scrutiny. "Not once did we find an avowed eye-witness to such things. Always our informant had heard of the torturing or the maiming or the murdering, but never had he personally seen it. It had always happened in another town—never in his own town." In fact, much to the contrary, Cobb saw examples of occupied villages in which German soldiers behaved properly and treated the civilian population with respect.

The train carrying Cobb's group of correspondents to Germany passed by Louvain prior to its destruction. It deposited them at Aachen, where flourishing sidewalk cafés, concerts, and plays stood in stunning contrast to the destruction just across the border. News of the war intruded there through official bulletins posted in shop windows and outside public buildings. Cobb mused on how people were shielded from real news of the war. In England and in Germany, governments fed people a meager diet of censored, positive news. Even in the United States, without wartime censorship, lies and misperceptions too often masqueraded as the truth.

It was this realization that prompted the reporters to set the record straight on the question of atrocities. The group of five—James Bennett and John T. McCutcheon (*Chicago Tribune*), Irvin Cobb (*Saturday Evening Post*), Roger Lewis (Associated Press), and Harry Hansen (*Chicago Daily News*)—signed a remarkable letter disputing the charges of German atrocities. Knowing that British censors would never allow it to go via the London cable to America, they submitted it instead to Berlin for wireless transmission to the United States, where it ran in hundreds of newspapers.

Their letter stated: "In spirit we unite in rendering the German atrocities groundless, as far as we are able. After spending two weeks with and accompanying the troops upward to 100 miles we are unable to report a single instance unprovoked.

"We are also unable to confirm rumors of mistreatment of prisoners or of non-combatants." It went on to list all the towns they had visited and mentioned the good behavior of the German troops, the lack of evidence for any of the charges from civilians, and the refugees they met who discounted atrocity stories.

Appearing in U.S. papers on September 7, the article created quite a sensation. It was so contradictory to reports coming from the Allied press that no one knew quite what to make of it. Nothing had been seen or heard of these five journalists since they departed Brussels on August 23. Richard Harding Davis's article about Louvain ran on August 31, and his article about his arrest and near execution by the Germans appeared on September 2. Convinced of the brutal tactics employed by the Germans, American readers had suspected that Cobb's group was either imprisoned or dead. Now theories turned to how they might have been tortured or forced to bargain for their lives or their freedom by writing such a letter.

In contrast to its reception elsewhere, the letter was so warmly received in Germany that the correspondents received a personal thank-you note from Kaiser Wilhelm. Quick to take advantage of suddenly being persona grata in a belligerent state, Cobb, McCutcheon, and Bennett (Lewis and Hansen had left for London) boldly wrote directly to the kaiser, suggesting that they might be able to give additional favorable coverage if they were allowed to travel to the German front lines. For three days they heard nothing, and then a colonel appeared with documents decorated with impressive seals and ribbons and signed by the kaiser himself. They permitted the reporters to go almost anywhere they wished in Germany and behind German lines.

It is tempting to find fault with these well-respected journalists for their anti-atrocities letter, if only for the fact that it was written in Germany and seemed an obvious attempt to curry favor with the authorities. Clearly they were holding to a narrow definition of atrocities, namely, the fabricated charges reported in the Allied press of bayoneting babies, mutilating captives, and raping nuns. In the scope of their limited observations, they had seen none of those things and could honestly report that fact. Deflating propaganda's more egregious diversions from the truth seemed a just cause. Other American reporters did the same. In fact, it ranks high among the achievements of American correspondents in the opening months of the war.

Having been virtually embedded in the German army, Cobb's group came to accept the justification for its severe treatment of civilians. The German army employed a campaign of "frightfulness" (*Schrecklichkeit*), a ruthless suppression of any civilians thought to be resisting the invasion force by sniping and other acts of aggression. In such cases the Germans considered it appropriate to deal with these civilians, and those who supported them, not as civilians or even as enemy soldiers but as illegal combatants, which placed them outside the protection of international agreements on the conduct of war. Punishment fell harshly upon them, and collective punishment might also include their families, houses, and communities. In a later article, Harry Hansen used that rationale to explain the letter: "Such shootings as have taken place appear to have been reprisals made necessary by hostile acts on the part of civilians." Of course Cobb's group had no way of knowing if all such killing of civilians fell into this category and with what justification civilians were labeled as combatants.

More than thirty-five years later, the topic was still on the mind of John McCutcheon when he wrote his autobiography, *Drawn from Memory*. In justifying the letter, he wrote: "Here we were, five American newsmen, who, by a set of curious chances, had seen much of the German army in its passage through Belgium, who had followed closely in its wake; here we were with a news story that Americans should hear. It seemed only fair to the Germans that we should say what conclusions we had reached, wholly independently and without coercion or bribe, about a situation that was stirring the world."

As for the other incidents, such as the destruction of Louvain, Cobb's group and others would eventually frame it in the larger context of the war. In focusing attention on such "technical atrocities," reporter Albert Rhys Williams explained, "we are apt to forget the greater atrocity of the violation of Belgium, and the whole hideous atrocity of the Great War."

Guests of the German Army

At the end of August, Granville Fortescue found himself Berlin-bound on a train of German soldiers wounded in the battles of Mons and Namur. Fortescue had quickly acquired the reputation of being the most opportunistic correspondent in the confused invasion landscape. His extensive military service also gave a depth of insight to his reportage missing from others covering the war. Why, for instance, had the Belgian army not utilized the splendid defensive positions offered by high ground at so many road crossing, bridges, and fords instead of making their stand in the towns along the invasion route? It was unfortunate from both a military and a civil point of view, because it offered a lesser defense and led to the destruction of so many towns and the sacrifice of civilian lives.

After he had been at both Mons and Namur and been arrested at Mons by the French, Fortescue's was recruited by the *New York American* for a special assignment. Little news made its way out of Germany, in large part because Britain had severed Germany's transatlantic cable on August 5 and interdicted its mail service to the United States. German wireless stations, which could reach the United States, could carry only a limited amount of official news.

Go into the heart of Hun land, the editor instructed Fortescue, and get to the bottom of the widely circulating rumors of social unrest that might presage an early end of the war. Germany would soon be torn apart by internal revolution, rumor held. Supposedly the poor were starving, antiwar riots and strikes crippled Berlin, the crown prince had been assassinated, and the country had nearly exhausted its supply of manpower. In this desperate first month of the war, when little could be done to slow the German rush to Paris, finding these stories to be true would be most welcome news indeed.

Fortescue found nothing in Berlin to give heart to the Allied cause. The city was the most cheerful of the capitals he had visited. Food was plentiful and moderately priced. Crowds gathered

6. Belgium authorities arrested Joseph Medill Patterson after he published an article debunking Allied charges of German atrocities. Source: George Grantham Bain Collection, Prints and Photographs Division, Library of Congress, LC-DIG-ggbain-01027.

outside newspaper offices eagerly awaiting each new edition, then wildly cheered their army's latest victory. Lively bands marched through the streets with each new unit of soldiers, a practice that had been abandoned in London. British soldiers seemed to be marching off to their own funerals, while Germans were heading to a festival. Fortescue himself felt the thrill of it merely watching them pass. In short spirits could not have been higher.

Although Germany shared the Allies' policy of not allowing correspondents at the front, that policy was evolving. If its well-oiled military machine faulted itself for anything at this point in the war, it was surrendering the journalistic high ground to its enemies. Most war stories found their way into the neutral press from reporters operating in Belgium or France and displayed decidedly Allied sympathies and prejudices. Public perception of Germans as the true descendants of the barbarian Huns, who despoiled Europe in the fifth century, had already taken root in Allied and neutral countries.

To address this imbalance in the news, Germany planned a charm offensive. It collected several neutral correspondents in Berlin and gave them access to military facilities, POW camps, and VIP interviews. Joseph Medill Patterson, scion of the Medill family that published the *Chicago Tribune*, happened to be in Berlin at the time, although now on assignment for the *New York Tribune*. Patterson published the Chicago paper jointly and contentiously with his cousin Robert R. McCormick. In politics and personality, the two were as different as night and day. McCormick held more conservative views and Patterson more progressive.

At the outbreak of war, Patterson had headed directly to Germany along with photographer-cinematographer Edwin Weigle. They planned to capture battles and behind-the-scenes action of the war with motion pictures and take the reality of the Great European War to theaters in America. McCormick, the other half of that publishing duo, would venture into war reporting and filmmaking in 1915 as the special guest of the Russian grand duke Nicholas, commander in chief of the Russian army.

While Weigle recorded moving-picture scenes of Berlin, Patterson landed an interview with Baron Mumm von Schwarzenstein. The lengthy article that resulted allowed the Foreign Office to lay out Germany's justifications for war. However, not all the reporting resulting from this enhanced access turned out as Germany wanted. Granville Fortescue's interview with "Lieutenant

Werner," the first aviator to drop bombs on Paris, exposed that aspect of German fighting that Fortescue found so distasteful.

Werner's account of air combat was thrilling. It might have been ripped from the pages of H. G. Wells's 1908 novel, *War in the Air*, which prophesized the new age of aerial warfare. But Fortescue could barely mask his revulsion at how nonchalantly Werner described bombing a city. Like Davis, Fortescue recoiled at war on civilians:

> What was in my mind during this conversation was, "Does this man know the cowardice of his deeds?" The dropping of a mangling, death-dealing projectile on defenceless women and children was not my idea of soldiering. . . . There was nothing in the outward aspect of Lieutenant Werner to make you suspect that he was the murderer of women and children, yet reduced to plain words, that is what he was. Germany is trying to hide too many crimes under the name of war; she cannot succeed in this case. How she can get her sons to do such things I cannot explain.

As a final bit of self-promotion, the Germans wanted to show the journalists the power of their new siege guns to level fortresses. No better place to do that than at Liège. On August 30 five correspondents, two U.S. Army military observers, and German officer escorts and chauffeurs all met at the American embassy and loaded into three automobiles. On the way to that captured city, the caravan stopped at Aachen to pick up Irvin Cobb, John McCutcheon, and James Bennett, on the opening leg of their blue-ribbon tour of the front.

As a military man himself, Fortescue took special interest in all the details of the battle of Liège, which German officers were only too eager to explain, in particular the damage caused by the Germans' massive, forty-two-centimeter siege guns. But Fortescue's strongest impression from the trip was roused by the destroyed villages he saw along the invasion route. "That motor trip told me more than all the stories of atrocities I had read in the Brussels papers," Fortescue wrote. "Here was the evidence of a crime that still cries to heaven for vengeance. Whole villages given to the flame. Towns once sheltering ten thousand peaceful people, now no more than blackened walls and rubble. . . . If there is a just God, Germany must pay heavily for this crime."

The journalists returned to Berlin, where Fortescue then headed to France. Joseph Patterson rushed out his own article denying atrocities. All the evidence he had seen spoke to the orderliness and discipline of the German army. The Germans were "stern, direct, and merciless" in the just pursuit of their military objectives, but they were not marauding barbarians, and the atrocity charges against them were rubbish.

Patterson and Weigle shifted their operations to Antwerp, where Weigle would realize his plan of capturing moving pictures of battles. Surprisingly, Patterson's no-atrocity story showed up in Belgian newspapers. The story had been copied off the London cable by the British press and from there was translated for the Belgian papers. Patterson and Weigle were subsequently arrested by Belgian authorities, and their passes and permits to travel and take pictures were confiscated. As Patterson would later explain it, "In the state of mind of Antwerp, to doubt that any German could ever fail to do the most depraved thing conceivable was to pronounce one's self a German sympathizer, perhaps a spy."

From Liège Cobb and his companions continued on a ten-day, whirlwind tour of the sites in Belgium and France where fighting had occurred or was occurring: Namur, Huy, Dinant, Chimay, Mons, Antwerp, Louvain, Tirlemont, and Rheims. The names of the towns along the invasion route already resonated with their role in the war: Battice, where "Belgian civilians first fired on the German troops from roofs and windows, and where the Germans first inaugurated their ruthless system of reprisal on houses and people alike"; Liège, where the Germans' siege guns pulverized the city's formidable ring of fortresses; Louvain, the beautiful university town whose famous library was burned; and Rheims, whose thirteenth-century cathedral had been damaged by shell fire.

This trio of correspondents might be considered some of the first tourists of the war, enjoying this escorted excursion to the scenes of the fighting. However, they shared that distinction with those already making pilgrimage to Louvain. When Cobb's tour stopped there in the first week of September, buses were already bringing sightseers from Aachen, Liège, and Brussels to see what the war had wrought. "They bought postal cards and climbed about over the mountain ranges of waste, and they mined in the debris mounds for souvenirs," Cobb reported. "Altogether, I suppose some of them regarded it as a kind of picnic." A widow who had lost her husband on the day the Germans took Louvain begged Cobb to buy the postcards she offered, with "all the best pictures of the ruins!" Enterprising photographers set up cameras by the more famous buildings. Photos of tourists or soldiers standing before gutted buildings could be mailed home as postcards.

More than mere tourists, Cobb, McCutcheon, and Bennett may well have experienced the most blue-ribbon tour of the entire war. Traveling with the kaiser's express authorization, the group got to see the full range of German military operations. Generals recounted for them the details of their victories. They visited a wireless station, a mobile cook wagon, a field hospital, and an artillery battery. They snapped pictures like excited tourists. McCutcheon took a ride in an observation airplane.

"Such Wanton and Wicked Destruction"

Standing on the once-crowded Place de l'Opéra, staring along the wide boulevards of the French capital, United Press correspondent William Shepherd could not see a single person or vehicle. Frederick Palmer, who had despaired of the British ever issuing him the promised credentials, arrived in Paris in the first week of September. In the hotel where he found lodging, he was one of only six guests in the establishment's five hundred rooms. The city reminded Richard Harding Davis of a "summer hotel out of season," except for the bustling business of tending to the thousands of wounded. By the end of August, a cloud of doom hung over Paris. The government had closed its offices and moved to Bordeaux. The Bank of France had shipped out its gold. Many citizens had fled the city. The last remaining stranded American tourists had departed. Nearly every shop had given up its staff to the army. The U.S. ambassador, Myron Herrick, won acclaim by choosing to remain in the city and keep the embassy functioning.

The correspondents who came to Paris in the hopes of seeing the climactic endgame of the war faced the all-too-familiar restrictions on their movements and access to information. They were forbidden from traveling to the front. The government issued them passes to visit army headquarters twice a day for bulletins, which gave vague details of encounters and movements. The *Paris Herald* cut its daily edition to a single page and ran war news in which words had been blacked out by the censor.

For the American journalists, such censorship seemed shameful. The French and British people, who were being asked to sacrifice so much for this war, knew virtually nothing about it. The fate of Paris, the outcome of the war, hung by a thread. A handful of Americans were the only correspondents in Paris, the rest having fled with the government to Bordeaux. Those remaining included Wythe Williams (*New York Times*), Paul Scott Mowrer (*Chicago Daily News*), Charles Inman Barnard (*New York Tribune*), Robert Dunn (*New York Evening Post*), and Elmer Roberts (Associated Press). As representatives for various press syndicates, the Americans represented nearly every newspaper in the United States, and all they could do was stroll the deserted streets of the French capital and listen to the rumble of distant guns. In a daring escape, Dunn loaded a bicycle onto a train and sneaked out of the city to find the war.

Every day, regular as clockwork, a German airplane flew over the city. If the reporters watched from the American chancellery on the side of the Trocadéro Hill, they had a wonderful view of what looked like a bug crawling across the sky, making long, leisurely turns in the face of crackling gunfire from the ground, to drop its three bombs and then depart. With binoculars they could even make out the face of the German pilot looking down on the city. Since this was the only fighting reporters got to see, the aerial bombing of Paris was featured in many news stories.

One quiet afternoon as the American correspondents lounged at their favorite outdoor café near the U.S. embassy, a man rode up on a bicycle, dismounted, joined them at the table, and ordered a whiskey. Even though he was dust-covered and drooping with weariness, they recognized him as their colleague Robert Dunn. All they could pry from him was that he had been a prisoner of the British army for several days and needed sleep. They then watched him trudge the short distance to the U.S. embassy and disappear inside.

After Dunn left the embassy, Wythe Williams paid a visit there to see what he could learn. Of course, Ambassador Herrick could not break a confidence, but based on other sources of information, and knowing that Williams could not get such information past the censors anyway, he did reveal that the situation was grave. Before he left the embassy that day, Williams knew the key facts: "The British army had been thrown back in disorder from Mons and the French beaten at Charleroi. The Germans had opened a gap in the Allied line, and the British and French armies were in full retreat."

Robert Dunn wrote a long account of the British army at Mons. He knew it would never pass French or British censors, so he slipped it into the mail. Not all mail was checked by censors. With any luck it would arrive at the *Evening Post* office in ten to twelve days. Williams wrote an innocuous story about the Red Cross and war charities but sneaked into it mention of the sudden wave of refugees that had descended on Paris from the direction of the fighting. He hoped some clever editor would put two and two together and embellish it with details.

Paul Mowrer managed to get out two carefully worded dispatches in late August about the German advance and the Allied retreat. But he burned to see action for himself. No one could buy a train ticket to any French town in the war zone, so Mowrer booked passage to London via the French port of Le Havre. But instead of traveling on to England, he left the train at Rouen, close to where he thought the fighting to be. Although well behind the lines, the city buzzed with the activity of war. He learned the basic details of the fighting from the U.S. consul and then managed to speak with British soldiers, officers, and wounded who had fought at Mons. They blamed the French for pulling back and leaving their flank exposed.

When Mowrer finally made it to London, he found the city buzzing about a newspaper that had published the first pessimistic hint of what was happening to the BEF. Its action was a matter of considerable public debate, yet no one in Britain had any idea what had happened to the country's army. British censors cleared Mowrer's story for transmission to America. Within two days the people of Chicago knew more about what had befallen the British army at Mons than did the citizens of Britain.

William Shepherd spoke the frustration of all the American correspondents still penned up in Paris:

> All we can do is to walk aimlessly about the deserted streets and listen to the rumble of the distant guns. We do not know whether these guns are French or German; we do not know how near the Germans really are; we do not know how long Paris can hold out. There is no one to go to for information. We cannot leave the city and make a try for the front, because we have no military passes. We know nothing about what is going on around us, and the United States must go without news so far as we are concerned.

Few doubted that German officers would soon be sipping wine in the cafés of Paris. But on the night of Sunday, September 6, a few of the correspondents witnessed a most unusual sight. A giant convoy of taxicabs left the city, each brimming with soldiers being rushed to the fighting in a last-ditch effort to save Paris and the Allied cause. The following day a government communiqué explained with maddening brevity this turning point in the war: "Our advance troops defending Paris have come in contact with the right wing of the Germans. The small engagement has resulted to our advantage." "Small engagement?" "Our advantage?" It took a fortuneteller to read between the lines. But when the German army did not appear in the city, it became clear that its advance had been stopped and Paris saved. That didn't tell the whole story, but for the moment at least, smiles returned to the faces of Parisians.

In the buoyant wake of victory, the French army tried its hand at a conducted press tour. Frederick Palmer, who in theory represented three American press associations, and veteran Associated Press correspondent Elmer Roberts joined several French officials for an automobile tour of the battlefield. On the banks of the Marne River, they passed through a blasted landscape marked with fresh graves that represented the furthest German advance. The French politicians on the trip could not contain their joy that the tide of war had turned and the Germans were in retreat. The more-objective, experienced correspondents read the situation differently. Standing in the ruins of the town of Soissons, peering into the hills beyond, Palmer got a glimpse of the next phase of the war. The Germans had chosen their defensive positions on the heights. "They had dug in; trench warfare had begun."

Meanwhile, those frustrated correspondents still bottled up in Paris reached the limits of their patience. They resorted to one of their most effective news-gathering strategies: bluff. Acting as if their meager pass to visit the War Ministry's daily briefings gave them carte blanche to tour the front lines, they sneaked from the city with the bravado of visiting dignitaries. Davis hired a limousine with a liveried chauffer to visit scenes of the fighting and see an artillery duel. Granville Fortescue rode a train far enough to gather details of the fighting from civilians.

Emboldened by these successful forays, a group of them decided to challenge the military with a large-scale expedition to the front. Instead of presenting themselves as war correspondents seeking to witness a battle, however, they would go under the guise of tourists on a pilgrimage to the city of Rheims to see what damage the Germans had done to its medieval cathedral.

A few months into the war, veteran reporters for the *Chicago Tribune* Robert McCormick and James Bennett would write a joint article in which they bristled at being labeled as war correspondents "if for no other reason than that the term [had] been insufferably cheapened by a crew of imposters and braggarts that [had] descended on Europe." Instead they considered themselves seasoned "war travelers" and "conscientious observers." This was precisely the role adopted by the Paris correspondents. Davis and Fortescue in particular had seen precious little of the actual fighting but had been staggered by Germany's war on civilians and nonmilitary targets. This trip would give them the opportunity to confirm the rumors of damage to one of Europe's most famous medieval architectural treasures.

Davis, Fortescue, Gerald Morgan, and British correspondent Ellis Ashmead-Bartlett loaded into Davis's limousine with food and wine and set off on the fifty-six-mile journey. They took a route that avoided the headquarters of the British General Staff at Villers-Cotterêts, since the British took special delight in throwing correspondents into jail. By Davis's reckoning the British had "bagged" thirteen journalists the previous week alone.

Their limousine and the War Ministry passes to attend press briefings proved impressive enough to get past sentries. The landscape resembled those they had seen in Belgium: destroyed villages, shell-cratered terrain, the debris of war, and hastily dug graves. When they arrived at Rheims, smoke still rose from the burning ruins. The Germans had occupied the town from September 4 through 12, then withdrawn across the Vesle River, where they directed a bombardment of the city once it was reoccupied by the French.

Despite the presence of a French unit in the city, the correspondents made their way to the cathedral without being stopped. There they gazed upon the cathedral's great tower, shell-damaged and blackened with smoke. Many of the exterior statues lay broken on the ground. Fire had gutted much of the interior. Rheims Cathedral had withstood six hundred years of warfare, until now. A favorite destination of tourists, the cathedral ranked as one of the grandest monuments in Europe. All but six kings of France had been crowned here. Its sculptures, paintings, tapestries, and stained-glass windows were a cultural and spiritual treasure beyond measure.

"Never have I looked upon a picture of such pathos, or such wanton and wicked destruction. A few days ago when you walked through the cathedral . . . you stood where Joan of Arc received the homage of France. Today you walk on charred ashes, broken stone and shattered glass," Davis told his newspaper readers.

For Davis the destruction of Rheims Cathedral fit the same pattern of German barbarity as the burning of the university library in Louvain. It was an attack on cultural treasures that belonged to Western civilization. Such savage behavior contrasted so completely with the all-too-human story told by the local abbot as he led the correspondents to the top of the bell tower. Wounded German soldiers were being cared for in the cathedral when it came under attack from German artillery, the abbot explained. Priests rescued the wounded from the resulting fire and then protected them from an outraged mob of citizens. Even as the abbot pointed out the location of the French and German artillery positions, visible from atop the tower, additional shells fell nearby.

As the correspondents studied the German positions through field glasses, another correspondent, this one behind the German lines, trained a telescope on the cathedral, far distant on the horizon. Irvin Cobb, enjoying the special attention lavished on him during his VIP tour, floated twelve hundred feet in the air in an artillery spotter's observation balloon. Cobb had heard many times from many sources the German version of the attack on Rheims Cathedral, an indication of how sensitive they were to the charges. They claimed they had spared the cathedral until the French posted artillery observers in its towers. And even then the Germans had warned the French to remove the spotters. Only when the French refused had the cathedral been targeted.

Cobb was clearly flattered to have been given this extraordinary opportunity. "I am probably the only civilian spectator who has enjoyed such a privilege during the present European war. . . . The distinction is worth much to me personally," he wrote. From his lofty perch in the balloon, the whole sweep of fighting under way along the Aisne River revealed itself. He could discern artillery shells in their flight paths in both directions. The lines of opposing trenches stood out clearly from this height, as did soldiers, small as insects, making their assaults. "For once in my life . . . I saw now understandingly a battle front," Cobb reported. "It was spread before me—lines and dots and dashes on a big green and brown and yellow map. Why, the whole thing was as plain as a chart. I had a reserved seat for the biggest show on earth."

For Davis, Fortescue, and companions, their trip to Rheims took a familiar turn when they were arrested on their way back to Paris. Their detention in a barn, along with suspected spies, German prisoners, and French deserters, gave one measure of French attitude toward correspondents. Returned to Paris under guard, they were held for a day and then "paroled" for eight days, during which time they could not submit any stories. This excursion finally exhausted Davis's patience with this war. "By gravy, this war is my Waterloo," he remarked to colleague William Simms. "I'm going home."

It seemed every serious correspondent trying to cover the war had been arrested at least once. For some, such as Will Irwin, arrest by one army or another became part of their modus operandi. They eluded or bluffed their way past the rear guard in a war zone and kept heading toward the grumble of artillery until they were arrested. When released they returned to Paris or London and wrote their story. And then repeated the process. They would always see troops and ammunition being rushed to the front and wounded returning, and if lucky they might snatch a conversation with a soldier or a civilian.

Richard Harding Davis returned to the United States with a wealth of experiences, but having seen very little of the pageantry, the noble personages, or the fighting. His adventures made good stories for his readers, but those readers were the ones being cheated by current restrictions on the news. "Never is the 'constant reader' so delighted as when the war correspondent gets the worst of it," Davis remarked. "It is the one sure laugh. The longer he is kept at the base, the more he is bottled up, 'deleted,' censored and made prisoner, the greater is the delight of the man at home. He thinks the joke is on the war correspondent. I think it is on the 'constant reader.'"

Irvin Cobb returned to America, numb to the challenge of reporting the war. When he saw his first dead soldier, he imagined that he could write an entire story about that tragedy. But soon the most horrible war scenes made little impression on him. How did you describe the endless battles, the deaths of one hundred thousand men, he wondered.

> We have used up all our adjectives on five-alarm fires, gang-murders, Slocum disasters [the steamboat *General Slocum* sank in 1904 with the loss of 1,021 lives], political conventions. We haven't got anything left for such a war. . . . You start out in the morning with the best intentions of grasping the facts of events and writing a bully story, and you come home in the evening dazed and brow-beaten. There never has been anything like it. Here you get a Gettysburg for breakfast, a Chancellorsville for lunch, Waterloo for supper, and, to make a good measure, they throw in a Sedan around tea-time.

Despite wartime restrictions on the news, American readers knew more about the war than their counterparts in any of the belligerent countries. In addition to receiving news reports from every country at war, they benefited from reports that evaded censorship by being mailed from neutral countries. Once American correspondents returned home from Europe, they could write with full candor about their experiences.

In his 1917 book, *Confessions of a War Correspondent*, United Press reporter William Shepherd reflected somewhat wistfully on the reporter's job in the opening months of the war:

> The harum-scarumness of those early freelance days is almost unbelievable, as one looks back on it now. Every word that a correspondent wrote for the news-hungry public was pure gold. Never, in the modern world, did news count for so much in the lives of so many millions of people as it did during those first months of the Great War. Not a word that a correspondent wrote in those days was overlooked by the news-seeking millions. News, lies, local color, human interest, fakes, all went down the great public gullet in Gargantuan gulps.

But those swashbuckling, free-for-all days had now ended. In the fall of 1914, searching for more fertile reporting locations, correspondents set off for other fronts in the war, in Serbia and Russia. However, the best opportunity for reporting the war now lay on the other side of the battle line, in Germany and the Austro-Hungarian Empire.

CHAPTER FOUR

The Central Powers Manage the News

I have seen men killed; I've seen men hanged; I've seen men executed at the wall, but this sight I happened upon by accident in Galicia is one of the most piteous that the sun could ever shine upon or that a human being could ever behold. (By mail to New York—Passed by censor)

—United Press correspondent WILLIAM SHEPHERD, Przemyśl, Austria, October 29, 1914

Berlin crowds stood twenty deep outside newspaper offices to read bulletins about General Hindenburg's victory against the Russians at the Battle of Tannenberg. Banners appeared around the city, and vendors sold photographic buttons with an image of the German hero. Even as the German advance stalled outside Paris in early September, victories continued on the eastern front. At the Battle of Masurian Lakes, Hindenburg pushed Russian forces out of German territory in East Prussia and advanced into Russian Poland.

From the start of the war, the Berlin correspondent for United Press (UP) and the *New York World*, Karl von Wiegand, had been reporting on the German side of the war for the hundreds of American newspapers that subscribed to the UP news service. He reported on scenes inside Germany and, with German officer chaperones, traveled around the western front. As UP's man in Berlin since 1911, he had developed a network of influential friends and acquaintances. He appealed to them now for permission to travel to the eastern front to report on German victories.

Western Europe overflowed with journalists, covering territory familiar to Americans, but no American correspondent reported with the German army in the East. The titanic battles being fought there had gone virtually unnoted in U.S. newspapers. How many Americans could even find Tannenberg on the map or trace their finger along the Vistula River from the Baltic Sea to Warsaw, General Hindenburg's next objective?

In the first week of October 1914, Wiegand traveled by auto with three German officer escorts from Berlin to Russian Poland. The German and Austro-Hungarian armies battled the Russians along a front that extended from the Baltic to Hungary's Carpathian Mountains. Wiegand caught up with the army just east of the town of Wirballen, the present-day city of Kybartai, Lithuania. Here the German advance extended a long, threatening arm north of Warsaw.

Wiegand shared a predawn breakfast with the German commander beneath the "whistling screech" of passing artillery shells and then climbed to a hilltop to watch the third day of the Battle of Wirballen. Twice the Russian infantry had advanced in force the previous day and been driven back. Now, as Russian artillery rained shells on the German trenches, the Russian infantry climbed from its trenches for another attempt.

It was an impressive sight. Thousands of soldiers formed into multiple skirmish lines at intervals of twenty to fifty yards and advanced with battle flags flying. German officers moved behind their trenches exhorting their men to brace for the attack. Well-aimed German artillery rounds tore holes in the Russian ranks, but "on came the Slav swarm—into the range of the German trenches, with wild yells and never a waiver." It was a scene from a Teutonic nightmare, the Slavic hordes that so haunted the national imagination, advancing in massed assault.

Wiegand felt a part of the nightmare: "As a spectacle the whole thing was maddening. I found my heart thumping like a hammer, and with no weapons more formidable than a pair of binoculars, I was mentally fighting as hard as the men with the guns."

Then Wiegand beheld a baffling sight. He saw a sudden "almost grotesque, melting of the advancing line . . . the men literally went down like dominoes in a row." Some fell backward as if blown off their feet. Even as he puzzled at the spectacle, the rattle of machine guns reached his ear. For the first time the Russian line hesitated, bewildered as to what was happening. Officers on horseback galloped forward to urge them on. Horses fell, and riderless animals galloped among the ranks. The continuous raking of machine-gun fire caused a panic, and the Russians fled back to their lines, leaving the field to the dead and dying.

Toward evening Wiegand crouched in the light cast by a shielded automobile headlight and scribbled out the notes for the biggest story of his career: "Today I saw a wave of Russian flesh and blood dash against a wall of German steel. The wall stood. The wave broke—was shattered and hurled back. Rivulets of blood trickled back slowly in its wake. Broken bloody bodies, wreckage of the wave, strewed the breakers. Tonight I know why correspondents are not wanted on any of the battle lines. Descriptions and details of battles fought in the year of our Lord 1914 don't make nice reading."

Wiegand had landed his eastern front scoop. It was the first time in this war that a correspondent had reported on a battle line, the first report of the awesome effectiveness of machine-gun fire against massed ranks, and the first eyewitness account of fighting on the eastern front. As with all his other German war stories, he now faced the challenge of getting his story back to America. Since August 5, when Britain cut Germany's transatlantic cables, all news stories to America passed through the London cable office, becoming subject to censorship. The blanket restrictions of Britain's Defence of the Realm Act, passed in the opening days of the war, guarded not only military secrets but also news that might threaten public support for the war, be that reports of Allied defeats, German victories, criticism of commanders, or problems with the conduct of the war.

The UP circumvented the London bottleneck by mailing its stories from neutral Holland, a process that took seven to ten days. The Wirballen story would typically have gone by mail, but U.S. secretary of state William Jennings Bryan had recently requested that Britain allow through stories from Germany for U.S. publications. So Wiegand crossed his fingers and sent his Wirballen battle story to London for cable transmission to the United States. He was pleasantly surprised to learn later that the article had passed through British censorship unedited, approved for publication in the United States but not in Britain. It ran on the front page of nearly every United Press newspaper.

Wiegand's coverage of fighting on the eastern front made him the darling of the German high command and caused it to reappraise its policy on journalists. Germany had been caught off guard at the start of the war by the avalanche of Allied propaganda and Allied influence on the coverage of the war. Germany had no similar apparatus in place to explain its actions, promote its successes, and handle the general publicity of war, particularly in neutral countries. It now appointed a single person to handle neutral correspondents.

Back in Berlin Wiegand was rewarded with a series of high-profile interviews that once again gave him and the German cause front-page headlines in hundreds of American newspapers. In November he landed an interview with Crown Prince Friedrich Wilhelm that allowed the prince to pronounce, "Undoubtedly this is the most stupid, senseless and unnecessary war of modern times. It is a war not wanted by Germany."

Wiegand followed that up in December by interviewing Grand Admiral Alfred von Tirpitz, who justified the looming submarine war to blockade England: "America has not raised her voice in protest and has taken little or no action against England's closing of the North Sea to neutral shipping. What will America say if Germany declares submarine war on all enemy merchant ships?"

As the first interviews with any German leaders since the start of the war, these stories ran in newspapers around the world, making Wiegand one of the best known correspondents reporting the war and proving to Germany the value of working with the press.

Austria's Kriegspressequartier

While Wiegand garnered headlines in American newspapers, glorifying German arms and giving voice to German leaders, report-

7. An American correspondent in German-occupied Belgium in the early months of the war. The German army was more tolerant of neutral reporters than were the Allied powers. Lettering on the door identifies him as working for the Newspaper Enterprise Association, one of the news syndicates that offered content to its member newspapers that could not afford their own war correspondent. Source: George Grantham Bain Collection, Prints and Photographs Division, Library of Congress, LC-DIG-ggbain-21756.

ing in the West entered what correspondents were already calling the "dark ages." The war of movement and siege had settled into the static trench warfare that would predominate for the next four years. This type of war was nearly impossible to cover without access to the fighting zone, and both the British and the French became even more determined to exclude reporters from their armies. Reporters were harassed and arrested if they attempted to get near the fighting. Most languished in London or Paris, virtual prisoners. The fall of Antwerp on October 10, 1914, robbed journalists of their last base of operations behind the lines, as the German army consolidated its hold on Belgium. For roughly an eight-month period, until June 1915, reporters were systematically excluded from reporting the war by the British and the French armies.

But the message came through loud and clear from Wiegand's headline stories that Germany and its ally Austria welcomed reporters from neutral countries. Another U P correspondent, William Shepherd, tested the waters by presenting himself at the Austrian consulate in Berlin and asking to go to the Austrian front. "We will be delighted to have an American newspaperman tell the truth about Austria," the consul said.

What a pleasant, shocking contrast from his treatment by the Allies. Just a month earlier French soldiers had arrested Shepherd when he stumbled onto the fighting at Soissons. They held him until he pledged not to divulge the name of the town or any details of the fighting in his articles. Germany and Austria, on the other hand, actually wanted the United States to know what was going on in their countries, wanted reporters to visit their front lines, wanted to tell their side of the story. It was enough to make a correspondent's head spin.

Shepherd was U P's "roving correspondent," sent to Europe at the start of the war to supplement its staff in the national capitals. He quickly proved his worth by landing a coveted interview with Britain's First Lord of the Admiralty Winston Churchill. Now he hoped to fill the gap in the coverage of Austria. Events in Austria had been almost totally absent from the world news. The country had been blamed for starting the war with its ultimatum to Serbia about Archduke Ferdinand's assassination, but Austria's story had never been told in the United States. Such an oversight seemed inexplicable given that Austria, more so than any other belligerent, had entered the war with a plan for dealing with the press.

On July 28, 1914, the day Austria-Hungary declared war on Serbia, it established the Imperial War Press Bureau, the Kriegspressequartier (K P Q), to handle all wartime press relations and propaganda. In the opening days of the war, it accredited 118 reporters with its army, including correspondents from Germany, Austria, Switzerland, Sweden, and Denmark. These reporters, photographers, artists, and filmmakers took up residence in a town about ninety

8. In October 1914 William Shepherd of United Press enrolled in Austria-Hungary's Kriegspressequartier (War Press Bureau), which conducted neutral correspondents on guided tours of the fighting. Source: Historic Images.

miles from the front, where Austria improvised a school for war correspondents. Reporters purchased horses, saddles, uniforms, and side arms and trained in their use. "Every morning they got on their horse and rode in a circle, riding-school fashion, around a riding-instructor. Later in the day they filled a near-by forest with the sounds of revolver practice." The ridiculousness of this preparation soon occurred to someone and it was abandoned, but the KPQ continued to operate as a quasi-military unit.

Austro-Hungarian and German correspondents could "enlist" in the KPQ for the duration of the war in lieu of military service. Correspondents from neutral nations accepted into the KPQ took up temporary residence and could not leave without military permission. Lodging, food, wine, and tobacco were provided for free, along with a soldier-servant to tend to each reporter's needs. They received a physical examination, inoculations, and the distinctive armband with the Austrian colors of black and gold marked with "Kriegspressequartier" that identified them as a KPQ correspondents.

On a somewhat regular basis, a group of correspondents would be taken on a tour, chaperoned by an officer "whose complex and nerve-racking task it was to answer all questions, make all arrangements, report to each local commandant, pass sentries, and comfortably waft his flock of civilians through the maze of barriers which cover[ed] every foot, so to speak, of the region near the front."

On these well-scripted excursions, correspondents might visit the scene of a previous battle, captured cities, munitions factories, prisoner-of-war camps, or the front lines during a lull in the fighting. They would meet officers, civil officials, or civilians. They could see reserve units heading to the front and the wounded being transported to the rear. The scenes were not all that different from what they had glimpsed in Belgium and northern France, but they saw more of them, and more importantly they saw them not as an outsider, resented or arrested by the soldiers, but as an official part of the army. Between such excursions the correspondents wrote up their adventures, submitted them to the censors, sent them off to their publications, and awaited their next tour.

When American reporters of the Great War returned home, they were often asked, "What did you actually see?" It was a good question, given that most people imagined that the job of a war correspondent was to cover . . . well, war, actual battles, and there had been little battlefield reporting coming out of Europe. "Since returning to New York every second man I know greets me sympathetically with 'So, you had to come home, hey? They wouldn't let you see a thing,'" Richard Harding Davis complained after returning from France. He penned a somewhat bitter rejoinder to those questioners.

> If I had time I told them all I saw was the German, French, Belgian and English armies in the field, Belgium in ruins and flames, the Germans sacking Louvain, in the Dover straits dreadnaughts, cruisers, torpedo destroyers, submarines, hydroplanes; in Paris bombs falling from airships and a city put to bed at 9 o'clock; battlefields covered with dead men; fifteen miles of artillery firing across the Aisne at fifteen miles of artillery; the bombardment of Rheims, with shells lifting the roofs as easily as you would lift the cover of a chafing dish and digging holes in the street with the cathedral on fire; I saw hundreds of thousands of soldiers from India, Senegal, Morocco, Ireland, Australia, Algiers, Bavaria, Prussia, Scotland, saw them at the front in action, saw them marching over the whole northern half of Europe, saw them wounded and helpless, saw thousands of women and children sleeping under hedges and haystacks while on every side of them their homes blazing in flames or crashing in ruins. That was a part of what I saw.

The flavor of the war came from more than the fighting. The massive logistics, the social and economic transformation of a nation, the psychology of a population, the story of one soldier, one refugee, or the contents of one ruined house told volumes. Two months into the war, the whole conflict still played out as a kaleidoscope of images, the first pieces of a puzzle being put into place that teased reporters with the slowly emerging picture.

In October 1914 William Shepherd and *New York Evening Post* reporter Robert Dunn became the first American reporters to join the KPQ. They settled into the quiet routine of the isolated village headquarters. Here the fighting on the western front might have been on the other side of the world. There was no mention of France or England, only Russia. Even the conflict with Serbia was only a proxy dispute for the true struggle against the Russian Empire. Six million men faced one another along the nearly one-thousand-mile battle line of the eastern front. It wound not through the garden-like countryside of France but through mountains and the wild, primitive landscape that stretched from the Baltic to the Black Sea.

Despite the carefully organized and orchestrated conditions of KPQ operations, the tours did not always prove so sanitized and the turn of events not always what Austria-Hungary would have preferred to be reported to the outside world. When Dunn and Shepherd arrived at the KPQ, the struggle with Russia raged around the fortified town of Przemyśl, in Austria's northernmost province of Galicia, near the present-day border of Poland and Ukraine. Russia had captured most of eastern Galicia in the opening weeks of the war, and now only the fortress at Przemyśl remained in Austrian hands. But Austria had recently pushed Russian forces back in some sectors, and it was this success that the KPQ wanted the correspondents to see.

A very clear picture emerged for William Shepherd and Robert Dunn during their two-month stay with the KPQ, October–December 1914. They saw, quite simply, the desperation and misery of the Austro-Hungarian Empire. They witnessed the empire suffer one of the most complete military routs of the war and were kept from seeing a second rout. The reporting of their KPQ tour made headline news in America and animated the memoirs they published during the war. Their experience on this conducted war tour provides an interesting example of what correspondents saw, what they understood of their experience, what they were permitted to see, and what they were permitted to report.

In the last week of October, the KPQ organized a tour for six journalists to the besieged city of Przemyśl. It was a war correspondent's dream come true, to be credentialed with an army, visiting an actual battle, in a theater of war that had received little eyewitness reporting. The sixty-mile, two-day journey from KPQ headquarters in the village of Neu Sandec to Przemyśl began with a sobering scene at the rail station. A trainload of wounded, on its way to hospitals in the rear, stopped at the station to unload a single body. On the station platform, men in rubber suits wrapped the body in a cloth. A Red Cross worker unfolded a large sheet of paper and fastened it to the railcar. It read in bold red letters: CHOLERA. The KPQ had inoculated the correspondents against the disease, but the incident served as a chilling introduction to the unknown dangers of the excursion.

Hour by hour a ceaseless line of trains moved toward the front, loaded with ammunition, food, and supplies. In the opposite direction rolled trains loaded with wounded and Russian prisoners. By three that afternoon Dunn had counted seven hospital trains, one with twenty-seven cars. Many bore the same cholera warning.

When the rail line reached its closest point to the battlefield, everything was transferred to horse-drawn wagons, including the correspondents. They fell in with the thousands of wagons plodding through the mud. Not one motorized vehicle to be seen. Horses worked to exhaustion, then fell dead. Bloodied and bandaged soldiers stumbled in the opposite direction along the side of the road. The sick and wounded were being sent from the city to travel on foot the fifty miles to a hospital in the rear. These pitiful creatures collected like moths around the numerous roadside shrines bearing a cross and a figure of Christ. Each shrine had its share of the dead and those praying for deliverance. In the grip of this atavistic scene, Dunn had to pause and remind himself of the year. The scene might have been Napoleonic or medieval.

The Russian army was tightening its grip on the beleaguered city. Creeping beneath a continuous exchange of artillery rounds, the supply wagons wove through successive defensive lines of trenches and barbed wire into a vast army camp. For the correspondents their KPQ armband served as a free pass to see everything and talk with everyone. They visited artillery positions, trenches, and forward rifle pits; talked to individual soldiers; and dined with officers. No one questioned their right to be there.

Of course, having a stranger in their midst barely registered with Austrian soldiers because they were an army of strangers. No American-like melting pot unified the hugely diverse Austrian Empire of Poles, Slovenes, Czechs, Hungarians, Slovaks, Croats, Ruthenians, Serbs, and Romanians. Military orders of the day occasionally had to be written in up to fifteen different languages to accommodate the various national and ethnic groups still using their unique languages. In some units English was the most shared tongue because so many of the men had been to America or had relatives living there.

Because Dunn wore a marine campaign hat and gaiters, he stood out in a crowd. "Are you an American?" many soldiers asked. They had worked in the Pittsburgh steel mills or waited tables in New York City. They were naturalized American citizens, went one often-repeated story. But it had been their misfortune to be visiting relatives in Austria without a passport when the war began. Unable to establish their U.S. citizenship, they were impressed into the Austrian army.

News about the thousands of American citizens serving voluntarily or involuntarily in the armies of the belligerent nations received little coverage during the war, except for the aviators flying for France. Unlike the news restrictions on the anonymous front-line soldiers, pilots could be mentioned by name. These American flyers would eventually form the unit known as the Lafayette Escadrille, and its members become America's first war heroes. News stories also glorified the role played by the many American doctors, nurses, and ambulance drivers volunteering with every army prior to U.S. entry into the war.

"What one writes for publication of life in Przemysl must be shorn of military verbiage, even of statements too strikingly human," Dunn pointed out in his war memoir, *Five Fronts*, published the following year. The explanation "Paragraph cut out by censors" appeared in Shepherd's syndicated accounts of Przemyśl. Censors removed details about the extent of Austria's battle with cholera. But they still allowed a good deal of the horror to get through. The nightmarish sights and sounds of battle clearly overwhelmed Shepherd—the continuous screech and explosion of artillery rounds, the dead and wounded, the struggles of doctors and priests to comfort the dying. "I've never learned any words that would tell such a story," Shepherd confessed in a newspaper account that went by mail to the United States. "I've found a story I couldn't write."

Missing from the newspaper accounts but made clear in Shepherd's 1917 memoir of his war experience, *Confessions of a War Correspondent*, was the sense of doom among the defenders and the journalists' dramatic departure from the city. With great fanfare the Austrian crown prince arrived in Przemyśl by automobile to attend a public mass for those soldiers selected to remain in the city. That night the crown prince, select army units, and the KPQ correspondents began the precipitous evacuation of Przemyśl. All order and planning broke down in the slow-motion tangle of wagons and trains moving away from the doomed city. In euphemistic military speak this was a "strategic move," a "shifting of forces," a "new plan," which was how it was explained to the correspondents. Dunn and Shepherd didn't believe it, but censors told them that any story depicting the departure from Przemyśl as a hasty retreat would not get through. Although no one suspected it at the time, the Austrian defenders held out for several more months.

The KPQ deposited its charges in Budapest to gather more-positive stories. The titanic struggle they had just escaped seemed a world away from the pleasant, business-as-usual capital of Hungary. Dunn visited a factory where women made munitions. He met American Red Cross volunteers, who were beginning to sour on the selfless zeal that first brought them here. He interviewed a Hungarian countess, who was the daughter of a Montana copper king. She worried about her husband away at the front, whether he had the right clothing for a Polish winter. There had been a trend before the war for socialites to marry impoverished nobility. Now these newly titled Americans were scattered across the warscape of Europe, on every side of the conflict.

The United Press particularly favored such human-interest stories to make the war more accessible for readers. Every day of the war was filled with complicated military and diplomatic developments, conducted by a cast of characters with unfamiliar names, happening in unfamiliar—sometimes unpronounceable—locations. People stories made it come alive.

Shepherd and Dunn wrapped up their KPQ experience with a second military excursion, this time to Serbia. They traveled with a successful Austrian advance into Serbia that later turned into a disaster when the Serbs rebounded and drove a broken Austrian army back to its own territory. Austria hustled the reporters back to Budapest, keeping from them the full truth of this disaster.

These two Austrian tours demonstrated some of the problems inherent in guided war tours, which would soon become the standard method for delivering and controlling the news for all the belligerents. Correspondents got a taste of the war but, for the most part, saw only what their hosts wanted them to see. The KPQ began to offer less traumatic adventures. When Arthur Ruhl joined the KPQ in early 1915, he described the experience as part "tourist's bureau, rest-cure, and a sort of military club" and complained of not getting close to the actual fighting. Learning how to handle the press was still a work in progress for all the armies, but Austria had learned an important lesson.

German War Tours

Journalists from the neutral United States had been popping in and out of Germany since the start of the war, needing only their passports for travel. But the flow increased after the fall of Antwerp in October 1914, and entry screening began to tighten. Horace Green, correspondent for the *New York Evening Post*, left Antwerp for Holland with the flood of Belgian refugees. In two weeks of news gathering, he had seen three armies in the field and watched the effect of war on the people of Belgium and France. Now he traveled to Germany to get the German point of view.

Green estimated that he had been stopped for questioning 130 times during his two weeks of news gathering in Belgium.

To ease his work in Germany, he made sure to get his passport viséd by the German ambassador in The Hague. To establish his credibility he carried letters of introduction from former president Theodore Roosevelt, Germany's U.S. ambassador Count von Bernstorff, and noted Harvard professor Hugo Münsterberg. Despite those documents, he still faced a grilling on entry to the country and was briefly abused by a crowd that thought him to be an English spy. England had become the focus of all hatred, and it was hard to distinguish an English-speaking American from the enemy.

Traveling around Berlin and into rural parts of the country on his own put him under constant surveillance. Green sensed that the war was beginning to weigh on the civilian population. At the Casualty List Office, he watched parents and wives scan the vast, posted lists of the wounded and dead. Outside Berlin he heard fervent wishes for peace. "Go home and tell your country what I think, and say, and many others like me," said the Frankfurt doctor he met on the train who thought peace must come now. He had been to Berlin to verify the death of his son and was now traveling to Aachen to claim the body.

Green became one of the first reporters to examine the impact of the war on Germany. Its leaders had predicted a rapid victory that would see the troops return home before the leaves fell from the trees in the autumn of 1914. Traveling outside Berlin gave Green a first hint of wartime frustration, "a glimpse through the veil of public optimism into the wells of sorrow hidden for the sake of public duty." To address this very issue, the German Foreign Office had just created the Central Office for Public Mood and designated an official to manage neutral correspondents.

Reporting on Germany's internal conditions would take on greater importance in 1915 and throughout the rest of the war, but for now at least, visiting the battle lines still served as the gold standard for neutral correspondents covering the western front. Robert Dunn arrived in the German capital in January 1915 with the best of credentials for such a tour, fresh from his visits to the eastern front with the Kriegspressequartier. He hoped to get a similar firsthand experience on the western front. He also had a cousin fighting in the German army.

The bar at the popular Adlon Hotel, where Dunn stayed, had become the gathering place for the cluster of Americans recently arrived in Berlin. Many of them claimed to be magazine writers waiting for a visit to the front. Most would never get there. Legitimate correspondents who were patient enough to work through the considerable red tape could expect to be taken on a war tour.

Dunn landed on a guided tour, along with a Hollander, a Norwegian, and several other American reporters, including Edward Lyell Fox (*New York American*) and John Reed. Dunn's cousin was added to the group for good measure. Unlike Dunn, Fox and Reed were not obvious candidates for such a tour. Fox established his reputation by collaborating on an autobiography of a German spy who had converted to the British cause, Armgaard Karl Graves. The book, *The Secrets of the German War Office*, was published the day before the war began. By the time Fox appeared in Berlin, the book had already gone through ten printings.

Reed, a socialist, wrote for *Metropolitan Magazine*. The publication liked its thoughtful articles on politics and social issues to be one exciting tick to the left of center. Reed had already interviewed the German socialist Karl Liebknecht, a member of the Reichstag controversial for his opposition to the war. Reed had soared to fame on the basis of his coverage of the Mexican revolution, when he traveled with the army of revolutionary Pancho Villa for four months, sending regular dispatches that enthralled the magazine's readers. The magazine rhapsodized about his literary brand of journalism: "The bursting energy, the continuous flow. . . . Such writing was like the sweep of sudden wind come to shake the closed windows of the literary scene out of their frames."

From Mexico Reed rushed to Colorado to cover the United Mine Workers' strike and its brutal suppression. Although Reed's framing of the strike in terms of class warfare with a capitalists-versus-workers interpretation gave *Metropolitan* editors pause, they still considered him the ideal candidate to cover the war in

Europe. When he arrived in the war zone, at the age of twenty-seven, he was among the best-known and highest-paid journalists in America.

Their tour of the Belgium war zone spent two days passing through "shot-to-pieces" villages, offering the sort of views of destroyed buildings that had become standard fare in American newspapers. They toured a hospital and watched a general award Iron Cross medals to wounded soldiers. Reed reported that one soldier, who had lost both legs, threw his medal on the floor. Always adept at finding the right detail to wring drama or poignancy from a scene, Reed added, "He was a famous long-distance runner."

From army commander Crown Prince Rupprecht of Bavaria, the correspondents received extraordinary permission to spend a night in the trenches, in the midst of active fighting. Sharing a night with the fighting men promised that degree of closeness that correspondents craved to understand the experience of combat. Of course, as Dunn's experience in Przemyśl had proved, it also came with risk.

One entered and left the trenches at night. The group of journalists fell in with rested soldiers and supplies flowing into the trenches near the town of Arras, while exhausted, wounded, and dead fighters were moved in the opposite direction. They slogged through the foot of standing water in the trenches while rocket flares outlined no-man's-land in harsh silhouettes and bullets flew like "swarming wasps."

The local commander, Colonel Meyer, welcomed the visitors to his battered farmhouse headquarters with a dinner of canned stew and beer. They finished just in time for the nightly concert. Through a telephone line connected to army headquarters came the exquisite sounds of a live piano concert. One by one the men passed around the telephone receiver to hear the notes.

In a warm exchange of toasts, Colonel Meyer made a request of his journalist guests. "Tell them that we are not barbarians. I have a sister who lives in Wyckoff, New York, and I'm afraid that by reading your newspapers, she thinks that I've become a terrible ogre." It was one measure of the effectiveness of Allied propaganda that Germany never shook the label of the barbarian Hun, enemy of civilization, that had been pinned on it early in the war.

"Everything seems to be in a daze. It is all too incredible," Fox mused about that outpost of warmth and creature comforts in such hellish surroundings. The food was tasty, the flow of Munich beer limitless. They were topping off the meal with coffee, cigars, a cordial, and now a concert amid the welcoming companionship of German officers. "And outside the sky is hideous with war," Fox observed, "and eight hundred meters away are the French. And this is war."

Back outside, word spread of friendly strangers in the trenches. The soldiers turned from their shooting to greet the reporters or shake their hands. "Amerikaner?" they called, and a few shared the names of relatives in the States.

Dunn felt a comradeship with these men, under assault from "them," the unseen French soldiers in the unseen opposing trenches who were trying to kill them. It brought him to a state of mind that led to one of the worst indiscretions possible for a war correspondent. At a spot just 140 meters from the French lines, a German soldier asked the correspondents, "Do you want to do something?" When Dunn answered, "Yes," the soldier offered his rifle. "The next moment it was in my hands, with the muzzle pointing through the eyehole atop the bank, across that short and hellish space. Be it on my head, I did it, fired twice," Dunn recalled.

Dunn offered a tortured rationale for this action in his 1915 war book, *Five Fronts*. Chances of hitting anyone were infinitesimal, he explained. It was in response to being under fire or in brotherhood with the brave Bavarian soldiers in the trench. He imagined that the neutral President Wilson, in these same circumstances, would have taken a shot. The incident brought him some infamy when it became known to the French. The French newspaper *Temps* labeled him an "assassin." Back in the United States, *Life* magazine voiced the general reaction to the incident: "For a newspaper correspondent to take pot-shots at men in battle merely to see how it feels to kill a man" was shocking. *Life* suggested that Dunn stay out of France unless he wanted to add to his wartime experiences by being stood against a wall and executed by firing squad. The last word on the incident came in Dunn's 1956 autobiography, *World Alive*, in which he said that he had fired "high into the air."

To give Edward Fox a better overview of the battle that extended far into the distance, an officer led him splashing blindly through the dark trenches to raised ground. Zipping bullets chased them from protective tree to tree until they gained a vantage point on the battle. Fox experienced it as "all color and noise—unearthly colors and unearthly noises." The reddish line of rifle fire and the yellowish flash of shells painted a ghastly scene. "I hear their fierce, harsh croaking and the deafening booms," he reported. Through the officer's binoculars, he watched the distant exchange of cannon fire continually brighten and dim and imagined the men climbing from their trenches under such an assault, and the bullets riddling their bodies. "I've had enough," he told the officer, and they descended into the relative safety of a bunker, where they spent the night. The correspondents' experience with the horrors of the trenches had come to an end.

Firsthand accounts of the fighting provided the sensational stories that sold newspapers. Those correspondents who reported on the fighting became the early celebrities of the war. They published under a byline, at a time when most reporters wrote anonymous stories. Their eyewitness accounts served as a first installment on the emerging character of this war. It had come to be understood as a "modern war," to indicate not simply the latest iteration of human conflict but some monstrous new incarnation spawned of the industrial age. Fifteen miles of cannon firing at fifteen miles of cannon, as Richard Harding Davis had observed. Aerial weapons and undersea weapons, larger and faster methods of slaughter, pushing the limits of human imagination and endurance.

The April 1915 issue of *Metropolitan Magazine* included both John Reed's account of his war tour, "In the German Trenches," and an excerpt from Richard Harding Davis's book *With the Allies*. They stood in stark contrast. Davis used his brilliant descriptive powers to portray the German war machine as an evil threatening civilization, an evil against which America must prepare itself. For Reed, the upstart literary war correspondent, the horrors and absurdities of war dehumanized the working-class men who fought it on both sides. By revealing the actual experience of the fighting man—the monotony, the desperate fatigue, the muddy trenches, the apocalyptic fighting, the earth-shaking artillery assaults, the complete horror of this new kind of war—Reed struck a vivid antiwar tone. In the issue Davis's excerpt received preferential treatment, along with a full-page photo of the dashing war correspondent.

Like Dunn, Arthur Ruhl also made the rounds of Central Power tours. Because he did it later in both Austria and Germany, however, he encountered a more sanitized experience. He described his German army tour in the spring of 1915 as a "Cook's tour" of the war, a reference to the popular Cook & Son travel agency famous for packaging European vacations. Along with several other Americans, a Greek, an Italian (Italy had not yet entered the war), a Spaniard, and a Swede, Ruhl's group raced through a well-orchestrated program as helpless as a "package in a pneumatic tube," traveling by express train and military automobiles, through a blur of "grey capes, heel clicking, stiff bows from the waist, and punctilious military salutes."

They might be under fire one minute and the next touring a palace, barracks, or a museum. Ruhl outlined a typical schedule: "At noon the guard is turned out in honor, at four you are watching distant shell fire from the Belgian dunes; at eleven crawling under a down quilt at some French hotel." The captain-guide, always perfectly attired, spoke all languages fluently and capably shepherded his charges through their dizzying schedule, past countless sentries and stubborn guards demanding papers and passes, and then delivered them back to their Berlin hotel.

To Ruhl's way of thinking, scripted tours were not the ideal way to see the war, but they gave journalists a piece of the story. "The front was a big and rather accidental place," he conceded. "You can scarcely touch it anywhere without bringing back something to help complete the civilian's puzzle picture of the war." Ruhl would later contribute an essay titled "The War Correspondent" to the first volume of the ongoing chronicle of the conflict,

The Story of the Great War, in which he made the case that correspondents could capture events in two ways. One was the personal experience of the eyewitness reporter as "he looks into the face of war." The other involved the correspondent sitting behind the lines and sifting through the cascade of reports and rumors that streamed in from a hundred sources, armed with atlases and maps, and a telephone call away from countless experts.

What had become patently clear at this point in the conflict was that correspondents no longer went to war; rather they were taken to war. No reporter could see or hope to understand a battle line that extended over four hundred miles in the West and nearly one thousand in the East. At most he could see a mile or so of that line, view one episode rather than the whole struggle. However, if one hoped for the personal experience, the "sensations of the individual as he looks into the face of war," the war tour was the way to do it.

The extent to which Germany controlled the war news flowing to the United States flamed to controversy in August 1915 with a series of provocative articles in the *World* that charged Germany with attempts to influence reporters, subsidize pro-German publications, and purchase newspapers and news syndicates. The article also charged Germany with financing professional lecturers and moving pictures and the publishing of books that promoted the German viewpoint. Edward Lyell Fox was specifically mentioned in regard to evidence that the German government had paid his expenses for a 1914 visit to the country and that it was willing to subsidize further visits because of his favorable coverage.

The charges were of little concern to Fox at the time. His book *Behind the Scenes in Warring Germany* had appeared to much acclaim, and as the *World* articles broke he was traveling on the lecture circuit with the movie *The Battle and Fall of Przemysl*, shot by American filmmaker Albert Dawson. Dawson worked for the American Correspondent Film Company, an enterprise secretly created by Germany to promote pro-German sentiments and help to maintain U.S. neutrality. The extent of German influence over Fox would emerge at a Senate hearing in the immediate aftermath of the war, when Fox admitted to fabricating stories of Russian atrocities. He had done so at the instruction of the German Foreign Office to counter the claims of atrocities being leveled against the German army in Belgium.

Germany's management of war news had been a work-in-progress through 1915. The War Press Bureau (Kriegpresseamt) had come into existence under the direct control of the military. It controlled all information about army operations for distribution abroad. It created and distributed periodicals, sponsored the publication of pamphlets and books, coordinated censorship, and guided correspondents on visits to the front.

Toward the end of 1915, the War Press Bureau summoned together all neutral reporters then working in Germany for a bit of good news. It had been decided to allow journalists to visit the front lines more frequently. They would be given more opportunities to witness battles and have contact with the troops. However, for this to be arranged, it would be necessary for correspondents to sign a pledge, agreeing:

1. To remain in Germany for the duration of the war, unless given special permission to leave by German authorities.

2. To guarantee that dispatches would be published in the United States precisely as sent from Germany, that is to say, as edited and passed by the military censors.

3. To supply their own headlines for their dispatches, and to guarantee that these, and none others, would be printed.

All the major correspondents permanently stationed in Berlin signed the pledge. Those few reporters who refused to sign were henceforth excluded from conducted tours.

Conditions inside Germany

As 1916 dawned, and the world stumbled wearily through the second year of the cataclysm, it was not greater access to German battlefield news that American newspapers desired; rather it was a clear assessment of conditions behind the battle lines. With access to raw materials and foodstuffs cutoff by Britain's stifling naval blockade, how much longer could Germany hold out? Given the murderous stalemate on the battlefield, were German leaders still intent on pursuing the war or desirous of peace? Were its people starving? What was the morale of the population and the troops? Would Germany's economic failures, rather than its military successes, be the determining factor in the war?

Two American reporters ventured into Germany in the summer of 1916 to visit the front lines in the economic war. Their articles about what they discovered ran that November in competing New York newspapers, and both found wider distribution in book form early in 1917, as the United States agonized over its entry into the war.

As a journalist, attorney, peace activist, and social reformer, Madeleine Zabriskie Doty seemed a good choice to report objectively on conditions in the German Empire. Carrying credentials from both the *New York Tribune* and the *Chicago Tribune,* she also traveled on a charitable mission to deliver funds to support German war orphans. For that reason it was thought she would be given official cooperation and enjoy unusual access to agencies supporting women and children.

Doty found life in Germany bleak. War suffering and privations weighed heavily on the people. "There are but two topics of conversation—war and food shortages," she reported. "That is the whole of life. . . . Life has become a mere existence, a prison existence." People assembled at two locations: food shops and the posted war bulletins that announced battlefield casualties. Walking the streets of Berlin one night, she came upon a small crowd of people gathered around the war bulletin, sliding their fingers along the list, searching for a familiar name. Doty estimated that the list, covering only the dates August 17–21, included forty-four thousand names of the dead, wounded, and missing.

Doty's subsequent book about her Germany visit, published only days before the United States entered the war, used the title *Short Rations,* which indicates the focus of much of her reporting. Meatless days, fatless days, artificial "ersatz" foods, meager portions, severe rationing—the obsession with food captured Doty as much as the people she wrote about. She reported a good deal on what she ate and what foods were available. She visited several tenements and described the travails of a typical family—a mother, nine children, and a grandmother, in two rooms and a kitchen. They could not afford to eat the subsidized meals at the public food kitchens. The mother had to run a gauntlet of shops and interrogations in government offices just to replace her worn-out socks. Everyone in the family was listless and undernourished. The six-month-old baby could not raise its arms. Only babies under six months of age received a milk allowance of a pint a day. The family was living on tea and potatoes. Doty encountered difficulty putting to use the five hundred dollars she carried for war orphans. She could not feed or clothe children when there was no food or clothing to be had.

After the war Germany's wartime ambassador to the United States, Count von Bernstorff, complained that German propaganda in America had been ineffective because Germany did not understand the psychology of the average American. They were not as dry and calculating as Germans but rather possessed a "great, though superficial, sentimentality." According to Bernstorff, Germany had tried to explain and justify its actions logically, whereas it would have been better served simply to have publicized the plight of its women and children, starving because of the British naval blockade.

Because they provided glimpses of a despondent population, wasting away physically and emotionally, Madeleine Doty's articles and book put a human face on the German population and empathized with their suffering. She provided some of the first reporting of the war to touch America's sentimentality. The German people are not "barbarians," she assured her readers. "They are like ourselves, just folks, kindly and generous, deceived and browbeaten by a ruthless military group."

One reviewer, commenting on Doty's book only a few weeks after American entry into the war, noted ironically that to fight Germany we had to hate Germany. "Hate and ammunition had to be manufactured in preparation of war. It doesn't do to let the supply of either run low. If we are to hate Germany, Madeleine Doty's book, 'Short Rations,' ought to be suppressed. You cannot hate starving women and children. You can ignore them, but you cannot want to make war on them."

Despite this reviewer's concern and the theories of Ambassador von Bernstorff, Doty's reportage on Germany's food crisis did not change U.S. support for the Allied naval blockade or weaken the resolve with which the United States entered the fighting. If anything Doty's implied linkage between food shortages and public unrest with the prospect of a revolution to topple military leaders gave logical, if not sentimental, support to the economic war.

In 1916 the *New York World* concluded that the reporting coming out of Germany had lost objectivity. The *World* already had a correspondent in Germany, Karl von Wiegand, but it was felt that through sympathy or censorship, his reporting had become too friendly to the German cause, whereas the reporting found elsewhere in the Allied press went to the opposite extreme of consistently demonizing Germany. The *World*'s energetic, young city editor, Herbert Bayard Swope, known for his scrupulous accuracy and objectivity, was just the right person to bring a balanced perspective to the issue. Also a visit to Germany early in the war had left Swope with a deep appreciation for the German people and the country's military capabilities.

Unlike Madeleine Doty's first-person narrator, buffeted by her German impressions, Swope adopted the detached tone of an objective observer. Although he reached the same superficial conclusion as Doty—"Life in Germany is not pleasant to-day"—he gave more weight to Germany's organizational ingenuity in sustaining its war effort. The somber mood that now gripped the country was in fact a measure of its strength.

Having been in Germany at the start of the war, Swope could compare the mood of 1914 to that in 1916. When he did, two major shifts in attitude became clear. The buoyant arrogance with which Germany went to war had disappeared. German thinking had shifted

9. Herbert Bayard Swope poses with German soldiers around an antiaircraft gun in 1916. Swope was the first recipient of the Pulitzer Prize for Reporting in 1917 for a series of articles titled "Inside the German Empire." Source: New York World-Telegram and the Sun Newspaper Photograph Collection, Prints and Photographs Division, Library of Congress, LC-USZ62-132306.

from one of confidence of certain victory to fear of defeat. The slogan on everyone's lips had gone from *siegen* (conquer or win) to *durchhalten* (stick it out or hold on), exposing an iron resolve that would certainly keep the country in the war. Not everyone in Germany had supported a war of conquest, but everyone, with all his or her fiber, supported a war for the continued existence of Germany.

The other dramatic shift in attitude since his earlier visit was a pronounced resentment of the United States, a contempt for its high-minded neutrality. Allied armies were fighting the war and killing German soldiers with American munitions. The chief of the War Press Bureau in Berlin referred all American correspondents to the three artillery shells sitting on his desk. They had been manufactured in the *neutral* United States. He would always add that he had been wounded by one of them. Swope endured rousing diatribes from officials voicing their contempt for the United States. German leaders did not fear U.S. entry into the war. They had little respect for the U.S. Army or Navy. However, whether America became a belligerent or not, its economic muscle would influence the outcome of the war.

Swope carried high-level endorsements, including letters from acting secretary of state Frank L. Polk, New York mayor John Mitchel, and even President Wilson, which allowed him to arrange interviews with leaders and gain access to the front. During his two-month stay, he interviewed Chancellor Bethmann-Hollweg and Minister of Foreign Affairs Dr. Alfred Zimmerman and visited the front at the Somme. He left the country in September convinced that Germany could not conquer Europe, but also that it could not be defeated. And contrary to Doty's conclusion, he felt the country was in a surprisingly good economic and emotional state.

During his journey home Swope accompanied American ambassador James Gerard, who allowed Swope's voluminous notes to travel in the diplomatic pouch in order to avoid censorship. After the ambassador made his report to the president, Swope visited Wilson himself to share his assessment of conditions in Germany.

Swope's articles began running daily on the front page of the

World on November 4, simultaneous with Doty's articles in the *Tribune*. His writing was notable for its thoroughness in assessing the military, social, and economic conditions without resorting to the sensationalism common in much war reporting. The overarching conclusion: Germany was hard-pressed, but its spirit was unbroken. When the Pulitzer Prizes were awarded for the first time in 1917, Herbert Bayard Swope received the award in the category of reporting for his series of articles titled "Inside the German Empire."

CHAPTER FIVE

Pushing the Limits of Reporting on the Western Front

The only real news written by Americans who are known to and trusted by the American public comes from the German side; as a result of this, the sympathizers with the cause of the Allies hear nothing whatever about the trials and achievements of the British and French Armies.

—THEODORE ROOSEVELT, letter to British foreign secretary Sir Edward Grey, January 22, 1915

On October 10, 1914, the *New York Times* reported the surrender of Antwerp, the capital of free Belgium. The brief article included a convenient map that outlined a considerable bulge in the western front along which the Germans pressed their advance hard against the French cities of Rheims and Verdun in the south and in the north against the Belgian city of Ypres.

The loss of Antwerp meant that E. Alexander Powell of the *New York World* had to find a new home. Since early in the war, Powell had been comfortably ensconced at Antwerp's fashionable Hôtel St. Antoine. Initially it served as a good base for daily forays from the city in search of the fighting. Each night he could return to the safe luxury of the St. Antoine to write his story and cable it off to the *World*. But soon the war came to him. From the St. Antoine's rooftop, he watched a giant zeppelin airship cruise malevolently above the city and drop bombs so close that they rattled the hotel to its foundation. It was the first aerial bombardment of a city in history.

As the city came under siege, the nervous Belgians briefly arrested Powell, then released him. He sheltered in cellars when

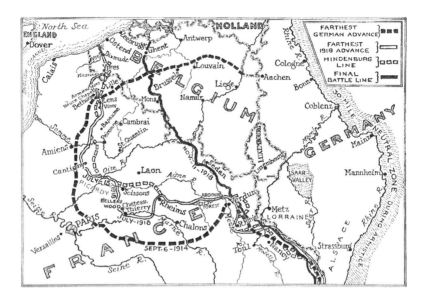

10. This map shows the area of Belgium and northern France that constituted the western front. Source: Frank J. Mackey, *Forward March* (Chicago: Disabled American Veterans of the World War, Department of Rehabilitation, 1934), 17.

the siege guns threw their 1,800-pound shells into the city. He saw Britain's First Lord of the Admiralty, Winston Churchill swoop in like a savior with a contingent of marines in a desperate attempt to forestall the city's inevitable capitulation. He fled the city with the panicky refugees and then returned as a diplomatic courier. When he discovered that the U.S. consul and his entire staff had left the city, Powell briefly occupied the consulate and took charge of American interests in the city, an action described by the U.S. embassy in London as "the damnedest piece of impertinence."

Antwerp was Powell's scoop. It had given him the fullest range of wartime experience imaginable. But even the best first-person war adventure did not count for much if you couldn't get it to your newspaper. At one point during the siege when the cable went down, a Belgian priest volunteered to walk eight miles to the nearest cable office to send off one of Powell's stories, stating, "The people in England and in America should learn what is happening here in Belgium and how bitterly we need their aid." Powell accepted his offer but realized that those pitifully inadequate, censored cables came as close to telling what was really happening in Belgium as a greeting card from the apocalypse.

Now that the German eagle flew over Antwerp, no reporting would be done from there. Things were not much different in London and Paris, where bottled-up reporters got their only war news from official War Office bulletins. Powell returned to America, so that he could tell the real story of what was happening in Belgium.

Magazine writer Will Irwin was still looking for his first big scoop of the war. After two months in the war zone, he had little to show for it. Along with Irvin Cobb, he had been detained by the Germans; with Richard Harding Davis, he watched from a train window as the Germans burned Louvain. But the newspapermen had reported on those events long before his own accounts appeared in *Collier's* magazine. Unfortunately, war news did not have a long shelf life. Weeks after an event—*days* after an event—American readers were already looking for the next big war story.

Operating out of the French port of Calais that October, Irwin learned about heavy fighting along the British line near the Belgian town of Ypres and set out in that direction by carriage. Relying mostly on London newspapers for his news of the war, he had no clear idea of the fighting in this western part of Belgium known as Flanders. Pervasive censorship kept England in a "fog of ignorance and doubt." Regiment after regiment vanished into the darkness of the war zone and were never heard of again. The British press continued with its vague reports of Belgian, French, and Russian victories and German atrocities.

Things looked promising as Irwin neared Ypres and fell in with battle traffic. Troops and ammunition trucks rushed past him heading toward the sound of artillery, while wounded soldiers flowed in a steady stream toward the rear. This northern edge of the front encompassed a confusing melee of battles. Where one ended and the other began was a matter of conjecture. Irwin paused at a high point along the road to get his bearings and was promptly arrested by a British officer. Having previously been arrested by both the Germans and the French, he was beginning to feel unwanted. After being searched, interrogated, and warned about returning to the war zone, he landed back in Calais. For several days he helped as a stretcher-bearer with the flood of British and Belgian wounded. Then, when it was announced that Calais would be closed to correspondents, he returned to London and joined the growing number of American reporters cooling their heels there as virtual prisoners. Irwin had been threatened with dire consequences if he returned to the continent or if he tried to tell American readers about what the British army was up to.

To Irwin Britain seemed unnervingly detached from the war. Perhaps it was the classic British stiff-upper-lip imperturbability, but "it grated upon us Americans," Irwin observed, "to come from stricken Brussels or Paris and see so many things running at their usual pace in London; to find the cafés open, the inhabitants dressing for dinner, the theatres running. . . . 'England is asleep,' we said."

Pervasive censorship that hid the war from the British public bore some of the blame. "Secrecy, dense and unfathomable, shrouds the whole military game as played out now in Great Britain," Irwin complained. In the first three months of the war, while the British War Office restricted reporters from the front, it issued exactly three brief official communiqués to keep the public informed. A battle that could influence the fate of the nation might be summarized in the most maddening brevity: "Yesterday as a result of a German attack in great force we were obliged slightly to readjust our lines." How could an Englishman become engaged in the war effort if he knew nothing about it? How could he appreciate the need for urgency and commitment if he had not heard rousing stories of heroism and sacrifice?

But it was not just the average citizen. At the highest levels, business continued as usual. For decades Britain knew that war with Germany was inevitable, and yet it had not prepared for war. It knew that Germany could mobilize millions of men overnight through universal conscription, yet Britain muddled along with its small volunteer army. New war policies that were announced were

11. In 1914 nearly all wartime activities were veiled under tight censorship. American journalist Will Irwin had to break the rules to tell Britain and America about how valiantly the British army fought at the Battle of Ypres. Source: Prints and Photographs Division, Library of Congress, LC-USZ62-106245.

not enacted; lessons learned were not implemented. Rather than enlisting the best and brightest minds to run things, hidebound retired army officers directed many government departments. The policy of "muddle through" had grown from "a reproachful catch-word to a creed."

Irwin had once admired in the British character the quality of confidence that Britons could prevail through any ordeal. Now he suspected it to be their biggest flaw. He wrote an article titled "England: The Puzzle, Are Her People Cool or Asleep? Brave or Blind?" Then he set aside war journalism and returned to the United States to help a friend from his undergraduate days at Stanford, a wealthy American engineer living in London named Herbert Hoover. Hoover had been tapped to run a huge relief operation to feed the starving population of German-occupied Belgium: the Commission for Relief in Belgium. The mammoth effort would involve the purchase, transportation, and distribution of food for some seven million people. Irwin accepted Hoover's offer to organize a publicity campaign in America to raise funds for the organization.

The *New York Times* bureau chief in Paris, Wythe Williams, had built up his own huge reserve of frustration trying to cover the war. The French War Office drove up his blood pressure with its senseless restrictions on legitimate news gathering. Like many other journalists, he had been arrested while trying to visit the front and been "paroled," which prevented him from sending any news to the *Times* for a week. Indeed, British monopoly of the transatlantic cable kept him from sending much of the news that he did gather at any time.

Before the war began, he had speculated with his colleagues about how the transatlantic cable would affect their profession once the anticipated conflict began. They had failed to foresee two developments. Unlike their prediction Germany had not cut Britain's cable, preventing news from reaching the United States; instead Britain had cut Germany's cable and could thus prevent all but its own filtered version of news from reaching America. Then, too, they had failed to anticipate that the cable would fuel America's voracious appetite for war news.

Topping Williams's list of wartime annoyances was the swarm of war correspondents who had descended on the continent, or as he called them the "special correspondents," as distinct from the "regular correspondents" such as himself or Karl von Wiegand in Berlin. The regular correspondents had been in Europe since before the war, had a deeper understanding of the culture of their temporary homes, and valued their network of contacts. "Mr. Special Correspondent" swept in like a wrecking ball, ventured out for his souvenir war adventure, and then wrote up a self-serving war exploit for the readers back home. Or, worse, he sat in a café in Calais and invented trips to the front.

In October 1914, three months into this litany of wartime frustration, Williams threw up his hands and took temporary leave of his profession to drive an ambulance at the front. He wanted to do something useful. It required the intervention of the U.S. ambassador, Myron Herrick, to arrange a position for him with the French Red Cross. This work took him exactly where he wanted to be: close to the fighting. But he had to pledge not to do any reporting while serving with the ambulance.

So as 1914 drew to a close, war correspondent Wythe William could be found racing an ambulance along the muddy roads near Amiens, France, dodging shell craters, weaving among lumbering food and ammunition wagons, transporting wounded from field hospitals to evacuation camps for the French Second Army. Will Irwin, living in New York, was publicizing the noble work of the Commission for Relief in Belgium, one of many war charities organized by Americans and competing for their financial support. Alexander Powell was busily telling the story of the war from the vantage point of America. He wrote an article on the fall of Antwerp for *Scribner's Magazine* and a book about the fighting in Belgium, and he also filled lecture halls telling about his war experiences.

But a portent of change came that month when both Irwin and Williams received a summons that would put their journalism careers back on track and involve them in major news stories that helped to change coverage of the war. At the hint of loosening restrictions on reporters, Powell would return to the war zone early in the new year and reveal to America the war in unprecedented, graphic detail.

Will Irwin Tells Britain about Its War

For Will Irwin opportunity knocked in the form of a long cable from an influential American businessman he had met in England, George Gordon Moore. Moore had made his fortune in railroads in America, then transferred his business interests to London, where he now moved in high society. He was a close friend of Sir John French, the field marshal commanding the British Expeditionary Force in France.

Moore's cable assured Irwin that if he returned to England, he would be given a chance to see the war and learn something about what was happening. To avoid the delays of magazine writing, Irwin arranged to work for the *New York Tribune*. The first inkling that something big was afoot occurred when he stepped off the train in London to be greeted by the U.S. ambassador, Walter Hines Page, who wished him well in his endeavor. Reporters generally did not receive such blue-ribbon treatment.

At dinner with Moore, conversation turned to oppressive British censorship, which was hiding the war from both the American and the British public; the secretary of war, Lord Kitchener, who hated reporters; operations of the War Office; and the fighting that occurred the previous fall around Ypres, from which Irwin had been booted. At Ypres the BEF and its commander, Sir John French, had performed well in preventing the German army from turning the Allies' northern flank and completing its link to the sea, Moore explained. Vastly outmanned and outgunned, the British made a valiant stand. Ypres had been the greatest British battle in history in terms of the numbers engaged and the losses sustained. During the fighting bits and pieces came in from various correspondents, but four months after the fact the public had still not heard the details of this glorious military achievement. The story had been "lost, fumbled, obscured in bureaucratic fog."

Moore had discussed the problem with Ambassador Page, Herbert Hoover, and others who were concerned about the state of Anglo-American relations and the abundance of war news coming from Germany. To rectify the situation, they wanted Irwin to tell the story of the British army at the Battle of Ypres. He would be given unprecedented access to information, and arrangements would be made to circumvent War Office censorship so that the story got published in both the United States and England. Journalistic scoops did not come easily in this war, but Irwin recognized one when it fell into his lap. He readily agreed to write the article.

Given access to General French's official reports, maps, and memoranda from the War Office, along with other confidential information, Irwin set to work. He interviewed officers who had helped to direct the fighting, every survivor of the battle he could find, U.S. military attachés, and newspaper men who had seen parts of the battle. The Battle of Ypres had run for sixteen days, beginning in late October. The fighting had been so continuous and jumbled that even those involved could not give a clear account of events. Irwin himself had seen a small piece of the action when he helped to carry the wounded in Calais.

At this point the influential British publisher Lord Northcliffe stepped into the conspiracy. He bought the English rights to the war news from Irwin's employer, the *Tribune*. Irwin's story would be mailed or messengered to the *Tribune* to avoid censors. Once it had been published in the United States, it would appear in Northcliffe's two newspapers, the *Times* of London and the *Daily Mail*. Northcliffe's objective was to force the War Office to change its censorship policy in a way that bolstered civilian morale and support for the war, without divulging any military secrets. He warned Irwin that they might face some heat for going against the War Office, a possibility echoed by Irwin's friend Herbert Hoover. "You'll get your fingers burned," Hoover cautioned. But on the scent of the major story, Irwin persisted.

Irwin shaped the chaos of facts into a coherent, heroic story about the BEF in the opening months of the war, how its meager force conducted a masterful retreat from Mons in the face of vastly superior German forces, helped the French army save Paris at the Battle of the Marne, and then moved to Flanders in October to halt the German attempts to capture the vital coastal ports. No story like this had been written in the war. No reporter had enjoyed this level of access. With the perspective gained by the passage of four months, Irwin could blend narrative with analysis to give a full picture of the battle:

> However heavy the German bombardment, the famous old Cloth Hall, the most beautiful of its kind in Flanders, went unscathed by shells. It was saved, we know now, for a particular purpose. Kaiser Wilhelm himself was moving forward with a special force to a special assault which should finally and definitely break the allied line at Ypres. To do this was to clear Flanders of the Allies; then, as by custom he might, he intended to annex Belgium in the Cloth Hall of Ypres. He came with his own Prussian Guard; it was the Guard which, on the 15th, led another terrible massed attack. It was no less vigorous than the attack of the 31st, but the English, reinforced now by the French, met it better. Again, the dense masses poured in; again the very officers fired until their rifles grew too hot to hold. When, that night, the strength of the German attack was spent, the better part of the Prussian Guard lay dead in a wood—lay at some places in ranks eight deep. . . . It had cost England 50,000 men out of a 120,000 engaged—a proportion of loss greater than any previous war ever knew. It had cost the French and Belgians 70,000. It probably cost the Germans 375,000. That is a half-million in all. The American Civil War has been called the most terrible in modern history. In that one long battle Europe lost as many men as the North lost in the whole of the Civil War.

When Irwin's article, "The Splendid Story of the Battle of Ypres," appeared in the prestigious London *Times* and the popular *Daily Mail* in February 1915, Irwin became an instant celebrity. This was the first real news the British public had received of any British battle, and it glorified the army and its sacrifice. Shopkeepers wanted to shake Irwin's hand; phone calls flooded his hotel switchboard with invitations to tea; and exclusive clubs invited him to speak. Irwin lunched with the Prime Minister Herbert Asquith at 10 Downing Street. One member of Parliament called the article "the greatest battle story in our language." Yielding to popular demand, Northcliffe reprinted the story in a penny pamphlet, with a run of half a million copies.

It was a curious fact during the first year of the war that the British public received much of its important war news from American newspaper reporters. British censors permitted U.S. correspondents to cable to their own newspapers stories that would never have been allowed into British papers. British papers could then justify reprinting these uncensored stories by citing their previous appearance in print. British newspapers published such stories often enough that some American reporters became better known in Britain than in their own country. Such was the case with Will Irwin.

While the Ypres story brought Irwin public acclaim, criticism came from other sources. Jealous reporters resented his special treatment, while they were forced to write stories off the official communiqués and had to play by the rules of censorship. They complained that he had written about a battle that he never even witnessed. The French and British War Offices were also displeased. The French thought Irwin's account gave too much credit to the British army. Additionally, he appeared to have stepped into the middle of a dispute over conduct of the war between the British war secretary Lord Kitchener and the commander at the front, Field Marshal John French. Irwin's story gave much of the credit for Ypres to the field marshal.

For the rest of 1915, Irwin managed several brief visits to France, including an April trip to be on hand for the Second Battle of Ypres, during which Germany introduced the use of poison gas. But after repeated frustrated attempts to operate out of Paris met with more threats of arrest, Irwin once again set a course for home.

Wythe Williams Unveils the French Army

While driving an ambulance for the French in December 1914, Wythe Williams received word to hasten back to Paris. The War Office had at long last decided to send correspondents to the front and would be preparing the list of authorized neutral reporters. When the new year dawned, circumstances had changed dramatically for the *New York Times* reporter. Instead of sneaking to the front, under constant threat of arrest, Williams found himself puffing a cigar in the back of a limousine with two other neutral journalists, being escorted to the front by solicitous army officers. Comfortable lodgings had been arranged in villages behind the trenches; meals awaited them at every stop. Everything they had conspired to see by trickery a few months ago now revealed itself through an orderly schedule of official visits—supply depots, transportation systems, commanding officers, artillery demonstrations, and soldiers in the trenches.

Most interesting of all, their officer escort provided daily briefings about current and past fighting, revealing the position of Allied and German units in the field and explaining German strategy in the opening campaign of the war and how the French army had countered it. The unprecedented candor and transparency seemed to reflect a new attitude of confidence that France finally had in place the war mechanism and the leaders to take it to victory.

Despite the blue-ribbon tour, Williams arrived back at his Paris hotel five days later with a profound sense of disappointment. He had just been accorded the most thorough view of the French war zone given to any journalist in the war, yet he had no urgent war news to cable back to the home office. He had not seen what he expected to see—the storming of forts, charging cavalry, or surrendering troops. "It was just the deadly winter waiting in the trenches, with the sentries who never slept at the port-holes and the artillery incessantly pounding in the rear."

Then it dawned on him that, in fact, he had one of the biggest war stories possible: the story of the French army. Less was known about it than any other fighting force. Because France had been so quiet about its army, few realized how large a role it played in the war, holding some 450 of the 500 miles of the fighting line on the western front. It had recovered from the initial German invasion and was now getting stronger and better organized every day.

Williams had fallen sick on his return from the front, but he was now filled with a sudden urgency to get out his scoop. He dictated the story from his sickbed, got it approved by the French censor, and cabled it off to his paper. The story that ran on the front page of the *New York Times* on March 8, 1915, stressed the French army's new capabilities and confidence. Williams could assure his readers that the French grand army of 1915 was "strong, courageous, scientifically intelligent, and well trained as a champion pugilist after months of preparations for the greatest struggle of his career."

Although Williams lacked the wealth of background information given to Irwin and Irwin's dramatic flair, his article signaled the sea change beginning in Allied attitude toward journalists.

Alexander Powell's Graphic War

In February 1915 *New York World* reporter E. Alexander Powell was publicizing the Allied cause in America by promoting his war book *Fighting in Flanders*, when he learned that the veil of secrecy on the fighting had begun to lift. Articles from Will Irwin, Wythe Williams, William Shepherd, and others showed that resourceful reporters were getting through to the front lines and writing hard-hitting articles.

However, when Powell arrived in Paris, he discovered that the veil of secrecy had not lifted very high. He lamented, "I wonder if you, who will read this, realize that, though the German trenches can be reached by motor-car in ninety minutes from the Rue de la Paix, it is as impossible for an unauthorized person to get within sound, much less within sight, of them as it would be for a tourist to stroll into Buckingham Palace and have a friendly chat with King George." For Powell getting permission to visit the front required the joint efforts of "three Cabinet Ministries, a British peer, two ambassadors, a score of newspapers—and the patience of Job."

As reporters won greater access to the front throughout 1915, they began to provide vivid descriptions of how this war was being fought. Civilian concepts of war were still predicated on past conflicts, but this war bore little resemblance to what had gone before. The locations, the weapons, the tactics, the experiences of the individuals doing the fighting, and above all the grand scale—all of this had to be explained to American readers who were more conversant with the U.S. war in Mexico, the Spanish-American conflict, or fifty-year-old memories of their own Civil War.

Photographer-artist Walter Hale, on his own French army tour that summer for the *New York Times*, painted a word picture of the physical layout of the fighting. "The Front," as Hale explained, was not one battle or one location, but a "shell-swept ribbon of No Man's Land" that stretched over four hundred zigzag miles of trenches, dugouts, and barbed-wire fences, from Switzerland to the North Sea. Life had been erased along this line between the two armies. No one and nothing lived there. It was a line swept day and night by artillery shells, rifle fire, hand grenades, and aerial bombs. Though it ran through what had once been forests and fields, it was now desolate of vegetation. Where it passed through villages, the villages had been reduced to broken walls and heaps of stone. Though it skirted wooded slopes, they now resembled wasted mining operations. Frederick Palmer thought the western front was less a war than it was "a competition in excavation; that these armies were not composed of men, but of rodents."

Alexander Powell narrowed the focus from that big-picture view to something personal and visceral. The circumstances of the actual fighting had yet to be properly defined, set in context, or pushed into the reader's face, a deficiency that Powell set about to rectify in a September 1915 article in *Scribner's*, in which he described his spring visit with the French army.

He huddled in cave-like dugouts with the soldiers while shrapnel whined overhead "like bloodhounds seeking their prey." Shrapnel, Powell explained to his readers, "sounds as much as anything like a winter gale howling through the branches of a pine-tree. It is a moan, a groan, a shriek, and a wail rolled into one, and when the explosion comes it sounds as though someone had touched off a stick of dynamite under a grand piano." Any millworker, farmer, businessman, or schoolchild understood something about this gruesome killer of the trenches after reading such description.

Powell's detailed narrative let readers peer with him through a sentry's peephole for a close look at the opposing trenches: "The so-called trenches are in reality concrete forts, with shields of armor-plate, protected by the most ingenious wire entanglements and other obstructions that the mind of man can devise, and defended by machine guns mounted behind steel plates and capable of firing a thousand shots a minute, in the enormous proportion of one to every fifty men. That is the sort of wall through which the Allies must break if they are to win the war."

Artillery was the primary weapon for breaking that wall, he explained. But this war's artillery was not remotely like the cannon exchanges from any previous war. The extensive cannon barrages at Gettysburg were like firecrackers by comparison. Modern armies used long-range artillery, thousands of such weapons hidden deep behind the lines. Powell visited an artillery crew that had been in position firing its weapon for three months and had never once seen its target or a single German soldier.

During one infantry advance, the British had not had sufficient shells to adequately soften up the enemy trenches, and the men were mowed down by German machine guns. For one assault by the Germans, they fired 700,000 shells in four hours. "There are no words between the covers of a dictionary which can convey what one of these artillery actions is like. One has to see—and hear—it," Powell wrote.

> Buildings of brick and stone collapse as though they were built of cards. Whole towns are razed to the ground as a city of tents would be by a cyclone. Trees are snapped off like carrots. Gaping holes as large as cottage cellars suddenly appear in the fields and in the stone-paved roads. Geysers of smoke and earth shoot high in the air. The fields are strewn with the shocking remains of what had once been men: bodies without heads or arms or legs; legs and arms and heads without bodies. Dead horses, broken wagons, bent and shattered equipment are everywhere. The noise is beyond all description—yes, beyond all conception. It is like a close-by clap of thunder which, instead of lasting for a fraction of a second, lasts for hours. There is no diminution in the hell of sound, not even a momentary cessation. The ground heaves and shudders beneath your feet. You find it difficult to breathe. Your head throbs until

you think it is about to burst. You feel as though your eardrums have been shattered. The very atmosphere palpitates to the tremendous detonations.

The following month (October 1915), Powell offered *Scribner's* readers an account of his visit to the British lines, providing stark descriptions of the impact of modern war on individual soldiers. At an evacuation hospital he found an injured man waiting his turn outside an overflowing operating room. "I hope that man is not married," Powell observed, "because he no longer has a face. What a few hours before had been the honest countenance of an English lad was now a horrid welter of blood and splintered bone and mangled flesh."

Censorship prevented British and French readers from getting this view of the war, stripped of its heroic, nationalistic glow, its fine uniforms, medals, and flags, and reduced to the starkest human terms. For the next two years, until the United States entered the war in April 1917 and imposed its own strict censorship, American journalists would continue to offer readers the most realistic assessment of the conflict, in newspaper articles that bypassed the British censors, via magazine articles, and in a succession of books on their war experience.

It annoyed Frederick Palmer that Alexander Powell, another American correspondent, was the first to get close to the British troops. Having been selected in the opening days of the war as the lone representative of the American press to be accredited with the BEF, Palmer had gotten nowhere near the British army. The War Office began its fledgling steps at expanded news coverage by having a military officer known as "Eye-Witness" provide regular, official accounts of war activities. The dry, vague details in Eye-Witness's reporting satisfied no one, so the practice was soon abandoned. Frederick Palmer and five British reporters received their long-awaited credentials in February 1915. The following month they took a trial visit to the British front, which included an interview with Field Marshall French.

No one was quite sure what to do with official correspondents or what they should be allowed to see. But that experiment went smoothly enough for the British to make the arrangement permanent three months later. American Frederick Palmer and the British reporters became part of the British army. They donned the uniform of a British officer, without insignia of rank. They took up residence in a small house near BEF headquarters in Saint-Omer. They paid for their own lodging, food, and automobile transportation. The officer overseeing their activities provided maps, daily briefings, and suggestions of what they might want to see. Each day the reporters divided up the front and went forth separately in their own car. Each night they sat around a table and shared their experiences with the others. Then they wrote up their individual stories and submitted them to the censors.

The censors had to "examine our screeds with microscopic eyes and with infinite remembrance of the thousand and one rules," Philip Gibbs, one of the British reporters with Palmer, complained of the Byzantine complexity of British censorship restrictions. "Was it safe to mention the weather? Would that give any information to the enemy? Was it permissible to describe the smell of chloride-of-lime in the trenches, or would that discourage recruiting? That description of the traffic on the roads of war, with transport wagons, gun-limbers, lorries, mules—how did that conflict with Rule No. 17a (or whatever it was) prohibiting all mention of movements of troops?"

British censorship of the press fell under the Defence of the Realm Act (DORA) of August 8, 1914. The government press office responsible for censorship, the Official Press Bureau, helpfully provided a list of more than seven hundred instructions on permissible content. To add further clarification, in the month the accredited journalists joined the BEF, new regulation under DORA put censorship violation in its own category, with six months imprisonment for each offense.

Before long the official correspondents settled into an understanding with the censors of what was permissible and what was not, and they steered their news coverage around forbidden topics. After the war Philip Gibbs and other British reporters received knighthoods for their service during the war. In later years Frederick Palmer was one of the few reporters to acknowledge that in a sense he and the other official correspondents became propagandists and "public liars" because they left out of their stories the important news. Apparently he saw the value of censorship, however, for after the United States entered the war, Palmer became the U.S. Army's chief censor.

New York Times illustrator Walter Hale and novelist-turned-reporter Owen Johnson arrived in Paris in the summer of 1915 with plans to motor to the front on their own. But a reporter's experience of the war was no longer subject to such chance exposures. There were no freelance excursions as there had been early in the war, only conducted tours. The handling of war correspondents had become "regulated, systemized, and standardized." Journalists arranged a visit to the front by presenting their credentials at a small office in the Ministry of Foreign Affairs and waiting impatiently for four to six weeks. During this time they usually received regular, nagging telegrams from editors back home, wondering when they were ever going to start writing anything about the war.

When Hale and Johnson finally got their war tour, it felt as choreographed start to finish as a summer travel excursion. "The precise duration of the trip, the precise route to be taken, the precise place at which each meal is to be eaten, the precise room in the precise hotel in which each night is to be spent, the precise General to be met and trench to be visited, are all inexorably fixed in the schedule of the trip," Hale complained. "The old-time freedom of the war correspondent has not only been curbed; it has been taken away from him and checked in the musty archives of the War Office." Reporters used to chase the scoop, he explained, tried to be the first to reach a besieged city or a certain battlefield, or to visit trenches under enemy fire. But now that reporters went on the same tour, in parties of four to seven at a time, it became nearly impossible to get an exclusive story.

The same sentiment caused Frederick Palmer to leave his post with the B E F. The proliferation of war tours robbed Palmer of the glory of being accredited to British army headquarters. Although his post had been created to be the sole representative of the American press associations, those press organizations each now had its own man with both the British and the French armies. Plus nonofficial reporters got the same, or better, visits to the British front as the official correspondents.

Opportunities to report the war were opening faster than anyone had imagined they would. Just as the competition over increasingly deadly weapons and effective tactics developed quickly, so too did the art of propaganda. If the Germans offered reporters tours of the front, then so too would the Allies. In fact they would go them one better and also offer tours to editors, novelists, statesmen, university presidents, and other "molders of neutral opinion." If the Germans gave reporters battlefield views from observation balloons, the Allies would do it from airplanes.

The British and the French officially attached correspondents to army headquarters. The French ran bus excursions from Paris to the scene of their greatest victory, the Marne battlefield. They opened a dedicated château where important visitors could stay near the front and enjoy excellent wine and cuisine while they awaited their tour of those sectors of the fighting where things were going well. Nothing proved as effective at generating positive publicity, nothing landed on more war tour itineraries, than a visit to Rheims, the "City of the Desecrated Cathedral."

In the fall of 1915, Richard Harding Davis once again stood before the great cathedral, now tightly packed with sandbags and devoid of its paintings, tapestries, and carved images. In the new era of French openness, he had returned and been taken to the Champagne region, where fighting was hot. He asked to see the cathedral again, and now that he gazed up at its barricaded facade stripped of all adornment, he waited to recapture the same outrage he had felt a year ago. A professional guide annoyed him with a set speech about the destruction of the cathedral, events that Davis himself had seen with his own eyes.

In one respect the visit was his wistful nod to the early months of the war, when a reporter could still have a jolly good adventure. But the original bitterness toward the Germans came back strong. For the past year it had fueled his irritation at the United States' continuing neutrality: "I feel the sooner those who introduced 'frightfulness' to France, Belgium, and the coasts of England are hunted down and destroyed the better."

Davis had become a staunch advocate for U.S. entry into the war and for American preparedness for that event. That summer he had participated in a curious military camp exercise in Plattsburgh, New York, conducted by the colorful General Leonard Wood, former army chief of staff and fervent advocate for American preparedness. Ostensibly the training was meant to provide a corps of men with the basic skills to become officers when the United States finally woke to its responsibility and joined the Allies. With a group of other middle-aged men, Davis hiked around with a forty-pound pack and a determination to prove his mettle. Instead he proved the limits of his middle-aged constitution and the dubious value of such freelance efforts at preparedness.

Rheims had become the perfect symbol to rouse such sympathies in the United States, and therefore any American who showed up in France was likely to be taken there. Alexander Powell explained how it worked:

> When the French have been pestered for permission to visit the front by some foreigner—usually an American—until their patience has been exhausted, or when there comes to Paris a visitor to whom they wish to show attention, they send him to Rheims. Artists, architects, ex-ambassadors, ex-congressmen, lady journalists, manufacturers in quest of war orders, bankers engaged in floating loans, millionaires who have given or are likely to give money to war-charities, editors of obscure newspapers and monthly magazines, are packed off weekly, in personally conducted parties of a dozen or more, on a day's excursion to the City of the Desecrated Cathedral.
>
> They grow indignant over the cathedral's shattered beauties, they

visit the famous wine-cellars, they hear the occasional crack of a rifle or the crash of a field-gun, and, upon their return, they write articles for the magazine, and give lectures, and to their friends at home send long letters—usually copied in the local papers—describing their experiences "on the firing-line."

Not that the war had become any less horrendous. Covering the Battle of Champagne, which began that fall between Rheims and Verdun, Powell feared that his readers would accuse him of imagination and exaggeration, "whereas the truth is that no one could imagine, much less exaggerate, the horrors that [he] saw upon those rolling, chalky plains." But could a constant litany of horrors move a distant reader in America as much as a ruined cathedral where nearly every king of France had been crowned? Where little girls now wandered among the visitors selling as souvenirs pieces of the cathedral's irreplaceable, thirteenth-century stained-glass windows?

The Allies had embraced the propaganda value of packaging their war to shape public opinion, an area of the conflict in which they enjoyed superiority over the Central Powers.

At an aviation station in the suburbs of Paris, Ralph Pulitzer struggled into a heavy leather flying suit and padded helmet, then climbed into the forward observer's seat of a twin-engine biplane. The French Foreign Office and the War Office were according him a "quite exceptional kindness" with an aerial visit to the fighting line. But then Pulitzer warranted such special treatment. Following the 1911 death of his father, legendary newspaper magnate Joseph Pulitzer, Ralph became president of the Press Publishing Company, which published the *New York World* and the *Evening World*, making him one of the most influential figures in American journalism. At age thirty-six, with dashing good looks, Pulitzer resembled a youthful Richard Harding Davis from the time of the Spanish-American War, when he was making heroes out of Teddy Roosevelt and his Rough Riders.

But dashing war correspondents did not go about on horse-

12. Ralph Pulitzer, reporter and owner of the *New York World* and the *Evening World*, was one of the first journalists to view the front from an airplane. Source: Harris & Ewing Collection, Prints and Photographs Division, Library of Congress, LC-DIG-hec-05235.

back anymore; they flew. At least those as prominent as Pulitzer did. From the air Pulitzer viewed the passing patchwork of landscape through a small observation window in the cockpit floor in front of his feet. While cruising at ten thousand feet, above a thick cloud layer, the pilot hammered on the partition separating them to get Pulitzer's attention. He was shouting something, but Pulitzer could not hear anything above the roar of the engines. The pilot pointed to the whiteness below and wrote an imaginary word in the air that Pulitzer could not decipher.

The situation became even more perplexing and frightening when the pilot suddenly stood the plane on its nose and corkscrewed down through the clouds. Pulitzer assumed engine trouble and thought he was breathing his last, until they punched through the clouds and leveled off. Again the pilot banged on the partition and pointed down to the now-visible earth. Pulitzer still didn't get the message, until the pilot made one final dive, then "stopped his motors for a fraction of a second, and in the sudden deafening silence he shouted, 'The front!'"

From three thousand feet, roads and trenches on the battlefield looked much the same. Pulitzer's unaccustomed eyes failed to distinguish all the sights to which his pilot earnestly gestured. The only evidence that it was a battlefield was the little puffs of smoke in the hazy distance from bursting French shells. As an exercise in battlefield reconnaissance, the trip was a bust; as a thrilling adventure for the influential American reporter, it paid dividends. Within months of returning home, Pulitzer published the book *Over the Front in an Aeroplane, and Scenes inside the French and Flemish Trenches*.

Seeing the front from three thousand feet may have been a disappointment, but not a serious oversight. By mid-1915 the first period of the war had ended, and with it the day-to-day suspense that some great decisive battle might bring a quick end to the carnage. It had settled into a static defensive standoff that offered little variety for news stories. "Modern war becomes a somewhat flat affair after the first impressions have been dulled," Wythe Williams thought. "Grinding monotony" was Frederick Palmer's term.

As with Wythe Williams, the French plan for Ralph Pulitzer had been to show him every component of their army. The key part of war strategy, the component in which the French could demonstrate the clearest progress, was not *on* the front but *behind* the front. Men and materials would win this war—organization, infrastructure, and resources. The stalemate on the front demonstrated that this would be a long war that would draw deeply on Allied resources, perhaps even require the entry of the United States for final victory.

Ralph Pulitzer, Wythe Williams, Owen Johnson, and Richard Harding Davis marveled at French activity in reclaimed territory: roads being upgraded, villages rebuilt, women and children working the land, and a high level of military preparation that indicated how completely Britain and France had built up their martial capabilities. Marching troops and transport trains crowded the roads for twenty miles behind the lines. France had brought in troops from its colonies in Somaliland, Madagascar, and Morocco. Endless lines of field artillery moved relentlessly toward the front. Every component of the army had been put on wheels and headed in the same direction: telegraph offices, butcher shops, bakeries, vehicle repair shops, giant searchlights, water tankers, herds of cattle and sheep, balloon units, and ambulances. Here a battalion of Zouaves practiced with bayonets; there a unit of African cavalry camped. No one seemed to know where everyone had come from or where they were heading, Alexander Powell observed, but everything was as well coordinated as traffic on Fifth Avenue in New York. Everything seemed like pieces on a chessboard being manipulated by unseen generals.

Powell saw the same level of methodical preparation behind the British lines. Britain did not begin the buildup of its war machine until after the war had started, "but what the British [had] accomplished in those twelve months [was] one of the marvels of military history." When the war secretary, Lord Kitchener, entered office at the start of the war, the army had been a joke, run by lawyers and politicians; now it had nearly three-quarters of a million volunteers prepared to do battle. Powell told his readers, "You don't hear him [the British soldier] singing 'Tipperary' any more or boasting about what he is going to do when he gets to Berlin. . . . He has buckled down with the grim determination of getting himself in condition."

On the whole 1915 had been a most disappointing year for the Allies. They had launched no great counteroffensive; their landing in Turkey had proved to be an ill-conceived disaster; hopes that a sea blockade would starve Germany of food and war materials had met with disappointment; and their ally Russia had been so pathetically manhandled that it might be effectively out of the war for a year or two. Yet despite those setbacks, every leader and military commander that the American correspondents met and every mud-caked soldier in the trenches, felt confident of ultimate victory. American reporters filled their dispatches with that message in the fall and winter of 1915.

1915 Wraps Up

In December 1915, sixteen months into the war, the New York Society of Illustrators held a special dinner at the venerable Brevoort Hotel on Fifth Avenue to honor ten wartime writers and artists. Irvin Cobb and Will Irwin were in attendance, along with Walter Hale, Arthur Ruhl, and Alexander Powell. No other group of Americans had more experience with the European war or were in a better position to assess where things stood.

Powell came off the lecture circuit for the occasion. He was touring with one of the French government's official motion pictures of the war, *Fighting in France*. "All phases of the war are shown," the newspaper ads promised: "The flight of bomb-loaded airships, great guns in action against enemy entrenchments, troops preparing to repel an assault, hand grenade action in no-man's land, prisoners of war, asphyxiating gas, and much more." The film was narrated by the correspondent who had been in every sector of the western front and seen more of the French army in the field than any other correspondent, who had marched and slept with the armies and been almost continuously on the battlefront since the war began. Powell's second book on the war, *Vive la France!*, had also just appeared.

Balancing Powell's focus on the Allied war efforts, reporter Edward Lyell Fox was touring at this time, publicizing German exploits by lecturing with the film *Battles of a Nation*. Fox had also written a well-received book about his travels with the German army, *Behind the Scenes in Warring Germany*. However, given the mood of the guests at the Brevoort, Fox's attendance would not have been appropriate.

A big-hearted evening of storytelling unfolded at the dinner, complete with stereopticon presentations. Everyone was on the same page about this war and what the United States' ultimate role must be. Reporters in the war zone had begun to detect a simmering contempt among the Allies for the United States' continuing neutrality. Allies ridiculed President Wilson's "too proud to fight" speech given after a German U-boat sank the liner *Lusitania* in May 1915, taking more than a hundred American lives and over a thousand others.

Fiction writer Gouverneur Morris explained to the gathering that he had asked former president Roosevelt the difference between a pacifist and a neutral, and Roosevelt had quipped that he had never learned to differentiate between the two brands of skunks. It got a laugh. Most correspondents had already surrendered their neutrality, if not their objectivity. It was the very sort of sentiment then hardening in the United States.

CHAPTER SIX

The Front Door and Back Door to Russia

Americans! What's the use of regulations when Americans are about?

—Russian prince VLADIMIR TROUBETSKOY to reporter
John Reed, *The War in Eastern Europe*

Everything changed for *Chicago Daily News* reporter Stanley Washburn when he met Alfred Charles William Harmsworth, 1st Viscount Northcliffe, two weeks after the start of the war. Washburn arrived in London with the first wave of American reporters, set on proceeding to the continent to attach himself to whatever army would have him. He might well have ended up with the other war correspondents who scrambled about Belgium and France, reporting on their adventures. Instead, in one brief meeting in August 1914, the trajectory of Washburn's war career took a dramatic turn. It diverted him to Russia, involving him in military strategy on the eastern front and in wartime diplomacy at the highest levels. It made him the confidant of generals, monarchs, and an emperor and established him as the most influential correspondent of the entire war.

Washburn came to the meeting with bona fides: journalistic experience, political acumen, and panache. The experience he had gained first as a police reporter in Minneapolis and then as a correspondent in assorted wars and revolutions. At the age of twenty-six, he commanded a dispatch boat in the South China Sea while covering the Russo-Japanese War. The instant that conflict concluded, Washburn hurried off to Russia for its revolution of 1905. He had an exceptional ability to befriend high-level military and political leaders, which helped him land numerous world

13. While reporting on fighting in Russia, journalist Stanley Washburn also operated as a quasi diplomat and strategist, influencing military and political policy in Russia and Romania. Source: National Photo Company Collection, Prints and Photographs Division, Library of Congress, LC-DIG-npcc-25010.

scoops. The political acumen may well have come from his father, a sixteen-year veteran of both the U.S. House of Representatives and the Senate. But onto that inheritance Washburn grafted his own brand of confidence and flamboyance.

When Washburn wrote a piece for the *Times* of London about the attitude of Americans toward the war, it came to the attention of Lord Northcliffe, legendary owner of the *Times* and many other newspapers in Britain. Within five minutes of the two men meeting, Northcliffe asked Washburn to go to Russia. The *Times* already had a correspondent stationed in Petrograd, so Washburn would be the paper's "special correspondent." The offer of a generous salary and an unlimited expense account sealed the deal.

From his initial contact with *Times* offices and staff, Washburn realized that he had stepped into a different world. They fairly exuded stuffy importance. When Washburn worked as a police reporter, his standard uniform had been an old rubber fireman's coat, a felt hat, and a detective's star pinned to his chest. The police reporter for the *Times* sported a morning suit, a silk hat, and a cane. *Times* editors were waited on by liveried servants.

"Young men of the *Times* are not the same as your reporters," the paper's foreign editor explained, "and our foreign correspondents have perhaps a different standing than do yours. Of course, they are all high-grade men and are expected to act as diplomats and meet our foreign services, both diplomatic and consular, on terms of equality."

The editor asked if Washburn had all the proper clothing for a *Times* correspondent: "a full dress suit, a tuxedo, morning coat, silk hat, black shoes and all the other essentials of a well-dressed gentleman." Washburn confessed that he traveled light when reporting wars—one small suitcase and a typewriter. That necessitated a hasty shopping spree.

Before Washburn set off for Russia, Lord Northcliffe gave him final instructions on the exact nature of his assignment: "I want you to thoroughly understand that perhaps the *Times* is different from any other paper for which you have worked. Of course, as I told you, we want the news, but I want you to realize this first and foremost, if you find you can do anything in diplomacy, in a military way, or through political intrigue, which I gather is a favorite pastime of yours, you are to forget the *Times* and serve the 'Cause,' which is more important to me even than exclusive dispatches."

In the Russian capital of Petrograd, Washburn joined a collection of Allied, neutral, and Russian journalists waiting for a chance to see the fighting. U.S. ambassador George Marye hosted a dinner for the American correspondents: Washburn, John Bass of the *Chicago Daily News*, and Granville Fortescue, then writing for the *Daily Telegraph* of London, a rival of the *Times*. The *Telegraph* advertised itself as the largest-circulation newspaper in the world, a claim Lord Northcliffe disputed.

Even though Russia had in place a 1912 law stipulating that a limited number of Russian and foreign correspondents would be allowed to travel with the army, Grand Duke Nicholas, commander in chief of the army, did not want reporters near the fighting. Requests would be considered on an individual basis.

Fighting in the East had received scant news coverage, so the U.S. military attachés at the embassy dinner brought the correspondents up to speed. At the start of the war, the Russian army made surprising advances into German Prussia and the Austrian province of Galicia, upsetting German war plans. The transfer of German troops from the west reversed Russian gains and led to a devastating Russian defeat, with some 160,000 casualties. However, the forced transfer of German troops from west to east, ten days before the Battle of the Marne, may well have saved Paris.

To understand the eastern front, they explained, one first had to make adjustments for scale. Less than two hundred miles separated Paris from Brussels. An observer could motor from Paris to the nearest fighting line in about an hour. The distance from Petrograd to Warsaw, on the other hand, was over seven hundred miles; to Czernowitz, on the southern edge of the front, was one thousand miles. These distances posed one of Russia's greatest challenges. The country's underdeveloped rail system could not adequately supply its armies in the field.

Washburn took it all in. He had an encyclopedic interest in the details of war. He used his idle time in Petrograd to study all the maps he could get his hands on. When he landed on one of the first organized tours ever arranged by the Russians, he had a good understanding of how geography and terrain impacted the movement of troops, supplies, and communications. Other reporters on the tour grumbled about not being able to visit the fighting or see anything worth writing about. However, Washburn cabled or mailed multiple stories every day.

For example, the many hospitals in the city of Lvov, swollen with some forty thousand Russian and enemy wounded, held a multitude of stories. For an estimate of the true strength of an army, a correspondent had to understand what was killing its soldiers. What percentage of hospitalizations resulted from illness or accident? What percentage of the wounded eventually returned to the fighting? What was the quality of their care? Few things had more impact on the morale of an army than the care received by the wounded.

On this tour Washburn practiced a news-gathering technique that he would utilize throughout the war: questioning everyone about morale. Although Washburn obsessed on military strategy and tactics, he believed that the most telling factors were those relating to the morale of an army or a people. He could become quite annoying with questions, stopping officers on the road, waylaying bedraggled refugees, or grilling wounded in the hospital. Did the old man in the village who had lost two sons regret the loss? What did soldiers think of the enemy fighters? Soldiers in trenches or in hospitals, citizens in occupied towns, and enemy prisoners—all were quizzed for their opinions. Washburn believed that "if one did not know what the common soldier was thinking, what he hoped for, and what he feared, one did not know anything about the army."

One startling fact emerged from his questioning of Austrian wounded. Most of them did not know why they were fighting and had no interest in waging war. In fact they asked Washburn if he knew what the war was about and why they were fighting the Russians. That one day in the hospital convinced Washburn that "Aus-

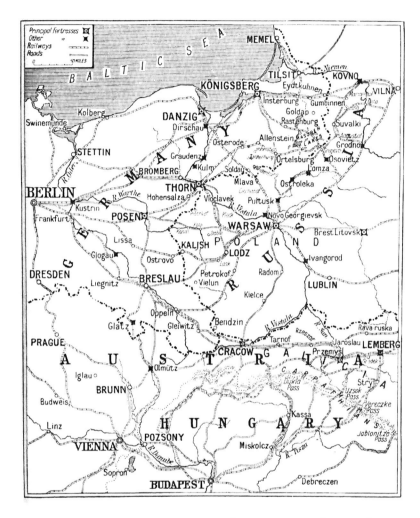

14. This map of the eastern front shows the strategic significance of
Warsaw. Source: J. A. Hammerton, ed., *The War Illustrated*, vol. 1 (London:
Amalgamated Press, Ltd., 1915).

trian morale was founded on banks of sand." At times such as this,
he recalled the advice of Lord Northcliffe: regardless of the news,
try to serve the "Cause." Back in Petrograd Washburn made his
first foray into wartime diplomacy. He met with the British ambassador and the Russian foreign minister Sergei Sazonov to share his

conclusions and discuss possible ways to break the morale of the Austrian army and drive a wedge between it and its German ally.

Granville Fortescue's first war tour in January 1915 took him to Warsaw, in Russian Poland. Warsaw stood at the crossroads between Russia and the battlefields, so through its streets funneled a parade of troops from throughout the empire: peasant soldiers from far-off Siberia and Turkestan, proud Cossacks, and men of unidentifiable origin in uniforms from the Napoleonic age. Their hard faces told of a life of suffering and privation. Fortescue wondered what an eye-opening experience it must be for these fighters, who had never before ventured beyond their villages, to now travel half a world away to fight for an empire of which they were only dimly aware. "One can almost perceive his brain grow under the stimulation of all that passes around him," Fortescue observed. "It is impossible to believe that when he returns to his home in Tomsk or Tashkent he will relapse into his original condition of mental vacuity."

Along with John Bass and their officer guides, Fortescue took a two-hour taxi ride to the fighting line. To reach the battle their auto had to push through the continuous line of supply carts hauled by hearty Siberian ponies. The Russians had set up a defensive line along the Bzura River. As far as Fortescue could see across the snow-covered plain, Russian artillery batteries ceaselessly fired out their shells. Back came the rain of German shells, falling relentlessly on the Russian lines, which looked less like trenches than prairie dog villages of scattered dugouts. Periodically, the Russians popped from hiding to make a valiant, suicidal charge, only to have the Germans answer with a countercharge. That deadly back and forth continued day and night. The wounded were carted off in the pony-drawn supply wagons; reserve troops took their place; and the scenario repeated itself. The ferocity of the combat made a deep impression on Fortescue, who had seen fighting everywhere on the western front.

Fortescue's reports were some of the first to single out the unique character of Russian peasant soldiers. So accustomed to privation and exposure all their lives, they remained steady in the face of bitter weather and the exhaustion of constant battle. "You can put a company of Russian soldiers into a trench," Fortescue wrote, "and they will stay there until they are all killed, captured or frozen. . . . The cold, the endless hours of battle, the smashing shell fire, and the rain of ripping bullets are met with what seems to be their universal answer to all the hardships of war— 'Nitchevo' [It's not bad]."

Forced to return home by a bout of illness, Fortescue missed out on one of the greatest victories for the patient, suffering Russian soldier, the recapture of the fortress city of Przemyśl. His absence handed the *Times* an exclusive on one of the biggest stories on the eastern front.

Being a correspondent for the prestigious *Times* of London conferred considerable stature onto Stanley Washburn. It took him beyond the bounds of a traditional war reporter, into policy, politics, and military strategy. Given that license to intrude, Washburn set about cultivating the contacts and procedures he would use to influence the internal workings of the Russian Empire.

In their first meeting, the Russian foreign minister Sergei Sazonov gave Washburn a thorough briefing on fighting on the eastern front. However, the conversation soon turned to conditions after the war. Before the war Germany had dominated trade with Russia. It flooded the market with cheap goods that suppressed the development of Russian industry. Its commercial agents throughout Russia worked with the pro-German party to keep Russia an agrarian economy from which Germany could buy food and raw materials.

Russia would be better off after the war, Washburn proposed, if it replaced German trade with British and American trade. He further suggested that Russia should stipulate in all its war contracts with the United States that those factories so busily producing war materials must quickly be converted to the manufacture of peacetime goods after the war. If Sazonov agreed with his thoughts, Washburn said, he would like to cable it to the *Times*. Sazonov did agree but did not have time to formulate a statement. Washburn would be happy to write it for him, he said, and submit it for his approval, to which Sazonov agreed. Washburn returned to his hotel, wrote a statement on Russia's postwar trade policy, and sent it to Sazonov. Within the hour it was back, authorized for publication. Washburn cabled it to London with the simple lead-in: "Sazonov authorizes me to quote him as saying." The statement appeared the next morning in the *Times* and a day later in almost every newspaper in the world. The *Times*' new special correspondent had scored his first exclusive.

Thus began Washburn's rapid climb to influence in the Russian power structure. He took another step in the climb in March 1915 when the Austrian fortress of Przemyśl surrendered to the Russian army after a siege of 133 days. The fall of this well-fortified city marked a major success for Russian efforts. The front lines were still officially closed to correspondents, but the Foreign Office requested from the commander of Russian forces, Grand Duke Nicholas, that Washburn be permitted to visit the city to report on this great victory. Washburn, the sole foreign correspondent in the city, reported on the lack of fighting will in the Austrian soldiers, the comfortable conditions and ample food the Austrian officers had enjoyed while the soldiers starved, how much the Austrians wanted the war to end, and how the population welcomed the Russian army.

Washburn now accepted that his job description included propagandizing for the "Cause." His goals became "first to increase the morale of the Russian troops and second, in such subtle ways as [he] could, to emphasize the growing weakness in the Austro-Hungarian cause, which fact of course, [he] wanted to have seep into Germany in every way that was possible."

Washburn cabled his Przemyśl scoop to the *Times* and was later informed that within forty-eight hours this story too ran in most world newspapers. The *Times* was so pleased to have another world exclusive that for the first time it gave Washburn a byline, which was nearly unprecedented. Being thus identified with this and future stories increased his fame and prestige. The story delighted the grand duke and made him appreciate the power of a friendly press. His imperial staff told Washburn that they believed his Przemyśl story hurt German morale more than would the loss of eighty thousand casualties. The seeds of a mutually beneficial relationship had been planted between the *Times* correspondent and the commander in chief of the Russian army. To commanders in the field, Washburn would soon represent himself as "attached to the General Staff," a claim that earned him considerable cooperation.

The Back Door to Russia

Typically, when a correspondent wished to visit the Russian front, he went to the Russian capital of Petrograd. He (no American women reported from Russia at this time) checked in with the U.S. embassy and then presented himself to the Foreign Office and showed his credentials. If he worked for a large newspaper or a wire service, or if he knew the right people, he might get his wish. His photo would be pasted onto an official pass, and an officer escort would take him somewhere in the general vicinity of the front lines. He would usually catch a glimpse of the fighting, interview a general, and get to view the beehive of behind-the-scenes activity that supported the troops.

Robert Dunn, waiting in Bucharest in neutral Romania, knew the procedure. He had recently jumped through the same official hoops in Berlin to arrange a visit to the opposite side of the lines, the headquarters of Germany's hero of the eastern front, General Paul von Hindenburg. He was about to embark on the final leg of that trip when he received an urgent telegram from the German Foreign Office withdrawing the invitation and barring him as well from traveling with the Austrian army. It had been determined, the telegram explained, that some of Dunn's previous dispatches had not been "friendly enough."

This news did not come as a complete surprise. When you broke the rules, you sometimes faced the consequences. The problem on this occasion stemmed from his time with the Austrian Kriegspressequartier. To avoid the Austrian censors, he had sent out a candid story on the Austrians' retreat from Serbia via a U.S.

embassy diplomatic pouch, a violation of his agreement to submit everything through their censors.

In his pursuit of war news, Dunn had previously been harassed, detained, arrested, imprisoned, and threatened with execution as a spy. He was blacklisted in France because he had fired a German soldier's rifle toward the French trenches. Now the Central Powers had also closed the door in his face.

A glance at a map of the Balkans revealed just how limited were his options. Neutral Romania was boxed in by warring nations, sharing borders with Serbia, Austria-Hungary, and Russia. The closest available fighting was a few hundred miles to the north in Austrian Bukovina, amid the wooded and craggy foothills of the Carpathian Mountains. Best case scenario, he might reach the provincial capital of Czernowitz and link up there with Russian forces. But the problems with this alternative plan were many: (1) the Romanian-Austrian border was sealed tight; (2) he might inadvertently link with the Austrians instead; (3) he had no pass to travel in this area; and (4) the Russian army banned reporters. A sensible person would have conceded defeat.

Instead, armed only with their passports, Dunn and another American reporter, Daniel Thomas Curtin, struck out for Bukovina. Finding the border guarded only by a Romanian customs official, the pair continued to the city of Czernowitz. The customs official assured them that Russians controlled the city, but peasants they met along the route told them that the Russians had fled. The peasants added in a fearful tone that Cossack patrols roamed the area. Cossacks served as the shock troops of the Russian army, often roaming in disputed borderlands where their legendary prowess as horsemen allowed them to range far over territory loosely held by one side or the other. German newspapers made much of their alleged atrocities against Jews.

A Russian flag still hung from a building in Czernowitz, but no soldiers greeted them. No city official or policeman appeared to ask who they were and what they were doing. They had stumbled onto the scene in that brief interval between the departure of the Russians and the arrival of the Austrians. They hired a peasant wagon to make their escape to the Russian lines on the opposite side of the Pruth River. Even as they hurried from town, they heard excited shouts and the clattering hooves of the Austrian cavalry entering some far corner of the city.

The departing Russians had blown the bridge across the Pruth River. Racing along the river, the correspondents passed two more destroyed bridges before reaching a wooden pontoon bridge still standing. It had been doused with gasoline and set aflame. Parts had been destroyed, parts still smoldered, but the river had extinguished the flames. A crowd by the bridge warned them against crossing. "Cossack! Cossack!" they shouted. They pantomimed shooting and pointed to a burned-out farmhouse on a hill across the river.

Dunn and Curtin faced a moment of decision. They did not want to be overtaken by the Austrian cavalry, which would shortly be on the scene. But to cross the river risked the dangerous and forbidden act in war of passing between enemy lines. Lacking proper papers, the best they could hope for from an illiterate Cossack sentry was to be arrested and taken to officers with whom they could plead their case. Many worse outcomes suggested themselves.

Crossing the bridge took all the courage the two men could muster. They laid boards over burned-out sections and still had to walk over fifty yards of ice to the far shore. As they scrambled up the hillside, a man appeared in what had been the doorway of the burned house, "a dark face under a shaggy shako, a carbine on his shoulder, straps crossed diagonally on his chest, with big leather knee-boots under the skirt of his brown coat." It was a Cossack sentry, the first Russian soldier Dunn had seen in the field since the war began. This vaguely malevolent image of the classic Cossack seemed a fitting cap to his hair-raising escape from the city and dash across the bridge. The adrenaline-seeking Dunn described the moment as "one of those rare, crowded eras of living which strips existence of your last vanity."

Dunn and Curtin found the fearsome Cossacks curiously indifferent to their presence. That night the *Amerikansky* reporters hitched a ride with a wagonload of Cossacks patrolling the roads for stragglers and spies. An illiterate sergeant studied their passports and accepted their legitimacy. The soldiers seemed more intent on singing gypsy songs than challenging stragglers. Cossack horsemen galloped passed them in pitch darkness at maddening speed. To Dunn the pointed hoods drawn over their heads against the cold made them look like headless horsemen. "It was the war business of romance, of story-books," Dunn thought, "as remote from the petrol, rocket-light horrors of the West as our old Indian fighting."

These were the kind of war adventures never available to those correspondents on conducted tours, who worked out of national capitals and consorted with diplomats and generals. Robert Dunn stood as a striking counterpoint to Stanley Washburn. Whereas Washburn delighted to share with readers his knowledge of how commanders thought, how battles unfolded, and how the psychological dynamic of a war played out in an army and a society, Dunn reported on what he saw and experienced. His stories were filled with individuals rather than strategies, hair-raising adventures instead of the morale of armies.

In 1912 Stanley Washburn wrote a book, *The Cable Game*, about his experiences covering the Russo-Japanese War. In it he identified two types of war correspondents: the "Feature" man and the "Cable" man. Washburn was the latter, the sort who traveled with the armies and regularly cabled back to the waiting world battlefield developments as they happened. Washburn disdained the other category of reporters, the feature man or "literary artist" who wrote about atmosphere and artistic impressions: "When the battles are over, they chronicle their impressions and send them by mail to their home offices. . . . Their names appear in large letters on the covers of magazines to which they contribute, and to the world they are known far and wide."

Cable men, such as Washburn, on the other hand, were the purveyors of "spot" news. They traveled in the "boiling vortex" of battle, where history was being made. Accuracy of fact and quick delivery were the essence of their work. "His paper require[d] him to be first on the spot where news [was] being made, and second to get a clear, concise, and correct report of that news to an uncensored cable, and do it before anyone else [could]." He must be constantly aware of two things: the hour his paper went to press and the line of communication to his cable office.

The cable man's exclusive stories might be printed in ten thousand newspapers in fifty different languages within twenty-four hours after he cabled them. "His version of affairs [was] read first by every foreign office in the civilized world. On his story the editorials on the 'situation' [were] based from London to Buenos Ayres." But because they typically wrote without a byline, cable men were virtually unknown to the general public.

Robert Dunn fell into the category of feature man. He was as different from Washburn as night from day but did not neatly fit Washburn's definition. Dunn wrote for a newspaper, the *New York Evening Post*, rather than a magazine, and he never hesitated to place himself in the "boiling vortex" of battle. An oversimplified comparison would be to label Washburn as cerebral and Dunn as emotional. But that would miss the difference in their approaches to reporting events.

Washburn had an agenda: "It was clear to those who read the *Times* that all my cables and mail stories were aimed at one objective; to shorten the war and make peace on legitimate terms as soon as possible. For this reason I carefully avoided the use of the personal pronoun 'I' in whatever I wrote," the only exception being when he wrote, "I know this because I was there and saw it."

For Dunn personal involvement *was* the story. He could convey to the reader the excitement, horror, tedium, and pathos of war only if he experienced it himself, if he filled his canvas with the characters and atmosphere that made the experience a real picture of war. Dunn dramatized his experience because he felt that "the good reporter, like the good soldier, must look upon war as the supreme adventure in the great drama of life." Dunn's next adventure awaited him on the opposite bank of the Pruth, in Russian Bessarabia.

At the Cossack camp the reporters' story about crossing the Pruth on a burning bridge caused consternation. The local commander, named Shechin, questioned them. The reporters had read about him in Austrian newspapers, "a notorious bandit of the first rank" who had "terrorized all Bukowina." When scouts brought back word that the Austrians were crossing the burned bridge, it set in motion a military encounter and made Dunn and Curtin feel just a little like spies who could now with justification be shot by the Austrians.

Adopted by the flamboyant Shechin, Dunn and Curtin tagged along with the Cossack regiment to the burned bridge to confront the Austrian incursion. They helped Shechin set up a captured Austrian machine gun in a mud house overlooking the hillside that sloped down to the river. He insisted that the reporters take a picture of him and his men beside the machine gun. Shechin pointed out to their untrained eyes the Austrians, a long line of black dots rising up from the river. He indicated with pride his six-hundred-man regiment arrayed across the hillside, already engaging the Austrians with rifle and machine-gun fire.

The two reporters tried to stay in the background, but Shechin kept calling them back to the action, to explain a new development in the battle or to elaborate on his military philosophy. For Dunn this "notorious bandit" loomed as large as the battle itself. One moment he studied Dunn's map of Bukovina, tracing the route he had taken, where he had camped and blown bridges. Then he would shout excitedly, "See them, see them!" and thrust his binoculars at Dunn so that he could watch the Austrian cavalry crossing a field. And next he expressed almost wistfully some deeper thought on the war: "The great existence. One night you sleep on the floor of a peasant hovel, eating black bread. The next, you are between linen in a château, after a supper of champagne."

From time to time a little yellow horse-drawn cart of the general staff climbed the hill, and a major checked to see how the fighting was progressing. Horseback couriers galloped up with notes for Shechin, who would scribble replies. To Dunn it felt "more like Buffalo Bill than war; no motor-scouts, no aeroplanes; the yellow wagon in place of a motor-car; instead of some lofty tactician with elegant entourage—our alert and garrulous friend, refined in the

15. Veteran war correspondent and ardent socialist John Reed became famous for writing about the Bolshevik Revolution, which took Russia out of the war, but he reported from many other locations during the conflict. Source: Prints and Photographs Division, Library of Congress, LC-USZ62-78094.

16. Illustrator Boardman Robinson traveled with reporter John Reed through the Balkans and along the eastern front in the spring of 1915 for the socialist magazine the *Masses*. Source: George Grantham Bain Collection, Prints and Photographs Division, Library of Congress, LC-DIG-ggbain-19361.

keenness of his mind, yet loving anger and action for their own sakes; loving his roving job and his loyal retainers."

Dunn's first newspaper boss had been the legendary muckraking journalist Lincoln Steffens. "Write it all down," Steffens used to tell him. "Put things down just as they happen, exactly." Which is what Dunn did—the Romanian official at the border became a character in the war narrative, as did the peasant wagon driver who helped him escape from Czernowitz and haggled over his fare, the dead body he found while crossing the Pruth, the Cossack commander who wanted his picture taken with the Austrian machine gun, and the destitute peasant family who gave him lodging and cooked him eggs.

Originally reported in the *New York Evening Post* and included in his book *Five Fronts*, published within months of these events, Dunn's Cossack adventure provided American readers with one glimpse of the Russian army. In this mammoth and monstrous conflict, one could no longer write accounts of great battles. The front was too huge, the strategies too confusing. One could only capture glimpses. Dunn had accomplished that with the British retreating at Mons, the Austrians fighting to hold Przemyśl, in the German trenches of Flanders, and now with the Cossacks skirmishing in Bukovina. Dunn seemed at his best when he floated as helplessly in the fast current of events as the soldiers and civilians he wrote about.

Three months after Dunn departed Bukovina, socialist reporter John Reed followed the same backdoor route into Russia. He would also have fallen into Washburn's category of "literary artist." When his dramatic war reporting ran in the large-format, well-illustrated *Metropolitan Magazine*, his name emblazoned the cover. However, an increasingly strong anticapitalist, anti-imperialist tone had crept into Reed's reporting, diminishing his standing with the magazine.

In April 1915 Reed set off with illustrator Boardman Robinson to see the fighting in the Balkans and Eastern Europe. They had worked together on the socialist magazine the *Masses*, a publication that advocated for labor reform and women's rights, and strongly opposed the war. They hoped to report on big developments brewing in the East—perhaps Serbia's heroic last stand or Romania's entry into the war. Everyone talked about Greece or Bulgaria joining in, on one side or the other. The reporters thought they might be on hand when the Allies took Constantinople or the Russian steamroller reached Berlin. In reality none of that occurred. In fact the war gods frowned on the whole venture. The two newsmen journeyed through the region for seven months, arriving at each location during a lull in hostilities.

May 1915 drew them to Bucharest on rumors that Romania was about to enter the war. When that did not happen, they headed north on news that a combined German and Austro-Hungarian offensive was pushing the Russians out of the Carpathian Mountains. The Russian ambassador would not give a pass to the front, but the U.S. legation, concerned about the safety of its citizens, gave Reed a list of names and locations of those Americans it knew to be in the war zone, along with a letter explaining he had been given the charge of checking on their well-being.

The broad Pruth River still held as the dividing line. Reed and Robinson went north by train, crossed the Pruth by rowboat, and hooked up with Turkmen warriors from the steppes of Asia. Their commander said that the Russians were in retreat due to a lack of artillery shells. But the Russians would advance and retreat again and again, he assured them, "as long as England gives money and the earth gives men."

By train and peasant cart, they made their way slowly over the "boundless Galician steppe," from one town to another. People gaped in astonishment at the two strangers dressed in Stetson hats, knickerbockers, and puttees. They were repeatedly arrested and released. Passes to the front could not be issued, Reed heard repeatedly. Such passes could only be obtained from an officer or a prince in Tarnopol, or Lvov, or Petrograd. So they continued north, swept along in the current of life behind the lines of the eastern front.

Soldiers in a mix of uniforms crowded the dilapidated towns, waiting on sidings, while trains rolled here and there in "utter disorganization." Here troops went hungry, while further up the rail line, mess-hall meals spoiled because there was no one to eat them. Supply trains rushed in opposite directions. Trains raced by with empty boxcars, while units waited for transportation. It seemed such a stunning contrast to the well-organized German military machine.

One town in which Americans were thought to reside had been captured, looted, and burned three times. The Russians had slaughtered most of the town's Jewish population, including some Americans named on Reed's list. Everywhere Reed found evidence of institutionalized anti-Semitism: filthy, crowded ghettoes; rumors of pogroms; and accusations that Jews were "traitors." He wrote an article on Russia's betrayal of the Jews.

Reed began to warm to being a behind-the-front war correspondent. During the excitement of war, men seemed to lose their "distinctive personal or racial flavor" in the "mad democracy of battle." But behind the lines, the population had "settled down to war as a business, had begun to adjust themselves to this new way of life and to talk and think of other things." It gave an insight not only into the psyche of a nation but into the war as well.

Like Dunn Reed too had been influenced by crusading muckraking journalist Lincoln Steffens, who had lectured at Harvard College while Reed attended. Steffens had recommended Reed for the job at *Metropolitan Magazine*. But it was Reed more so than Dunn who took naturally to the fight against corruption and social injustice, writing well-received articles about New York's Tammany Hall corruption and antilabor violence. So when Reed discovered that graft in Russia existed on a monumental scale and threatened the war effort, it became a natural target for his pen.

Even minor transactions required payoffs to officials and middlemen, but malfeasance could also function on an epic scale, such as ships paid for by the government but never built. The corruption extended up to high military officers, the nobility, even the imperial court. An English arms dealer told Reed about a shipment of artillery shells stranded at the northern port of Archangel in 1914. It had been critically needed to stop the loss of a Russian army, but the dealer refused to bribe the Russian railway and ordnance officials to ship it to the front.

On the train Reed struck up a friendship with several Russian officers on assignment to investigate the disappearance of seventeen million bags of flour—thirty train carloads. The vital commodity had started on the eighteen-mile journey from Kiev to Tarnopol and simply vanished. The officers had no proof but believed that it had been sold to the Romanians and then shipped to Austria. "Such things will happen," one confessed.

The correspondents' unauthorized entry into the country finally caught up with them in the town of Cholm, where they were arrested as German spies. Confined at the local hotel under Cossack guard, they were permitted one telegram to American ambassador George Marye in Petrograd, seeking his help. Eight days later came the curt reply: "You have been arrested because you entered the war zone without proper authority. The Foreign Office notifies this embassy that you will be sent to Petrograd."

Having been informed about Reed's socialist background by the State Department, Marye provided no help for Reed. The Jewish names on Reed's list persuaded Russian officials that he had an antigovernment agenda. While Reed sorted out his problems in the capital, he became fascinated with the Russian people and the widening gulf between them and their leaders. His focus shifted from the war to social unrest—strikes, mass marches, food shortages, petitions to the Duma and the czar, and the wholesale dismissal of government officials. "Is there a powerful and destructive fire working in the bowels of Russia," he wondered, "or is it quenched?" In articles such as "The National Industry" about corruption, "The Betrayal of the Jews," and "A Patriotic Revolution," Reed tried to capture the mighty currents that flowed through the "vast, restless sea of Russian life."

Eventually forced to leave the country, Reed and Robinson made their way back to their point of entry. Russian border officials thoroughly disassembled and searched their luggage and clothing and confiscated their notes and sketches.

Reed wrote seven long articles for *Metropolitan* during his seven months in the Balkans, Russia, and Turkey, which were collected into a book the following year. His accounts often read like travelogues of war, not the fighting war but the disparate characters populating the background. "History of grandiose and unprecedented character," one reviewer enthused. "Everywhere they went they made friends with all manner of people and had through these acquaintances the most intimate, revealing, and instructive glimpses into the life and character of the people and into the present conditions in Russia."

By expanding the scope of his war reporting to include conditions within the countries at war, Reed helped to shift the focus of war reporting, a change that became increasingly popular and revealing during the remaining years of the war. Such reporting would attempt to answer the growing question about how long countries would be able to sustain their war effort. How long would manpower and resources hold out? How long would public opinion support an increasingly costly, senseless, and unpopular war?

News on the eastern front could scarcely have been worse for Russia in 1915. In May a combined Austro-Hungarian and German force launched a massive offensive in Galicia. As it unfolded, Stanley Washburn was a figure in constant motion. Outmanned and outsupplied, the Russian army was pushed back everywhere. Preceding one attack the Germans fired seven hundred thousand artillery rounds in five hours, while the poorly supplied Russians suffered from a severe shortage of shells and even rifles. Washburn rushed to the front to confirm reports of the first use of gas in the East and learned that chlorine gas had caused four thousand casualties in ten minutes. Always looking for the positive spin, Washburn could report that many of the attacking Germans had been drawn away from the western front and that the use of gas inflamed Russian morale and caused the Russian soldiers to fight more brutally, preferring now to kill rather than capture German prisoners.

But any uptick in morale proved temporary. In June enemy forces recaptured the fortress town of Przemyśl and then broke the Russian lines to force them completely out of Austrian Galicia. Washburn traveled over a thousand miles by auto, visiting the Russian lines everywhere they were threatened. When pressure next turned to Warsaw, he made repeated trips from Petrograd with American military attaché Sherman Miles along the narrow corridor remaining open to the city. He fired off a continuous flow of cables to the *Times*, remaining in Warsaw even when German artillery shells reached into the city and airplanes dropped bombs. When the Russians attached explosives to the city's bridges, to be blown at the last minute, Washburn made his exit.

Amid the refugees and military transports crowding the roads, Washburn reported one of the most extraordinary sights he had ever seen in war—two girls in white duck dresses carrying tennis rackets. They typified the nonchalance of the refugees and echoed Reed's observations about life behind the lines. "War becomes simply a matter of a day's work," Washburn wrote, "and even the civilians get so used to hearing the shells burst and planes on air raids that it does not even interest them, much less create a panic." Unfortunately, the refugees from Warsaw did not get used to hiking out of Poland, along roadways through terrain scorched barren by the retreating Russians. On subsequent trips Washburn saw their bodies in fields and roadside ditches.

On his flight from Warsaw, Washburn paused to send off a brief cable announcing the fall of the city, estimating that Russia had lost between half to three-quarters of a million men defending the city over the past ten months. It was the first word to reach the outside world about the abandonment of Warsaw. Once again Washburn had proved his worth to the *Times*.

He did not have time to explore in his cable the mix of emotions that gripped him at this latest development. He had already noticed with concern the erosion of Russian morale in the army from the string of defeats and the chronic supply problems. How could the Russians keep the Germans from taking Petrograd and forcing a separate peace, thus taking Russia out of the war? He turned these questions onto the Russian colonel traveling with him. The colonel took the questions calmly, indulgently. "You in the West do not understand my people," he responded. "You think we are a race of barbarians, uneducated, without culture and without intelligence. . . . But my people have a culture of simplicity, fortitude and faith, and it is in the hearts of a hundred and eighty million peasants."

Actually, that assessment closely matched Washburn's own impression of the Russian peasant soldier. Like Fortescue he admired how their simple stoicism made them formidable fighters, able to endure horrendous conditions and endless abuse and still continue to fight. If the German army fought as a highly organized industrial machine, the Russians fought as hardened, individual men. And just as Germany could expend a million shells without blinking, Russia could match that with another million-man army drawn from across its vast empire.

Washburn had been concerned about morale in the army since May, and now rumors circulated in Petrograd that the government would seek a separate peace with the Germans. If such a rumor reached the men at the front, it might easily cause the complete collapse of morale. Foreign Minister Sazonov angrily denied the rumor but told Washburn he was powerless to stop its spread. It presented Washburn with yet another opportunity to use the power of public relations to control a bad situation. As he had earlier, he wrote up a statement for Sazonov denying the truth of the rumor and stressing confidence in the army. After getting Sazonov's approval, he sent it to the *Times*. Also reported in the Petrograd papers, the statement had the effect of eliminating the dangerous rumors or at least holding them at bay for another year.

The following day Washburn received a letter from Sazonov along with a small red leather box containing a medal. The letter stated that Czar Nicholas had conferred the medal on Washburn in appreciation of his efforts for Russia. As a follow-up to this honor there occurred one of the most telling moments for Washburn in the course of the war, one that unlocked for him the highest level of influence in the Russian government. He received an invitation to dine with the czar and his general staff.

He found it a stiff and pitiful affair. The heir to three hundred years of Romanov rule was reportedly a simple, approachable man, but the luncheon guests of generals, the grand duke, and a bishop went through the meal as frozen and silent as statues. After lunch, with everyone standing at attention in an anteroom, the czar spoke with Washburn, who took the occasion to stress to him the importance of developing public opinion and support in the minds of the common soldier, a concept that seemed to puzzle the czar. Apparently no one had ever talked with him about the morale of the troops or given any opinion about the army. "You are always writing and talking about public opinion" the czar said, "but we have no public opinion in Russia."

"Sire"—Washburn raised his voice a little—"the difference between developing public opinion and ignoring it, is the difference between evolution and revolution." The entire room shuffled, "as though they expected a bolt of lightning would surely strike [him] dead. Evidently, the word 'revolution' was also a forbidden one in the Imperial Staff." Washburn explained what he thought should be done regarding handling publicity for the army and offered to write up a plan if he could get the cooperation of the staff. The czar received the suggestion without comment and then crossed the room to leave but paused at the door to remark in a voice loud enough for all to hear, "Mr. Washburn, until I see you again I want to assure you of my personal appreciation for what you have done for Russia and for me personally. I thank you."

The simple remark might as well have been an official edict. When the czar left the room, everyone else, from the highest generals to the grand duke, came over to Washburn, clicked their heels, and saluted him. The following day a colonel was assigned to be his personal aide. Henceforth, Washburn was nominally attached to the czar's staff. His travel permits came from the imperial general staff, and his automobile bore its license plate.

Being a *Times* correspondent had always carried the dual responsibilities of journalism and diplomacy, but Washburn had now ascended to a lofty plane where no war correspondent had ever tread. He had just been given unprecedented access and influence in the Russian government and military. Diplomats and foreign leaders wanting a clue to Russian policy now sought his opinion and followed more closely his dispatches from the eastern front.

Never was that more apparent than when he took a break from the war late in 1915. The frantic pace of his reporting had taken a toll on his health. Early in November, with the war settling into a winter lull, Washburn headed home to the United States for some rest. A stop in Britain filled quickly with meetings with diplomats and government ministers wanting his appraisal of Russia. Washburn stressed that the Russians needed eight hundred thousand rifles immediately to continue the fight. He had seen Russian soldiers charge from their trenches without weapons. Lord Northcliffe chided him for the overly optimistic tone of his recent reports, as did his publisher, who felt the same about a book he had sent in on the Russian fighting. In an open letter to the *Times*, Washburn recommended that the government provide money for refugees and open a propaganda bureau in Petrograd. Bring members of the Russian government to England, he urged, and send lecturers and moving pictures to Russia to explain Britain's war effort to the soldiers.

During the several months he spent in the United States, Washburn had little time for "rest." He was a man on a mission—meetings with the State Department and the Russian ambassador, a lecture at the War College, and lunch with Colonel Roosevelt. With the help of a stenographer, he sent out fifteen to twenty letters a day and managed to write sixteen articles for the *Chicago Tribune*. He collected those articles in a hastily published book, *Victory in Defeat*, in which he justified his optimism for Russia in the new year: "I believe the Russian reverses have been so costly and demoralizing to their victors that history will judge them as the greatest single source of the German downfall, whether it be in six months or two years."

In spring 1916 he returned to Russia to see his optimism rewarded. To the surprise of nearly everyone except Washburn, the Russian army launched a major offensive all along the eastern front, led by General Aleksey Brusilov. In his new role as advisor to the czar, Washburn rushed to Brusilov's headquarters and studied the battle maps. His affiliation with the general staff now paid dividends, as most commanders shared with him their plans. Through June and July he visited all the zones along a two-hundred-mile front, rarely sleeping more than two nights in any one location and writing a column a day for the *Times*. Particularly in the south, against the Austrians, Russia made astonishing gains, breaking their lines, sweeping up prisoners by the hundreds of thousands, and taking vast stretches of territory.

From enemy prisoners and wounded, Washburn again learned that large numbers of troops had been transferred from the western front to halt the Russian advance. Austria had been forced to halt its offensive in Italy and Germany to draw off divisions from its long assault on Verdun, giving the Allies much-needed breathing space. Washburn also made a curious observation about captured German soldiers: their height and age had begun to vary. Early in the war, they had all been young men of similar height, but now their ages ranged from nineteen to forty-nine, their height from five feet two to well over six feet. Germany had used up its young men and had begun to draw off men from factories, many of them skilled workers. The impact would certainly be felt on its war effort and for a generation after the war. Reprinted in the *New York Times*, the headline on his story read, "Teuton Reserves Used Up."

The infusion of German troops stiffened Austrian resistance, slowing the Russian advance. Both sides suffered staggering casualties. One night Washburn watched from his hotel room in a small town as an endless flow of wounded passed by in peasant carts, four abreast, hour after hour. He had seen so many of these unfortunates that he could now tell from their wounds what type of fighting they had been doing. Wounds to the head and left hand meant they had been firing through loopholes. Shattered limbs and body wounds meant they had been caught in the open during an advance.

At this point in the war, Washburn may well have been more knowledgeable about conditions on the eastern front than anyone in the Russian command. He knew all the commanders and their strengths and shortcomings. He had visited their battle lines and studied their maps. He knew the fighting quality of the various Russian armies and the psychology of the general staff. In August he took a break on the estate of an English woman in Poland, staying in the bedroom where Napoleon had slept during his invasion of Russia in 1812. There he put the finishing touches on his third book about the eastern front, *The Russian Advance*. He hurried it off to his New York publisher, and it appeared the following month. While he worked on the book, Romania entered the war on the Allied side, in time for him to mention it in his preface as "the turning point in the war." It was yet another example of his boundless optimism running ahead of reality.

On August 28, the day after Romania joined the war, Washburn received a telegram from the *Times* telling him to report from Romania. He also received a request from the Russian general staff that he visit Romania and report on the morale and combat effectiveness of the Romanian army. Cables went from the Russian government to Romania to lend Washburn every assistance. Washburn made the 1,300-mile trip by auto, visiting battle zones along the way, often exposed to danger. His stamina was wearing down, but the lure of a news scoop and the opportunity to influence events pushed him relentlessly.

In Bucharest he convinced Romanian King Ferdinand and his influential Queen Marie of the need for a statement explaining Romania's reasons for entering the war, expressed in such a way as to win the strongest Allied sympathy and support. Following the usual scenario, Washburn wrote the statement, got approval, and cabled it as an exclusive to the *Times*.

A survey of the Romanian front left Washburn pessimistic about the army and its chances of holding off the Germans gathering on its border. He persuaded the queen to write to her cousin the czar requesting that several Russian armies be sent to assist Romania. In Bucharest Washburn became the center of a whir of activity: advising the Romanian National Bank on how to protect its gold reserves, helping to draft an evacuation plan for Bucharest, repeatedly visiting and advising Romanian commanders in the field, and recommending the destruction of the Ploeşti oil fields. Zeppelins and airplanes made almost daily bombing runs on the city, raising anxiety. Romanian fighters had already been pushed out of the mountain passes that granted access to the country. It was only a matter of time.

It is not clear how delusional Washburn remained about Russian chances. He certainly knew that things were hopeless in Romania. When he returned to Brusilov's headquarters, he found the general furious about Romania's entry into the war. A neutral Romania had been a bulwark on his southern flank; now he had to stretch his reserves and his limited inventory of shells to support Romania's tottering army.

The outlook appeared gloomy when Washburn studied Brusilov's war maps. But ever convinced of the power of publicity to galvanize public opinion, he convinced Brusilov to issue a statement praising Romanian entry in the war and Russia's solidarity with its new partner. The statement, which Washburn wrote, began with a bold quotation from Brusilov on the value of Romania joining the Allies: "The war is won today." The story did not run in the *Times* until November 10, by which time new German victories reclaiming Brusilov's hard-won gains gave the quote an especially hollow ring.

Washburn caught up with Czar Nicholas in late November at the Kiev train station and informed him of the situation in Romania. The czar looked "haggard and worn," a description that also applied to Washburn. The emperor informed Washburn of the reelection of President Wilson on a promise to keep American out of the war. "I do not understand your politics," the czar confessed. Washburn admitted that he too was terribly disappointed.

The emperor of Russia shook the hand of the American war correspondent, who reported for the most prestigious newspaper in the world, who had been intimately involved in Russian politics and its prosecution of the war over the past two years, and who had seen more of the fighting on the eastern front than any other person. And whose faith in the character and soul of the great empire ranked only a step down from the emperor's. It was the last time they would see each other.

As usual Washburn's desperate need for rest was thwarted when he arrived back in Petrograd. He had to place ten chairs in the hallway outside his hotel room to accommodate those waiting to see him. Appointments began at 7:00 a.m. and often went until two in the morning. Everything seemed so important at that juncture, and no one else had any firsthand knowledge of developments in the south. The Foreign Office, the War Office, embassies, and civilians sought his knowledge and advice. British engineers on their way to destroy the Romanian oil fields stopped by. As he had recommended, the British had opened a propaganda bureau in Petrograd, and the director wanted him to write some material. Oh, and could he use his connections in London to get the ten thousand pounds they needed to do their work?

Exhaustion finally got the best of Washburn and kept him bedridden for two weeks, while political events added to his distress. The latest reverses of the army and food shortages in the city made the situation tense in Petrograd. Articles in the press called for a reorganization of the government. He could only speculate about the incendiary speeches being made in the Duma because only heavily censored versions appeared in the papers. Conspicuous blank spaces dotted the text in the newspapers, where censors had removed details too sensitive for the public to know. Other correspondents complained that the Russian censors stopped almost everything they tried to send out.

The time had come for Washburn to leave Russia. Early in 1917, as he traveled along the leisurely cross section of the empire cut by the Trans-Siberian Railroad, the man who had proved so adept at reading the Russian tea leaves and championing the cause of the empire reached an unsettling conclusion: "For the first time I began to envisage the possibility of a revolution."

CHAPTER SEVEN

Gallipoli and Greece

With the evacuation of Gallipoli, the British forces had come to Saloniki. The bay was jammed with warships, battleships, transports and
hospital ships. The big hotel was thronged with officers. The ancient
Thessalonian city had become an important news center.

—Reporter-artist JOHN McCUTCHEON, *Drawn from Memory*

I n February 1915 the *Chicago Daily News* heard rumors that the
British fleet intended to force its way through the Dardanelles,
the heavily fortified straits that served as the gateway to the
Turkish capital of Constantinople and the Black Sea. If the fleet
could capture the city and knock Turkey out of the war, it would
open a water passage to Russia and likely convince wavering Balkan states to enter the war on the side of the Allies. In other words
it just might be the biggest news story of the war.

The newspaper rushed its Berlin correspondent, Raymond
Swing, to Constantinople to cover the event. There he joined
the only other American reporter in the city at the time, George
Schreiner from the Associated Press. Turkish authorities were cool
to the pair, having recently been burned by unscrupulous American reporters who repaid Ottoman hospitality by publishing false
accounts of "riots, arson, bloodshed, and wholesale executions"
in the Turkish capital.

Fortunately, the Turkish minister of war, Enver Pasha, was a
strict but reasonable man. The correspondents could travel anywhere and see anything they wished, with the understanding that
they were subject to Ottoman military law. Any violation of that

law could mean a summary execution, without appeal to their embassy. Overall it wasn't an unreasonable restriction, common on all fronts. Journalists knew the rules. As long as they stayed in the country, their dispatches had to go through the military, where eagle-eyed censors would delete their smallest indiscretions, saving them from the firing squad.

During the quiet weeks of waiting for the Allied assault, the newsmen toured fortifications on the Gallipoli peninsula and met with German and Turkish officers. The Turks had lined the straits with an impressive number of large-caliber guns in well-fortified emplacements that would pose a serious challenge to an Allied intrusion. Swing parked himself at the town of Çanakkale on the Asian side of the straits with a clear view of the waterway and the peninsula on the opposite shore. It was the narrowest and most heavily fortified point on the Dardanelles. There he awaited the fireworks.

One day, as a diversion, Swing and a German correspondent took an excursion by camel to the ruins of the ancient city of Troy. Some three millennia earlier, another invasion fleet, led by the Mycenaean king Agamemnon, landed an army of Greeks to capture the city that guarded this vital waterway. Little of the site had been excavated, but they were able to identify the seven layers of occupation that testified to how far into the past stretched the effort to control the Dardanelles. But the most remarkable occurrence of the visit happened when they climbed to the nearby heights that overlooked the Aegean Sea approach to the Dardanelles and saw a British ship anchored there, a vintage pre-dreadnaught battleship with the name—of all things—HMS *Agamemnon*. "It was a strange example of the depth of history," Swing noted.

History presented itself for Swing's personal inspection on March 3, when eighteen British and French warships, bristling with large cannons, sailed into the Dardanelles, aligned themselves for battle, and commenced pounding Turkish fortifications.

There had been precious few naval engagements in this war, and rare was the occasion when a reporter could watch the mighty guns of a battleship in action. For two and a half hours, the ships bombarded Turkish batteries near Swing's location, their shells blasting out great geysers of earth and spraying the area with shrapnel. The answering shells from the Turks exploded in the water and struck home on a few of the ships.

The scene repeated itself several times over the next two weeks. Ships returned to sweep mines and shell fortifications on both sides of the straits. Swing got as close as he dared, watching from an ancient tower, a waterside tea shop, or a trench behind one of the besieged Turkish forts. On each occasion, when the ships withdrew, he rushed to the sites under attack and found relatively little damage to the fortifications. It seemed to cast doubt on the Allied strategy to knock out the guns lining the strait.

The climactic battle played out on March 18 with a massive display of Allied naval power. Twelve battleships entered the waterway. Sailing in two circling formations, they rained a continuous bombardment on the shore batteries. The blast of the guns, the whistling flight of the massive shells, the deafening explosion when they impacted, and the shriek of flying shrapnel blended into a cacophony of battle. Several times Swing changed his location when shells fell too close. A Turkish shell set one ship ablaze. It soon rolled and sank. A destroyer and a minesweeper that rushed forward to rescue survivors also fell victim to Turkish shells. By nightfall, when the fleet withdrew, two additional battleships had been sunk.

Swing hurried to inspect the Turkish fort near his location. Its gun remained operable, but the German gun crew was distraught about their depleted supply of shells. An insufficient supply had been laid up before the battle, they complained. When the Allied fleet returned in the morning—and no one doubted it would—the shore batteries would not be able to hold it off. It would sail up the Dardanelles and capture the Turkish capital.

As an indication of just how desperate circumstances had become, the correspondents received orders that they were to be packed and ready in the morning for evacuation into the interior. That night, at what might be a breathtaking turning point in the war, Swing wrote a story and sent it by courier to Constantinople. He reported the action of the battle and the sinking of the Allied battleships. He did not mention that the Allies were poised to win the battle the next day and that the Turks knew it, or that he had been ordered to move inland. Had that information managed to get past the Turkish censor, it would have earned Swing a date with Enver Pasha's firing squad.

To the great surprise and relief of the defenders, the fleet did not return in the morning. The Allies chose that exact moment to abandon their plan to storm the straits in favor of landing troops on the Gallipoli Peninsula. Swing considered it the greatest missed opportunity of the war. Half a century later, at the close of an illustrious journalistic career, Swing reimagined that moment in his autobiography as "the hinge on which history turned." King Agamemnon had returned each year to battle Troy for a decade before that impregnable city fell. Had the Allies returned just one more day, forced the Dardanelles, and captured Constantinople, "the Gallipoli landing would never have been made, Turkey would have been plucked from its German Alliance, the water route to Russia would have been opened, Russia would have fed the Allies with its grain, and the Allies would have stocked Russia with their artillery and ammunition. . . . There would have been no Bolshevik Revolution—certainly not as early as it occurred—the United States would not have entered the war, and the history of the human race would have been vastly different."

Landings on Gallipoli

Turkey's Asian shore juts into the mouth of the Dardanelles directly opposite the tip of the Gallipoli Peninsula. From that vantage point Granville Fortescue looked down on the "most fascinating war picture" he had ever seen: an amphibious landing of British troops. Dozens of transports and warships dotted the sea at the entrance to the straits. He recognized the battleship *Majestic*, which carried his British colleague and fellow correspondent for the *Daily Telegraph* Ellis Ashmead-Bartlett.

The land phase of the Gallipoli campaign had begun a month earlier, in April, with the landing of British and ANZAC (Australian and New Zealand Army Corps) troops. The first troops that went ashore at this location made little progress. Around the peninsula on the north shore, ANZAC forces battled valiantly and at great cost to hold a sliver of beach. This infusion of reinforcements was meant to turn the tide.

The battleships first softened up the Turkish defenses along the crest of the peninsula with a rain of fifteen-inch shells. The boiling smoke and fire of the explosions reminded Fortescue of spewing lava. Certainly nothing could survive in that blasted kill zone.

Then the transports, former passenger liners, moved close to shore. Fortescue adjusted his binoculars to pull into focus the deck cranes swinging outward and back, unloading ammunition cases, dismounted cannon, and all the supplies of war. Crowds of soldiers descended ladders into the small boats that ferried them to shore amid the splash of Turkish artillery rounds. Fifty yards from the beach, the boats hit ground, and the men jumped into the water to wade ashore.

It lasted all morning. He could see the troops already on shore, crouched in a ravine at the base of a cliff, on which sat the Turkish defenders. At midday, the battleships and cruisers pulled closer to shore and unleashed a final volley on the hilltop and the hillside, every location that might shelter defenders. Even miles away on the opposite shore, the cannons boomed so loudly that Fortescue could scarcely shout a conversation with his Turkish translator.

The instant the bombardment ceased, the landing beach sprang to life with tiny figures scrambling forward and charging up the hill. "As if from their graves," the Turkish soldiers came out of hiding and from their hilltop vantage point poured down on the attackers murderous rifle and machine-gun fire. Turkish artillery dropped shrapnel rounds into their midst. The fighting continued well into the night, when the warships again took their turn at bombarding the Turks.

"Exhausted, depressed, filled with melancholy visions of the fate of the men who had fought so gallantly that day," Fortescue fell asleep in his observation trench. He woke to his interpreter's excited report that a battleship had been sunk during the night.

Down in the straits, a tight cluster of ships was sailing away from the shore, leaving the landing force unsupported. Already the Turks directed a concentrated fire onto the landing beach. What would the troops do now, without naval support when they ran out of food, water, and ammunition?

Hotly indignant at the abandonment of the troops, Fortescue wrote an impassioned article. A small bribe assured that it passed the Turkish censor without being mangled. It would travel from Constantinople to Bucharest and from there onto London. No telling how it would be received by British censors or by his editors at the conservative London *Daily Telegraph*.

Three other American journalists on the scene had opted to get a closer view of the fighting on the peninsula. Two of them, Arthur Ruhl (*Collier's*) and Henry W. Suydam (*Brooklyn Eagle*) rode a supply boat from Constantinople to the town of Gallipoli on the peninsula at the upper entrance to the straits. They had visited that sleepy little town earlier that month, after British ships shelled it from miles away in the Aegean. The town had served as a military outpost, but the attack also took civilian lives. Incensed, the Turks rounded up fifty English and French nationals living in Constantinople and transported them to unfortified towns on the peninsula. Turkey notified England and France and left it up to them whether they wanted to shed the blood of their citizens with further bombardments. Ruhl and Suydam accompanied the group to the peninsula to chronicle the whole affair. They sat in abandoned houses for several days, until the U.S. ambassador, Henry Morgenthau, interceded and quietly ended the ill-conceived standoff.

Otherwise, May had been a busy month on the peninsula. Repeated waves of reinforcements attempted to break out of the landing beaches. A massive Turkish counterattack against the ANZAC beachhead failed miserably. The Turks brought thousands of wounded into Constantinople in the night to minimize public reaction.

The correspondents returned now to see where things stood. As was customary, they first presented themselves to the commandant of peninsular forces, German Field Marshall Liman von Sanders. He had designed the peninsula defenses, and German officers manned the artillery, but he praised the Turkish soldiers, not the same fighting men who had lost the Balkan wars and been forced out of Europe. Westerners had heard for so long about the Ottoman Empire being the "sick man of Europe," poised to collapse, but the Turks were formidable fighters. To see for themselves, the correspondents received a pass to the ridgeline on the north or Aegean Sea side of the peninsula.

The terrain reminded Ruhl of the California foothills in the dry season, tangled valleys with sparse pines and scrub oaks and rocky slopes. Except that here they swarmed with camel trains and carts transporting supplies and wounded. The Turkish command post nestled in a camp dug into a hilltop with a view of the waterways on both sides of the peninsula. The Turkish commander explained with great satisfaction how he had watched the sinking of the British battleship *Majestic* by a German submarine. It had been a once-in-a-lifetime sight to watch the great ship roll over like a stricken whale and go under. To the commander the implications were clear: the English and French navies had not been able to force the straits; after a month of fighting, their land forces had been checked by Turkish defenders; and now German submarines had arrived to deal with the enemy fleet.

The commander directed the two reporters to the observation periscope that poked through a screen of pine branches and offered a view over the edge of the parapet, down onto the front-line trenches and the sea. Ruhl made out a narrow, curving rim of beach and the yellow line of British trenches twisted along the base of the cliff. Directly facing them—in some places not more than fifteen or twenty feet away—ran the first-line Turkish trenches. They stood so close that they could have fought with revolvers and shovels. The view supported the commander's optimism. With the sea to their backs and a well-manned, well-fortified cliff before them, "the position of the English did not seem enviable."

Reporter Raymond Swing missed the transport ship that carried his colleagues Ruhl and Suydam to the peninsula but caught a later paddleboat loaded with supplies. One hundred miles of the Marmara Sea separated the Turkish capital from the top of the Dardanelles. During his three months covering the Gallipoli front, Swing had made the voyage numerous times, but this time he was in for a surprise. Midway in the journey, a British submarine, the *E11*, suddenly surfaced in the path of his boat. A British officer appeared on deck and yelled, "Who are you?" As the only English speaker aboard the supply boat, Swing was appointed spokesman for the vessel.

"I'm Swing of the *Chicago Daily News,*" was the prompt reply.

"Glad to meet you, Mr. Swing, but I mean what ship is that?"

"The Turkish transport *Nagara,*" the reporter answered.

"Are those marines?" asked the submarine commander, referring to the fez-topped crew scrambling about the *Nagara*'s decks.

"No, they're just sailors," said Swing.

"Well, I'm going to sink you."

"Can we get off?" piped the journalist.

"Yes, and be damned quick about it."

A wild scramble ensued to launch all the lifeboats. Some frightened sailors jumped into the sea. Swing climbed into the last small boat, helped to rescue those in the water, and then headed for shore as an officer from *E11* boarded the *Nagara* and planted explosives to scuttle it.

Swing wrote up his exciting encounter with the submarine for the *Chicago Daily News* and elected to mail the story rather than cable it, a move that ended up embarrassing the newspaper. While his story made its leisurely, multiweek journey to Chicago, *E11* returned to England. The submarine had conducted a highly successful operation in Turkish waters, sinking several ships. Its skipper, Lieutenant Commander Martin Eric Dunbar-Nasmith, received the Victoria Cross. When the editors of the *Chicago Daily News* read the account of *E11*'s exploits in the London papers, they were surprised to see mention of its encounter with the American newsman Raymond Swing. Why was the *Daily News* keeping Swing in the Dardanelles, they wondered, if he could not even scoop a war story that involved himself? Swing's own story of the encounter arrived at the newspaper office two weeks later.

In hindsight Swing explained his decision to mail rather than cable the story as a reflection of his concept of the proper role for a newspaper correspondent, "which [he] considered to be to report the facts and not to recount his own personal adventures." Since the work of most correspondents appeared without a byline, such modesty was not out of line. However, modesty did not feed the appetite of American newspapers for novel war coverage.

Swing's encounter with *E11* survived in British submarine lore for some time and in fact came to an interesting conclusion in the next war. Swing went on to gain fame as a foreign correspondent in the 1920s and 1930s and rose to international acclaim after becoming a radio news commentator on European affairs in 1936. In the late 1920s, while stationed in London, Swing once again crossed paths with the *E11*'s skipper, Martin Dunbar-Nasmith, then an admiral. The admiral mentioned that it had been an *E11* officer named Guy D'Oyly-Hughes who boarded the *Nagara* to plant the explosives, and that he had returned to the submarine carrying Swing's typewriter. D'Oyly-Hughes eventually went on to captain the aircraft carrier HMS *Glorious* and lost his life when that ship sank during a naval engagement off the coast of Norway early in World War II.

As Swing took up the story in his autobiography, D'Oyly-Hughes's widow eventually came to work for the British embassy in Washington, and the two of them had lunch. Mrs. D'Oyly-Hughes shared that her husband spoke often of Swing and was pleased that the newsman who gave the American commentary on the British Broadcasting Corporation was the same man he had met in the Sea of Marmara in 1915. She told Swing that her husband carried the typewriter with him wherever he went, and that it had gone down with him on the *Glorious*.

But the exploits of one daring British submarine did not change the untenable position of the Allies in Gallipoli. One day after *E11* sank the *Nagara*, the German submarine *U-21* prowled off Gallipoli in search of larger targets. The sub had just completed a five-thousand-mile voyage from its base in Germany, when Kapitän-leutnant Otto Hersing spied British battleships formed in a line bombarding Turkish positions. He centered the HMS *Triumph* in his periscope and sent off one torpedo that hit the bow. The explosion drew the attention of both the ANZAC and the Turkish soldiers on shore, who stood up in their trenches to watch until the mighty battleship slipped beneath the surface, then resumed their fighting. Two days later Hersing repeated the extraordinary achievement by sinking the battleship *Majestic*.

When *U-21* arrived in triumph at Constantinople on June 5, Raymond Swing landed his biggest Gallipoli scoop by interviewing the U-boat captain. "Since Odysseus sailed from Troy bound for rocky Ithaca no more extraordinary voyage has been chronicled than that of Capt. Lieut. Otto Hersing and his thirty-two companions," Swing wrote. He was able to report that Hersing had just received a congratulatory telegram from the kaiser, conferring on him the prestigious medal the Pour le Mérite. Originally created in the eighteenth century, the medal retained its French name.

Hersing regaled the reporter with his harrowing, record-setting forty-two-day voyage. Coming just one month after a U-boat sank the passenger liner *Lusitania*, with the loss of 1,191 lives, Hersing's story gave added proof of the lethal, long-range capabilities of German U-boats and the additional danger facing the British effort at Gallipoli. This time Swing cabled the story.

Summer fighting on the peninsula featured failed Allied assaults and futile Turkish counterattacks. Stories given an Allied slant could be cabled through London and were sure to make it to America. Those reporting a Turkish achievement often went via Berlin for wireless transmission to America. When the Allies' all-out "August Offensive" achieved only small and costly victories, reporters began to draw comparisons to the stalemated trench fighting on the western front.

Granville Fortescue's employer, the *Daily Telegraph* of London, a paper that strongly supported the government, published only censored versions of his frank accounts of the fighting to downplay the desperateness of the British position. The hard truth of Fortescue's accounts reached the British public and its leaders in a more roundabout way. The American International News Service took Fortescue's articles off the London cable and sent them uncensored for publication in New York. Those stories were then republished in Paris and Berlin and then finally in their uncensored form in England, where they inflamed debate in Parliament about the Gallipoli campaign.

Lord Northcliffe's *Times* and *Daily Mail* began to openly grumble about the handling of the campaign and how the government used censorship to cover its mistakes. The Gallipoli campaign had been the brainchild of the First Lord of the Admiralty Winston Churchill. The *Daily Mail* called for the dismissal of the "inefficient bunglers among the politicians and at the War Office."

Fortescue was recalled to England, where members of Parliament, including Lord Northcliffe, sought his assessment of the situation. They pressured Fortescue to write a hasty book summing up his impressions of the fighting, his analysis of the tactics, and conclusions about why the campaign would not succeed. The book, *What of the Dardanelles? An Analysis*, appeared in October 1915, and in it Fortescue came down hard on the planning and conduct of the campaign, with chapter headings such as "The Initial Blunder" and "The Second Miscalculation." The book appeared only weeks after Germany, Austria, and their new ally Bulgaria began a combined attack on Britain's ally Serbia. Fortescue stressed the urgency of withdrawing from Gallipoli in order to address that more urgent crisis in the Balkans. The following month the commander of the British war effort, Lord Kitchener, conducted an inspection tour of Gallipoli, and the withdrawal of British forces soon followed. Churchill resigned from government that same month.

As late as 1937, when Fortescue wrote the memoirs of his war experience, he had not lost his disgust for the Gallipoli campaign and the man responsible for it. "When the cost of that gigantic failure is counted it must weigh heavily on one man: Winston Churchill," he asserted. "How can he lift his head among his countrymen?"

Salonika, Gateway to Serbia

One year into the fighting, correspondents on the western front began to receive nagging telegrams from their editors to find some new angle on the war. Once the savage possibilities of the trench stalemate had been reported a dozen different ways, they became quite boring. Write about what was happening *behind* the front, some suggested. Or cover the fighting in some new location. Italy had just entered the war in May 1915 on the Allied side. Its alpine encounters with the Austrians might offer novelty. The dark hole of Serbia always held surprises. Or try the Caucasus in eastern Turkey, where no reporter had been.

Comfortably ensconced in Paris in October 1915, war reporter-artist John McCutcheon received a telegram from his editor at the *Chicago Tribune* that read, "Go to Saloniki [alternative spelling] stopping Athens for interview with Venizelos [Greek Prime Minister]." McCutcheon's colleagues, United Press reporter William Shepherd and *Collier's* photographer James Hare, thought it was a good idea and joined him on the journey.

On his way to Salonika, McCutcheon had only a three-hour layover in Athens to get the requested interview with the prime minister, write his dispatch, and cable it home. With the help of the American embassy, he set up a hasty meeting. It was symptomatic of Balkan politics in general and Greek politics in particular that Venizelos was no longer prime minister when McCutcheon arrived.

Venizelos lost his post by mobilizing the Greek army when Bulgaria entered the war on the side of the Central Powers, a move opposed by the Greek king. Venizelos assumed correctly that Bulgaria would attack Greek's ally Serbia, but the king wanted Greece to remain neutral. Venizelos stated emphatically to McCutcheon, "If I return to power, I shall make war against Bulgaria."

McCutcheon hurried to the cable office to fire off his short summary of the interview. There was no censorship in neutral Greece to slow things down. Then he took a blazing taxi ride to the port, where his ship had already raised anchor. He had to climb the boarding ladder of the moving ship from a rowboat to get onboard. Another day in the life of a war correspondent.

"If ever a stage was set for trouble, it is here," McCutcheon wrote in his first cable from Salonika. By early November 1915, Salonika had become an Allied base and a key news center. Typically a bustling, crowded port city of 120,000 souls, Salonika now had 100,000 Allied troops quartered in the city, along with 100,000 mobilized Greek troops and their families.

The three correspondents took over the only available accommodations at the Olympus Palace Hotel, a vast open space that had previously been the hotel dining room. Its large windows looked directly onto the harbor and the stone landing steps of the main pier. It provided the perfect viewing post for the drama of Salonika's waterfront. Passenger liners, fishing boats, cruisers, submarines, freighters, hospital ships, and mammoth battleships crowded the water. Transports unloaded troops, artillery, ammunition, and supplies. Throughout the day small boats tied up at the pier, "marines came ashore for the mail, stewards for fruit and fish, Red Cross nurses to shop, tiny midshipmen to visit the movies, and the sailors and officers of the Russian, French, British, Italian, and Greek war-ships to stretch their legs in the park."

A steady flow of soldiers disembarking from transports climbed the stone steps outside the hotel window. British and French soldiers arrived from Gallipoli, French colonial fighters from Africa and China, and Hindus come to serve with the British. Salonika's wildly diverse population and refugees newly arrived from Serbia jostled on the street with trolley cars, oxcarts, donkeys laden with grain and potatoes, military automobiles, carriages, motorcycles, vendor pushcarts, mounted officers, and marching soldiers.

Martial law did not govern this neutral city. No one censored the news. The consulates of all the belligerents remained open, and the citizens of any country came and went freely. Turkish or German officers and consular officials encountered British and French officers in the cafés. The 170,000 Allied troops in the city and at the front were merely guests in the country. No one had ever before seen a war situation like this.

The unmatched openness and ease of access made the job of spying that much easier. Spies collected in Salonika like nowhere else in the war zone. When John Reed had passed through the city the previous month, he described it as an espionage comic opera, with a most colorful cast of characters: "Germans with shaved heads and sword-cuts all over their faces pretending to be Italians; Austrians in green Tyrolean hats passing as Turks; stupid-mannered Englishmen who sat drinking and talking in the cafés, eavesdropping the conversation in six languages that went on about them; exiled Mohammedans of the Old Turkish party plotting in corners, and Greek secret-service men who changed their clothes fourteen times a day and altered the shape of their moustaches."

The correspondents developed their own network of news-gathering "spies" who reported rumors overheard in the bazaar, the café, or the Turkish bath. Journalists or spies trying to monitor Allied intentions could also read the city's four newspapers, two pro-Allies and two pro-German. These papers published detailed reports on the military traffic passing through the city.

Even the commander of Allied forces in the region, the French general Maurice Sarrail, practiced an unusual transparency by conducting daily briefings for the newsmen. Although the sessions were short and the general could not be quoted or interviewed, they provided an authoritative view of events.

The indisputable truth remained that just fifty miles to the north, tiny Serbia was swiftly being overrun by three invading armies. "I'm afraid Serbia is done for," a British officer confided to the correspondents. When William Shepherd traveled into the southern edge of Serbia, he ran out of superlatives to describe what he saw. "The world war ha[d] developed no scene of greater horror" than the tragedy unfolding in Serbia. Dead bodies lined the road from Nish to Monastir, the "highway of agony"—men, women, and children who had succumbed to starvation, exhaustion, and disease while fleeing the invasion. What was happening in Serbia was the "blackest page in human history!" The thousands of Serbians making it to Salonika brought additional stories of the unfolding tragedy.

Would those invading armies cross into Greece when they had finished with hapless Serbia? Would that motivate Greece to join the war, and if so on which side? Days after arriving in Salonika, McCutcheon could already report that Venizelos had returned to power. If Greece should declare for the Allies, and perhaps even with that gesture influence Romania to join as well, it could tip the scales against the Central Powers. However, no rational person ever placed a bet on what would happen next in the Balkans.

When the dean of American war correspondents, Richard Harding Davis, drifted into this chaos in late November 1915, he increased the size of the American community in the city to six—four correspondents, the U.S. consul, and a man representing Standard Oil Company. Davis was forced to lodge with his colleagues in their spacious room with its window onto the city. Like the seasoned campaigner he was, he adapted to circumstances. He arranged several chairs for a bed and unfolded his collapsible, rubber bathtub that went with him everywhere. His splashing cold-water baths became the first sound to wake his companions each morning.

At dinner with his companions, Davis always took center stage. He would drink deeply of the seasoned Greek liqueur mastika and then regale them with stories. His daring adventures spanned the past thirty years of world history, from his early newspaper days in Philadelphia to personal exploits covering conflicts in Manchuria, Cuba, Central America, South Africa, and Mexico. All of it he generously sprinkled with a cast of famous and colorful characters whom he had met and interviewed along the way.

It seemed to an outside observer that Richard Harding Davis sometimes loomed as large as the events he covered, as if the full import of a battle or a famous personage could not be fully appreciated unless interpreted by the master storyteller. Reporters drawn into his orbit did not just cover a battle or a war, but they covered it "with Richard Harding Davis." His name, idiosyncrasies, and distinctive writing became elements of their own experience and were often mentioned in their news stories.

Davis had been in Salonika only a few days when General Sarrail, summoned reporters for a special announcement. When McCutcheon and his companions arrived in Salonika in early November, they had been virtually the only correspondents in the city. But then a series of setbacks turned Salonika into the hottest news spot in southeast Europe. When Austria and Germany forced Russia out of Galicia, Gallipoli turned into a fiasco, and Bulgaria allied with Germany, regional focus shifted to the tottering Balkan ally of Serbia, which bordered Greece. The Allies had just rushed in troops and supplies to stiffen Serbian resistance. Some two dozen foreign reporters now crowded the small room to hear General Sarrail's update on the situation.

For a long moment the general leaned casually against a windowsill, as if nothing special would be offered that day. And then he stated that British and French troops were withdrawing from Serbia. It no longer made sense to maintain an advanced and dangerous position in that country, he explained. Better strategically to withdraw to a more defensible line. Sarrail spoke in an even, measured tone that made everything seem obvious and reasonable. Bridges and tunnels were being destroyed and equipment and matériel being removed. The retreat was orderly and remarkably free of casualties. A moment of weighty silence filled the room. Reporters waited with pencil and paper in hand as though straining for the words that would make sense of this development that would explain why, after only two weeks of fighting, the Allies were abandoning Serbia.

Realizing this might be their last chance to catch the fighting before the final collapse, the American reporters got permission to enter Serbia. They rode an empty freight train, passing by units of the retreating French army. Davis and photographer James Hare transferred to a truck that bounced and skidded over roads churned to mud by heavy traffic. At an advanced supply depot, they watched British soldiers load supplies onto trucks and wrestle them over the mud-clogged roadways.

Learning that some rearguard units remained in the mountains holding off the Bulgarians, Davis and Hare arranged for a French staff car to take them in search of the last Allied fighters in Serbia. Davis filled his account of the excursion with vivid details of suntanned soldiers fresh from Gallipoli and soldiers breaking through ice-covered lakes to wash mud from their uniforms. The mountain vistas and numbing cold became part of the story, as did peasant fishermen and the resemblance of the village houses to those he had seen in Cuba during the Spanish-American War.

They finally located an English artillery unit dug into a hillside. It was in fact the only military unit in sight, in a landscape of barren, snow-covered mountaintops, operated by a handful of men and commanded by two boy officers, one eighteen years old and his superior aged nineteen. There was no enemy in sight, no village or fortification, no troops, trench, or other artillery. From somewhere in the surrounding hills, a spotter telephoned instructions—eight degrees to the left, four thousand yards. The men adjusted the gun and then blasted away.

Davis pointed out to the young officers that they appeared to be holding out on their own. "The child gazed around him. It was growing dark and gloomier, and the hollow of the white hills were filled with shadows. His men were listening, so he said bravely, with a vague sweep of his hand at the encircling darkness: 'Oh, they're about—somewhere. You might call this,' he added with pride, 'an independent command.'"

When Hare set up his camera to take a picture of the gun firing, the French driver insistently honked his horn, urging the reporters to return to the car. Davis felt a heart tug of guilt at leaving the boy soldiers, writing, "At the door of the car we turned and waved, and the two infants waved back. I felt I had meanly deserted them—that for his life the mother of each could hold me to account."

Davis titled his story of that visit "The Deserted Command." A handful of boys had been abandoned in that menacing landscape to protect the rear of a retreating army. Maybe they withdrew before the Bulgarians rolled over that mountaintop. Maybe not. A journalist rarely learned the end of a story. All Davis could do was to write a snapshot of that war moment and capture a small measure of the guilt a journalist felt when he removed himself from the danger.

Despite the Allies' strategic withdrawal from Serbia, they gave every indication of settling in at Salonika. Engineers built new roads. Shiploads of reinforcement and supplies continued to arrive day and night. The French constructed a camp outside the city, and new warehouses appeared at the waterfront. The shattered remnants of the Serbian army straggled into the city and joined with the French.

Throughout December Davis peppered his employer, the Wheeler Syndicate, with more-traditional news stories that reported the quickly evolving scene. Syndicates provided war coverage for hundreds of smaller newspapers that could not afford their own correspondents. They needed a continuous flow of short articles that monitored the pulse of events. Davis reported on defensive preparations around the city and speculation about which of the three armies then in Serbia would invade Greece. He told about *Chicago Tribune* reporter Mildred Farwell trapped at a Red Cross hospital in Serbia when the Bulgarians overran the town; about a visit to an artillery outpost in Bulgaria; German and Bulgarian planes bombing the city and the retaliatory closing of their consulates; and the thousands of residents fleeing from Salonika.

The Deserter Hero

While Salonika awaited the enemy at its door, a wild collection of individuals continued to appear in the correspondents' room at the Olympus Palace Hotel. Americans in trouble who needed a bed for the night or enough money to cable home knocked on their door. British correspondents and Allied officers wanting to relax with a cup of tea or a whiskey stopped by, as did whatever human flotsam drifted in on the tide of war.

The hotel porter got in the habit of nabbing people in the lobby and conducting them to the correspondents, if he thought them newsworthy. He would knock on the door, announce, "A man to see you, misters," and then usher in the confused person to be grilled by the resident reporters. In such a way they met a British gentleman just arrived in the city after escorting a group of nurses through twenty days of hardship and danger during the Serbian rout. Other visitors brought grisly stories of escaping through the Albanian mountains, hiking through waist-deep snowdrifts, past the frozen bodies of those who had fallen. One visitor agreed to sell a state secret for five francs; another wanted the world to know that he had invented a new type of poisonous gas for use in the trenches.

But no other story of the war ever unfolded like the one brought to their room by a young American who was a sergeant in the British army. Four of America's most renowned war correspondents were drawn into the personal life of an individual soldier and counseled him through a moment of crisis in his life. This individual's predicament came to represent that of all servicemen at that point in the war—indeed, of the nations themselves. Correspondent Stanley Washburn would have called it a morale problem. The story became the most famous war story written by the most famous correspondent and also his last.

Like so many other stories of Salonika, this one too showed up at their door. The subject was a son of the American Midwest, an idealistic college boy who had gone to Canada, lied about his citizenship to enlist with the British, and been in continuous action with them for the past fifteen months. He was homesick and just wanted to spend a moment with some Americans.

Having seen action at Mons, the Marne, Ypres, and Gallipoli, he exuded a war-weariness. Soldiers sometimes got a rest from battle, he groused, but not the medical corps in which he served. He had been a hospital steward, a stretcher-bearer, and an ambulance driver nonstop.

"I don't believe there's any kind of fighting I haven't seen," he declared; "hand-to-hand fighting with bayonets, grenades, gun butts. I've seen 'em on their knees in the mud choking each other, beating each other with their bare fists. I've seen every kind of airship, bomb, shell, poison gas, every kind of wound. Seen whole village turned into a brickyard in twenty minutes; in Servia [alternative spelling] seen bodies of women frozen to death, bodies of babies starved to death, seen men in Belgium swinging from trees; along the Yser for three months I saw the bodies of men I'd known sticking out of the mud, or hung up on the barbed wire with crows picking them."

And for now, he just sat in a wet, muddy, and brutally cold tent camp six miles from Salonika, doing nothing and was so god-awful sick of war. He worried whether he could ever become a quiet, decent American citizen again. He wanted to go home and write a book about the war, he said, maybe give lectures.

When he could get another leave of absence, he planned to visit the U.S. consul in Salonika to get a passport so he could prove that he was an American citizen. Maybe then he could get out of the British army. But he didn't think he could do that in a British uniform, so if he came back again, could he borrow some civilian clothes from the correspondents to visit the consul? The correspondents assured him that he could. McCutcheon offered shoes and a cap, Shepherd had an extra suit of clothes, and Hare had spare socks. When the young man left, the reporters thought they'd never see him again. Rare was the soldier who didn't grumble about the war. Once he got busy again, he would be distracted by his duties.

"A man to see you, misters," the hotel porter announced early next morning, while the correspondents sat around breakfast in their room. In walked the soldier, come to borrow their clothing. "Don't let me take you from your breakfast," he told them. "I'll just shave in the wash-basin, if you don't mind."

When Davis later wrote about this young man, he did not use his real name, instead calling him Billy Hamlin. The others would follow his example. So it was Billy Hamlin who with a sense of purpose removed his whiskers and shaved off his moustache. None of the reporters realized the gravity of that moment for the soldier, who by this seemingly simple act was breaking a rule in the British army that required moustaches. It was an offense that alone could land him in the guardhouse for ten days.

The drama resumed that afternoon, when the correspondents returned to their room to find an anxious Hamlin. He had learned he could not get a passport from the consul in Salonika but would have to go to the embassy in Athens, which is what he planned to do. He had a ticket for a boat that departed in two hours.

Davis was the first to state the delicate but obvious fact.

"I suppose you know it's desertion."

"It's not *my* army," Hamlin said. "I'm an American."

"But wouldn't you be shot for desertion in war-time, if you were caught?"

"Yes, but any fellow 'll be shot if he sticks to the war game long enough, so what difference does it make?"

The arguments grew more insistent and Hamlin more agitated. "What do you fellows know about it?" he countered. "You *write* about it, about the 'brave lads in the trenches'; but what do you know about the trenches? What you've seen from automobiles. That's all. That's where *you* get off! I've *lived* in the trenches for fifteen months, froze in 'em, starved in 'em, and I've saved lives, too, by hauling men out of trenches." He lifted his shirt to reveal a scar across his stomach where a bullet had caught him when he rescued a wounded soldier from no-man's-land.

He said the correspondents talked as though he was a coward afraid of danger, but it was the discomfort he hated more than anything. He had lived in a hole like a prairie dog in Gallipoli, with sand in his boots and his food, and then they shipped him to the brutal winter in Serbia in his summer uniform, where the wet fabric froze to his body, and the only thing he treated men for now was pneumonia and frostbite, and when they took guys out of their blankets, their frozen toes fell off.

The reporters urged him to stop and consider the consequences of what he contemplated. A deserter would never be able to hold up his head in society, could never sell a book to a publisher or give lectures of his war experience. He would be an outcast. Hamlin had been through hell and should be proud of that; he should be able to show that marvelous scar as a badge of honor, not hide it as a deserter.

"We'd give our eye-teeth to see what you've seen," Davis added, "and to write the things you can write. . . . When this war is over you'll have everything out of it that's worth getting—all the experiences, all the inside knowledge, all the 'nosebag' news; you'll have wounds, honors, medals, money, reputation. And you're throwing that all away." It was hard to know what registered with Hamlin. He seemed too wound up to be persuaded of anything except catching that boat to Athens.

To deflate the tension, McCutcheon suggested that the other correspondents go take in a motion-picture show, while he talked with Hamlin. They took his advice, and when they returned, they found Hamlin standing in the middle of the room once again dressed in his mud-caked uniform, looking distinctly uncomfortable. For being away from camp without leave and shaving off his moustache, he knew he would go straight to the guardhouse. "Tell them you got drunk, and shaved it off because a girl wanted you to," one of them suggested.

Hamlin paused at the door and glared at the reporters. "I hope when you turn into those beds to-night you'll think of me in the mud. I hope when you're having your five-course dinner and your champagne you'll remember my bully beef. I hope when a shell or Mr. Pneumonia gets me, you'll write a nice little sob story about the 'brave lads in the trenches.'"

Davis described the correspondents standing "like school boys, sheepish, embarrassed, and silent," until McCutcheon chimed in with "Don't forget, if there's anything we can do for you, let us know."

"Well, there is one thing you can do," Hamlin said. "You can all go to hell."

The door slammed, and Hamlin was gone. The correspondents sat in silence for a moment, until Davis broke the mood. "This is my story!" he yelled. "Best war story I ever knew." Davis left Salonika a few days later. His account of the incident appeared in the September 1916 issue of *Metropolitan Magazine* as "The Man Who Knew Everything" and later was published as the book *The Deserter*.

Correspondents had certainly portrayed the gritty sides of the war before, but never such a bitter, disillusioned soldier, never an individual who represented the disenchantment felt by so many at this point in the war. A conflict that was supposed to last for a few months had entered its second year. The enthusiasm that motivated a generation of young men to rush to arms for lofty causes had died somewhere amid the slaughter. Now only bitter resolve seemed to animate soldiers and armies.

The Deserter marked a turning point for Davis, moving him away from his heroic, civilization-saving conception of war and closer to the more modern realism of such reporters as John Reed and William Shepherd. It also served as an indictment of his profession. The correspondents' advice for Hamlin to bravely endure the hardships and dangers of soldiering, rang with the empty echo of an earlier age. It exposed the war reporters as comfortable, behind-the-scenes hypocrites.

Davis never saw his story about Billy Hamlin in print. In April 1916, back home in the United States, while talking on the phone to his editor, Davis died of a heart attack at the age of fifty-one. It fell to John McCutcheon and William Shepherd to tell the final chapters in the story, the part that Davis never knew.

Three days after Davis sailed home from Salonika, a note came to the correspondents from Hamlin. He was down on the pier with the Red Cross, on his way to a hospital in Alexandria, Egypt. He asked them to hurry down so he could say good-bye. They found him on a litter, about to be ferried out to a hospital ship anchored in the bay. He had been busted to private and docked two months' pay for his little escapade, he explained. But then his old stomach wound acted up, and he had been sick ever since. He gave them a letter to mail to his girl in New Orleans, then he sailed out of their lives for a second time.

Three months later William Shepherd discovered that the story had one final scene to play. Some scholars have since questioned the veracity of Shepherd's neat and coincidental closure to the story, but according to Shepherd, he ran into Hamlin in London, still in uniform, and over lunch learned the rest of the story. At the hospital in Alexandria, the doctors discovered that his gut had grown together from his old wound, and it took two operations to straighten it out. Then he was sent to England to convalesce. When he was released from the hospital in England, the British military restored him to the rank of sergeant, and a major told him he would be awarded the Distinguished Service Medal for rescuing that guy in no man's land.

Hamlin recalled the experience. "'It can't be me,' I told him. 'Why, I wanted to desert in Salonica, and they degraded me.'

"'Wanting to desert isn't a crime, my boy,' says the major. 'You didn't desert, did you? Well, there you are.'"

Hamlin proudly wore his DSM ribbon and showed Shepherd the award citation. "If it hadn't been for you fellows in Salonica I'd have missed it," Hamlin conceded. "I almost threw it all away . . . and besides, you know, I still think I was sick and didn't know it. And you fellows stepped in, just when I needed help, and made my decisions for me. I never can thank Davis and you fellows enough for steering me the right way."

Hamlin's regiment was heading to France in a few days, and he was going with them. "My girl wants me to come home, but I don't want to quit in the fifth inning." Two days later, Shepherd accompanied Hamlin to Charring Cross Station, where hundreds of soldiers were boarding a train to go back to the war. That's where the correspondents finally lost track of the deserter-hero from Salonika.

CHAPTER EIGHT

A Revolution in the Midst of War

The people can say what they please, but I smell trouble. And thank God I am here to get the photographs of it! If there is a revolution I hope it comes now, for although I hate to see bloodshed, if it has to be it might as well come while I am on the ground with plenty of film.

—Photographer DONALD THOMPSON, Petrograd,
March 8, 1917, *Donald Thompson in Russia*

The telegram Arno Dosch-Fleurot received in the last week of October 1916 said simply, "Suggest you might like to go to Russia." Such was the courteous manner with which his editor at the *New York World* sent him on new assignments. Dosch-Fleurot read the telegram in the harsh light of a bunker, beneath a hundred feet of rock and masonry, in the French fortress complex at Verdun. Throughout 1916 hundreds of thousands of French and German soldiers soaked Verdun with their blood. Dosch-Fleurot had been drawn there when the first French offensive of the campaign recaptured forts that had been taken by the Germans in February. It portended a shift in this endless battle, but it could not compete with developments in the East.

A circuitous, several-day journey by way of France, England, Sweden, and Finland, by boat, train, and horse-drawn sleigh over a frozen river, brought the *World* reporter to Petrograd, capital of the Russian Empire. He spent his first night on a hotel billiard table, the only accommodation he could find in the crowded city. During that sleepless night he realized how ill-prepared he was to cover this mysterious country. What little he knew about it came from novels and the writings of the American explorer and war correspondent George Kennan. (Kennan should not be confused with his distant cousin George F. Kennan, 1904–2005, American diplomat and Cold War strategist.) Kennan had a complicated relationship with Russia, which was generally conceded as the only sort of relationship one could have with the empire. He wrote warmly about the country's isolated tribal groups, but after meeting exiled dissidents in Siberia, he became an ardent supporter of Russian democracy, for which view he was banned from the country. Other than that Dosch-Fleurot's restless imagination ran with "nihilists with bombs, corrupt functionaries, Red Sundays, and cruel Cossacks."

Dosch-Fleurot followed the usual protocol after arriving in a new country: he conferred with colleagues, presented his papers to the Foreign Office, and visited the U.S. Embassy. The Reuter's correspondent, Guy Beringer, confessed that he had lived in Russia for ten years before he realized he didn't understand Russia. French journalist Ludovic Naudeau stroked his beard and offered some advice: "You will see in Russia every epoch of European life, from the monks of the Dark Ages, through the awakening sense of nationalism of the Renaissance, to a more modern and enlightened understanding than you will meet in Western Europe. You will find yourself tempted to compare Russia with other countries. Don't."

Dosch-Fleurot's application for war correspondent status with the Ministry of Foreign Affairs accomplished nothing more than to put a spy on his trail. When he protested, he was told to think nothing of it; everyone in Russia was followed by a spy. The U.S. ambassador, David R. Frances, told him that during the military victories of 1916 the people gave strong support to the war, but the recent catastrophic reverses had turned the public mood ugly. He introduced the reporter to Russian politics by taking him to a session of the Duma, the Russian parliament. There he heard the leader of the Constitutional Democratic Party argue that Russia risked defeat in the war because its efforts were hampered by "dark forces." The time had come, he said, for Russia to have a government responsive to the Duma. Dosch-Fleurot noted that the remark "fell like a bomb—a blow at the absolute power of the Czar. The Duma vibrated with excitement. There was a recess, deputies and spectators poured into the immense gallery area to discuss the audacity of the proposal." One of the delegates came up to the ambassador, livid that the authority of the czar had been attacked in public. "Mistakes we can correct, but let authority be questioned in the midst of war and we are lost," he insisted.

"Dark forces," Dosch-Fleurot would learn, was a thinly veiled reference to German influence in the economy, the war effort, even the court of the czar. Suspicion fell on the German-born czarina and the enigmatic monk named Grigory Rasputin, who exercised a mysterious power over her. Everywhere Dosch-Fleurot went in November and December 1916, Rasputin's name worked into conversation. Dosch-Fleurot and several other correspondents made arrangements to interview the influential monk, but the day before the scheduled meeting, the monk was poisoned, shot, and then stuffed through a hole in the frozen Neva River. The longer Dosch-Fleurot stayed in Russia, the more he too believed in "dark forces."

The sensational new of Rasputin's death reached news photographer Donald Thompson two months after the fact. It came on the human telegraph of news and rumors accosting him as he traveled the breadth of the empire on the Trans-Siberian Railroad. The army planned a new offensive in the spring, he heard from travelers. Food shortages in Petrograd would cause problems if the government didn't do something about them. And the much-reviled Siberian monk had been killed.

Thompson came to Russia at a critical juncture in the war. When he arrived in Petrograd on February 26, 1917, the German army stood only one hundred miles from the city. There was talk of fortifying or evacuating the city, moving the government to Moscow. *Leslie's Illustrated Weekly* wanted Thompson and reporter Florence MacLeod Harper to report on the climactic battle for the Russian capital, perhaps something on a par with the Battle of the Marne, which had saved Paris at the eleventh hour in 1914. If such a battle occurred, Thompson was the man to capture it.

17. Being wounded and arrested multiple times did not stop photojournalist Donald Thompson from covering the war on many fronts. His photographs and movies gave Americans some of their first views of the fighting. Photo courtesy of David Mould.

Few journalists had done more to bring the war home to America than Donald Thompson, who not only reported on the war but *showed* it, through dramatic photographs and motion pictures. Simply witnessing a war was dangerous enough, but only a true daredevil would stand up in the midst of whistling bullets and exploding shells to take its portrait.

The French arrested him eight times for trying to reach the front from Paris before he finally succeeded and got the first film of British troops in action. Lord Northcliffe sent him to Germany in 1915 for the *Daily Mail*. He once halted an advancing column of German infantry to take its picture, nonchalantly puffed a cigar until the dust settled, and then snapped his photograph and allowed the war to continue. In 1915 he accompanied Robert McCormick, publisher of the *Chicago Tribune*, on a VIP tour of the Russian lines. McCormick introduced the American public to fighting on the eastern front with cinematic lectures that featured Thompson's movie *With the Russians at the Front*.

By the end of 1915, Thompson could report to the trade publication *Motion Picture News* that he had worked with every army in Europe, had been in thirty-eight battles, lost three cameras, been arrested many times, and suffered several wounds. The *Topeka Daily Capital* referred to its hometown boy as "the photographic hero of the war." Thompson had been recuperating at home from a fractured skull caused by a shell fragment in France when he got the assignment from *Leslie's* to hurry to Russia. Before departing on yet another dangerous adventure, he had to promise his wife to write her every day. If that request was made to give her comfort, it failed miserably. The letters began as breezy notes about his journey but quickly changed to detailed accounts of a revolution, an internal war in the middle of a world war that put him at greater risk than any of his time in the trenches.

Once he arrived in Petrograd, Thompson made a hasty visit to the Russian front. Allied commanders lost sleep worrying about the Russian army. With the disastrous collapse of its Brusilov Offensive the previous summer, many believed the army had lost its will to fight. If Russia could no longer occupy the attention of the million German troops along the eastern front, those troops would move quickly to the West and tip the tide of the war. Thompson found things relatively quiet at the fighting line, but he saw supplies and artillery shells stockpiled everywhere, in preparation for a planned spring offensive. An officer promised Thompson lots of opportunities for good pictures in the spring. But opportunities for good pictures came sooner than that and not at the front but on the streets of Petrograd.

Food shortages were stirring protests and strikes in the capital. "If you could see these bread lines," Thompson wrote his wife. "You would hardly believe that this is the Twentieth Century." People dressed in rags stood for hours in freezing temperatures to get the terrible war bread. Thompson felt guilty walking past them in his heavy fur coat. A bread shop near his hotel had to call for police protection when people smashed the windows to get bread. Thompson's candid letters home had to be smuggled out through special mail pouches or via courier to Norway.

An official at the U.S. consulate warned Thompson and Harper to expect trouble. Proclamations posted around the city prohibited demonstrations and parades. Cossacks patrolled the streets to maintain order. Followed by his ever-vigilant spy, Dosch-Fleurot visited the factory sections of the city and learned about the secret worker groups that promoted strikes and protests. A servant at Thompson's hotel whispered that workers planned to march to the palace and demand food and work. Thompson hired as a translator a young man named Boris, who told the photographer there would be a revolution. In fact an eruption of some sort seemed so imminent that Florence Harper wandered around town, "watching and waiting for it as [she] would for a circus parade."

That parade appeared for Harper one day in the form of fifty women gathered in the street. One made an angry speech about her factory-worker husband. He was on strike, and she could find no bread to buy to feed him. Others spoke up with their stories, and their numbers grew. When they began to sing the wobbly notes of "La Marseillaise" and march down the street, Harper followed. The women stopped several streetcars and scattered a unit of army recruits drilling on a parade ground. By the time they reached Nevsky Prospect, the city's main boulevard, their numbers had swelled to nearly five hundred. A line of police finally succeeded in breaking up the march. Harper later noted it as the "first riot of the revolution."

City streets became venues for the unrest. Crowds gathered every day, growing progressively larger and uglier. They broke windows and scuffled with police. Repeatedly, Thompson and Harper landed in the middle of churning marchers, jostled, knocked down, fleeing mounted police and Cossacks. Harper received two sharp jabs from the butt end of a Cossack lance for moving away too slowly from one march. Thompson worked with his small camera to be less conspicuous. Still his translator had to explain repeatedly to protestors that he was not a police spy but an *Americansky* reporter.

Word came of rioting on the outskirts of the city. Streetcars had been overturned, phone and electric wires cut. The next day the crowds included a rougher element that smashed shop windows and stopped traffic. One man tried to force his way through, but he was dragged from his sleigh and beaten to death. Dosch-Fleurot wrote several stories about the "bread riots," but none of them made it past the censor.

Given the flashpoint of tensions in the city, the crowd that gathered on sunny Sunday, March 11, looked surprisingly peaceful. It reminded Harper of "Circus Day" in a small American town. Street marches had become a bit of a spectacle for the curious, and on this day many children brought a light-hearted mood to the crowd. But heading back to their hotel, Thompson and Harper encountered a large group of determined marchers singing "La Marseillaise." Something made the two reporters apprehensive. They hung back rather than following along. "Those poor devils are going to get it," Thompson said.

When the protestors reached the next cross street, there came an explosion of gunfire. Many fell dead or wounded, and the crowd wheeled around in panic. As the terrified men, women, and children ran screaming, a storm of gunfire greeted them from the opposite direction. Soldiers along the street fired, and rooftop snipers opened up. A well-dressed woman standing next to Harper groaned and sank to the pavement. A little girl ran past, clutching her throat where a bullet had struck.

Harper and Thompson hit the ground. "Pretend you are wounded," Thompson advised. "The ambulances will pick you up." Freezing and paralyzed with fear, Harper waited until an ambulance removed her to the hospital, and then made it back to the Astoria Hotel. When she told people at the hotel what had happened and that hundreds had been killed, no one believed her.

The following day word reached Dosch-Fleurot that soldiers had refused the orders of an officer to fire at a crowd. He tried to visit a barracks but was refused entry. Meanwhile, marches, demonstrations, and riots popped up around the city. Street-corner orators exhorted passersby to protest food shortages. The whole city seemed captured by the unrest. Moving along with a crowd, Dosch-Fleurot found it impossible not to be caught up in its enthusiasm. "It was a moving spectacle when they stopped before the palaces and the burnt police stations, which symbolized the autocracy to them, and sang of their freedom," he wrote.

He came upon a crowd breaking into an arsenal. They loaded rifles into cars. As he watched, a truck wheeled around a corner, filled with soldiers, sailors, and civilians, "faces radiant." "Freedom!" they yelled enthusiastically. One waved a red cloth. That's when the true significance struck Dosch-Fleurot. This was not a "bread riot" or an uprising by mutinous troops; it was a revolution.

That night a group of soldiers and civilians visited the Astoria Hotel and met with the Allied officers living there. The officers assured them that no antirevolutionary meetings were being held in the hotel and that they would observe a strict neutrality, after which the revolutionists pledged to leave the hotel alone. But next morning a regiment crossing the square came under fire from a machine gun believed to be on the roof of the Astoria. An angry mob gathered in the street, and a few Russian officers staying at the hotel fired on them with their pistols. The mob answered with a fusillade of shots, killing some curious hotel guests standing at their windows. The crowd surged into the lobby and spread over the lower floors. A fire in the lobby sent smoke through the elevator shaft to the upper floors, further alarming the terrified women rushing around begging to be saved.

Early in the melee Harper slipped from the hotel and mingled with the crowd, which gave her the novel experience of assisting in the attack on her own hotel. "When it was over I found that

I had rather enjoyed it," she recalled. The women hotel guests were allowed to leave with whatever luggage they could carry. As the foreign officers left, the crowd cheered them, but most of the Russian officers were killed.

Dosch-Fleurot marked the end of the revolution on the day he saw a huge street march of unarmed civilians and soldiers surge toward a unit of soldiers that still held out. The dense crowd ran forward, shouting and waving red flags. Dosch-Fleurot watched apprehensively as the soldiers raised their rifles and took aim. The crowd did not hesitate but came straight on, yelling, "Brothers, comrades, don't shoot. We are free, free, free." It was a most remarkable sight. Dosch-Fleurot counted the seconds as the mob covered the final yards. No shots rang out. The crowd enveloped the soldiers in warm greetings and continued its tidal surge into other parts of the city to win over the last pockets of soldiers.

Dosch-Fleurot ran into an official from the French embassy on the street and waved him down. All winter long correspondents had heard about German influence paralyzing the army and how bureaucracy and corruption had hampered it as well. Surely the Russian army would now fight with the enthusiasm of free men.

"What a day for the Allied cause," Dosch-Fleurot gushed to the French official.

Wearing a crestfallen expression, the official took the reporter's hand. "Don't deceive yourself," he said. "We have lost the war today." His remark reflected the concern of many that the revolution increased the likelihood of the unthinkable: Russia leaving the war.

However, when news of the revolution broke in America on March 16, press reports were almost uniformly optimistic. Accounts stressed that the transition to democracy had been faster and easier than any would have predicted. Bloodshed had been minimal. Capable men had stepped forward to lead an interim government. Pro-German influence would now be eliminated. There would be a renewed commitment to the war effort. And within days news also came that women had been given the vote. The warm afterglow of the revolution barely outlived the spring, but for that brief moment it all seemed "beautifully logical, gloriously unanimous. Everyone wanted it; everyone was glad when it came."

The United States entered the war the following month, comfortable in the notion that its new sister democracy would continue to tie up the million German soldiers on the eastern front.

Women Report the Revolution

The March Revolution served as a clarion call for a new crop of American reporters who appeared in Petrograd the following summer. (According to the Julian calendar then in use in Russia, the revolution occurred on February 23. All dates in this chapter refer to the Western, or Gregorian, calendar, according to which the revolution occurred on March 8.) Those journalists who championed social causes such as labor reform and women's suffrage, who fought against poverty, political corruption, and social privilege were inspired by the birth of democracy in Russia. Conspicuous among them was the largest group of female reporters ever assembled in the war. Most could not be labeled as war correspondents. They had cut their journalistic teeth by exposing corruption in government and the exploitation of women and workers. They felt in sympathy with the socialist values of the revolution and its provisional government.

Florence Harper had arrived to cover the war and ended up covering a revolution. But the other women who appeared in Petrograd in the spring and summer of 1917 were drawn by the revolution itself. The well-known journalist Rheta Childe Dorr (*New York Evening Mail*), champion of labor reform and women's suffrage, arrived in Petrograd in May. Dorr had always been an admirer of the French Revolution, and she saw in Russia a birth of liberty greater than the French had ever imagined. Louise Bryant arrived late that summer, along with her famous socialist war-correspondent husband John Reed. The Bell Syndicate assigned her to report on the war "from a woman's point of view." Translated from journalese that meant to report on conditions on the home front. How was the civilian population—largely women and children—adapting to the privations of war? Reed's impeccable leftist credentials gave him and Bryant access to revolutionary leaders and placed them at locations where critical events unfolded. Bryant's articles and subsequent book on the revolution established her journalistic reputation.

Women had played a minor role in reporting the war, largely through freelance magazine assignments, Mary Boyle O'Reilly being the most notable exception. Covering the early years of the war for the News Enterprise Association, O'Reilly had been expelled from Belgium along with Richard Harding Davis, Arno Dosch-Fleurot, Gerald Morgan, and Will Irwin. With them she recorded her horror at watching the German destruction of the city of Louvain.

No woman was ever accredited by any of the belligerent armies, but women found ways to report on the fighting and what happened behind the lines. Madeleine Doty traveled to Germany in 1915 to distribute charity funds to war orphans and wrote about internal conditions. Novelist Mary Roberts Rinehart became one of the first civilian eyewitnesses to visit the trenches on the western front in February 1915. Novelist Edith Wharton, who lived in France during the war, visited several battlefields for *Scribner's Magazine* and wrote and edited books championing the cause of France.

Even before revolution stole headlines from the war that spring, the *San Francisco Bulletin* sent its reporter, Bessie Beatty, globetrotting to write a series of articles called "Around the World in Wartime." The stunt was a nod to the famous exploit of Nellie Bly, who in 1889 raced the fictional record of Phileas Fogg, protagonist of the Jules Verne novel *Around the World in Eighty Days*. Bly accomplished the feat in seventy-two days and garnered months of front-page stories for her newspaper, the *New York World*.

Beatty swept westward over half the globe, reporting on social and cultural issues in Hawaii, Japan, and China. Like many reporters who traveled to Russia, she journeyed from the Pacific port of Vladivostok to Petrograd aboard the Trans-Siberian Railway. A fair proportion of any war correspondent's reporting involved travel writing. Good stories often emerged as the reporters moved

18. Rheta Childe Dorr, pictured here in 1913 when she was editor of the *Suffragist*, traveled to Russia in 1917 to report on the revolution for the *New York Evening Mail*. Source: Harris & Ewing Collection, Prints and Photographs Division, Library of Congress, LC-DIG-hec-03403.

under difficult and dangerous conditions, thrown together with the wild mix of those forced to flitter along the edges of the conflict.

Riding the rails for twelve days through the vastness of Russia, Beatty glimpsed the warm afterglow of revolution. She traveled with soldiers heading to the front, political revolutionaries returning from exile in Siberia, the son of the famous novelist Leo Tolstoy returning to his homeland from America, and members of the Committee of Workmen's and Soldier's Deputies traveling to a meeting in the capital. A mood of optimism and great potential animated everyone. "The heavy heart of Russia lifted with a mighty shout of joy: 'Svoboda! (Freedom) We are free!'" Beatty reported. "For the moment this was enough. That single word, with its age-old power of placing man on the mountain-tops, made Russia happy." When Beatty reached Petrograd, her round-the-world excursion ended.

The first thing that greeted Bessie Beatty when she arrived in the city was a "war demonstration" of legless, armless, and blind soldiers, exhorting their able-bodied brothers to fight the war to a victorious conclusion. Rheta Dorr saw these castoff victims all over Petrograd. Missing limbs, horribly disfigured, clad in tattered uniforms, they begged on street corners or on church steps. No soldiers' homes or pensions supported the forgotten wounded in Russia.

When Dorr checked into the Military Hotel, formerly the Astoria Hotel, she discovered that the revolution too had left physical scars. Pockmarks from revolutionary bullets still adorned its exterior, and two bullet holes marked the wall above her bed. On the floor beneath the window in her room was a "pool of blood as big as a saucer." These were the harsh reminders that the two great forces of war and revolution were trying to find accommodation with each other. War had already pushed Russia beyond its limits, and now revolution challenged it for dominance.

Dorr began her coverage of the revolution by hiring a translator, then set out to take the pulse of Petrograd. An amazing number of soapbox orators on the streets harangued passersby with strong opinions about the war and the government. Dorr talked to people on park benches, in trams and trains, and at other public places. She met Russians from every walk of life and every political persuasion. In factories she spoke with workers and employers. She talked with the last Romanov left in freedom.

Political factions had already emerged to tug at the fabric of the revolution and challenge the Provisional Government. Prisons had been emptied of old radicals, and exiles were welcomed back from

Siberia and abroad. Socialist visionaries from the United States arrived to pursue their dream to refashion society. A profusion of councils, congresses, and committees gave voice to those who had never had one. Dorr watched young men march in the street with banners demanding "All Power to the Soviets." The soviets were councils of workers, soldiers, and peasants that appeared everywhere in the wake of the revolution: in cities, factories, and the military. They arose along with the Provisional Government as a parallel, competing political power.

The Petrograd Soviet launched the postrevolutionary period by issuing Order No. 1, which declared an end to military discipline. Soldiers' councils could now challenge orders of officers. As a way of preventing military units from being used against the revolution, it made perfect sense. As a policy for maintaining fighting order, it proved a disaster.

For reporters from the world's greatest democracy, the chaotic democracy of the workers' and soldiers' councils went beyond reason. Radicals controlled the council, Madeleine Dorr concluded. The war did not matter to them. Some were well-meaning theorists and dreamers but generally reasonable. Others were a "noisy and troublesome" minority known as the Bolsheviks, who had their own vast dream of establishing a "new order of society not only for Russia but for the whole world." They demanded that dream immediately and would not compromise.

"They say that everyone is to be equal," Donald Thompson noted with incomprehension, predicting that it would never work: "90 per cent of them cannot read or write," and they are the "orneriest bunch of devils I have ever met. . . . They are handing out proclamations every five minutes to appeal to the rabble they represent."

"Russia is sick," Dorr concluded. "She is gorged on something she has never known before—freedom: she is sick almost to die with excesses. . . . She is not even morally responsible for what she is doing." A sharp tone of frustration emerged in Dorr's reporting, as she tried hard to explain developments that she did not fully understand herself.

Like some of the other correspondents, Dorr had been drawn to

Russia by the March Revolution and its potential to reshape Russia, and she expected an upward trajectory. "The Russians want us to help them establish public schools; to show them how to build and operate great railroad systems; to farm scientifically; to do any number of things we have learned to do so well," she observed. An American commission visited Russia that June with a full complement of experts, including correspondent Stanley Washburn. But U.S. assistance was contingent upon Russia remaining in the war, a prospect that diminished by the day.

"We mustn't despise the Russians," Dorr wrote as she wrestled to put things in context. "We must learn to help them. And we can't do that unless we understand them. Take, for example, the army situation. It is very bad. The mass of soldiers are in rebellion against all authority. But consider the past history, the very recent past history of those soldiers. Aside from brutal treatment at the hands of some of the officers, they were cheated and starved and neglected by the bureaucracy in Petrograd."

In the seven-month period between Russia's two revolutions, the army became the center of attention for both those who wanted to protect the homeland and honor the commitment to the Allies by continuing to fight (the Provisional Government) and those who wanted to stop fighting because it only served the interests of capitalists and the bourgeoisie (the Bolsheviks). While the Provisional Government tried to maintain discipline in the ranks and political support for the war, the Bolsheviks visited the trenches to promote disobedience and desertion.

The Women's "Battalion of Death"

In the wake of the March Revolution, it was reasonable to expect that the granting of freedoms in Russia would soon extend to women's suffrage, the issue dearest to the heart of Rheta Dorr. Her journalistic career had been built on championing women's issues, including a series of articles investigating the grim conditions of working women. She served as the first editor of the publication *The Suffragist*.

War, revolution, and suffrage came together in one of the most publicized news stories of that momentous summer. It happened one day in early June, when an illiterate peasant woman from Siberia named Maria Bochkareva knelt in the great square in front of Petrograd's St. Isaac's Cathedral while priests sprinkled her with holy water. Along with thousands of other spectators, Rheta Dorr and Bessie Beatty watched with fascination as Bochkareva rose to her feet to have a sword buckled about her by three generals. This was a banner day for women's rights. Bochkareva had just become an officer in the Russian army, the first woman army officer in the world. Behind her 250 female soldiers stood at rigid attention, members of Bochkareva's newly formed "Battalion of Death." Each of them wore a red-and-black ribbon arrowhead on her right sleeve, red for blood and black for a death that was preferable to dishonor. Many news stories called Bochkareva "Russia's Joan of Arc."

The details surrounding this incredible story played out over the summer and attracted the interest of the world press. Drawing on threads of Russia's desperate military situation and the expectations for empowerment unleashed by the revolution, the story resonated with every segment of the confused and conflicted Russian society, except for those who opposed the war. Every foreign female reporter in Russia captured a piece of this story, but none more fully than suffragist Rheta Dorr.

Dorr visited the Women's Battalion during training to learn the stories of these inspiring women who had taken center stage in Russia's war effort. A product of Russia's long-suffering peasant class and a widow of the war, Bochkareva had been determined to fight in the army. After many rebuffs and appeals that rose to the czar himself, she was allowed to join the army in November 1914. She served for two years, receiving three wounds and several medals for bravery. Although an ardent revolutionist, she was disgusted by the conduct of soldiers after the revolution. When the men of her army unit began to lose their discipline, riot, and desert, she asked permission to form a women's battalion. "We will go wherever men refuse to go. We will fight when they run. The women will lead the men back to the trenches," she vowed.

Leaders of the Provisional Government saw the great symbolic value of a women's battalion. During this difficult time at the front, some battalions of male soldiers had formed "Death Battalions," composed of men committed to fight to the death to defend Russia. Bochkareva's innovation was to form a women's Death Battalion in the hopes of shaming men to return to the fighting, from which so many had fled.

At first Petrograd took the Women's Battalion as something of a joke. Thousands of men and women, civilians and soldiers on leave, traveled out from the city each day to see the "female soldiers" in training. Its recruits came from all ranks of society— peasants, factory workers, servants, also women with education and social prominence. The youngest was fourteen, the oldest a mother who, after losing four sons in the war, walked a hundred miles to Petrograd to join the battalion. Only the most physically fit were accepted. Only those who held up to Bochkareva's demanding standards and iron discipline survived the training. Dorr found them totally sincere in their conviction that they could rally a demoralized army. "Our men," they told her, "are suffering from a sickness of the soul. It is our duty to lead them back to health."

While the battalion trained that June, Dorr applied to the War Ministry for permission to travel with the battalion to the front. Before approval came, the women received orders to ship out immediately. In a panic Dorr rushed between government offices seeking emergency permission, without success. In desperation, only hours before the battalion was scheduled to depart, Dorr stopped by the U.S. Embassy, where she ran into veteran correspondent Arno Dosch-Fleurot. Don't worry about a permit, he advised. Just get on the train and stay on until they throw you off or you get where you want to be. Either way you will have a story. He told her how William Shepherd of the United Press once traveled all over the western front with nothing more to show than a worthless mining stock certificate. But it looked impressive and when waved with authority under the noses of those who didn't read English, it worked just fine.

So, without official permission, Dorr and Bessie Beatty joined the battalion on their train ride to the front. At every station along the route, crowds gathered to cheer them and to demand to see Bochkareva. Many were women—nurses, peasants, and working girls—fascinated by the battalion and all that it portended for women in Russia. However, the further the train traveled from Petrograd, the more apparent it became that "things were terribly wrong with the empire." The character of the station crowds began to reflect the widespread disruption in the army. Men in uniform crowded the stations, but they were soldiers in name only. "They slouched like convicts, they were dirty and unkempt, and their eyes were full of vacuous insolence. Absence of discipline and all restraint had robbed them of whatever manhood they had once possessed. The news of the women's battalion had drawn these men like a swarm of bees. They thrust their unshaven faces into the car windows . . . 'Who fights for the damned capitalists?' they screamed. 'Who fights for the English bloodsuckers? We don't fight.'"

The women shot back scornfully, "That is the reason why we do. Go home, you cowards, and let women fight for Russia." The taunts of the men reminded Dorr of New Yorkers watching a suffrage parade in the early days, when suffragists were taunted and ridiculed.

Dorr and Beatty spent a week with the battalion while it underwent additional preparation. But they were back in Petrograd when word came that the women soldiers had seen their first engagement. Dorr pieced together the story by interviewing wounded survivors in the hospital, including Bochkareva. When the men in their unit waivered, the women stormed the German trenches and took prisoners, the proud survivors reported. But the men would not advance to support them, forcing them to withdraw. Of the two hundred who went into action, twenty were killed, eight taken prisoner, and most of the rest wounded.

Because it was such an inspiring story, news accounts of the Women's Battalion made it past the censors and briefly painted a positive face on Russia's war effort. But the battalion saw action as part of what had been named the "Kerensky Offensive," after the

19. Correspondent Bessie Beatty visits with Russian soldiers at the front. Photo courtesy of Occidental College Special Collections and the Beatty Family.

leader of the Provisional Government, Alexander Kerensky. Meant as a last-ditch effort to change the momentum of the fighting and rally the army with a victory, it experienced initial success that quickly turned to defeat and a virtual collapse of the army. Tens of thousands of deserters flooded Petrograd or commandeered trains to take them back home. Kerensky published numerous deadlines for soldiers to rejoin their units, called them traitors to the revolution, and threatened to deprive their families of a share in the distribution of the land. Nothing worked. An unpopular war had now become unthinkable. "Anarchy pure and simple reigned on all the fronts and in the rear," Dorr noted. No one called louder for immediate peace than the Bolsheviks.

Dosch-Fleurot felt obliged to point out to his readers in a July article that while most outsiders believed that the Russian Revolution had already occurred, the toppling of the czar was only a political revolution. The real revolution, the social-economic revolution, had yet to occur.

The July Uprising

The telephone rang in Florence Harper's hotel room. "Hurry up!" came the excited voice of Donald Thompson. "They are shooting up the town, and there's hell to pay!" Harper donned her hat and a sturdy pair of walking shoes and made her way through hallways and lobby, which were suddenly alive with anxious women and officers. One lesson that Russia's foreign visitors learned from the revolution was that one never knew what kind of fighting was occurring, who exactly manned the machine guns and armored cars, and for which faction they fought.

Thompson and Harper walked miles through the city that night, dodging armed soldiers and civilians and the isolated crack of sniper fire from rooftops. Rheta Dorr and Bessie Beatty arrived at the hotel in the middle of the excitement, still caked with mud from a visit to the frontline trenches. They paused long enough to change, then hurried onto the street. The Bolsheviks were making their move against the government. Carloads of their supporters, the Red Guard, raced through the streets armed with rifles and machine guns. They fell into clashes with the Cossacks, who supported the government. Dorr counted seventeen dead Cossack horses.

The following morning Thompson picked up Harper with his hired car. His uniformed driver and an orderly rode in the front seat, while he set up his motion-picture camera tripod in the back seat with Harper. Looking very much like one of the threatening armored cars patrolling the city, they took up a position at a crowded street corner. They didn't have long to wait before Bolshevik and Cossack forces clashed there, sweeping the street with machine-gun fire. People in the crowd fell to the ground or ran for safety, but Thompson kept cranking his camera. The war correspondent E. Alexander Powell once remarked, "[Thompson had] more chilled-steel nerve than any man I know." Thompson needed such bravado for the street fighting in Petrograd. When his driver showed signs of panic, Thompson drew his revolver and threatened to blow his head off if he moved. That incident, later reported to the U.S. ambassador by another reporter, portrayed a crazed Thompson filming in the middle of a street battle, while clutching a revolver in each hand, which wasn't far from the truth.

Fueled by adrenaline and fear, Thompson and Harper chased the fighting and fled from it for the rest of the day, as the Cossacks began to get the upper hand. After making it back to the hotel that night, Harper, Thompson, and the orderly flopped onto a couch, physically and emotionally drained. Harper was shaking from head to foot. Thompson too. His orderly was crying. The next day word came that their driver had been killed the previous night after dropping them off.

Thompson's letters home did not shield his wife from worry. "I have had more narrow escapes today than I have had for the last few months," he reported on July 20. "Now that I am sitting here in the hotel I can't for the life of me figure out why I am not lying dead on the streets. I am a nervous wreck for what I have gone through today. On top of this I have the blues, for I see Russia going to hell as a country never went before."

Thompson's frank assessment to his wife did not appear in any of the news stories from the foreign correspondents. As Bolshevik sympathies continued to spread in the population, correspondents wrote about the true state of affairs, but their articles never made it past the Russian or British censors. Harper concluded that "not one newspaper man [or woman] who was in Russia during that summer had a single serious article published."

When the Provisional Government temporarily closed the borders in late July, Thompson and Harper decided that if they didn't get out of Russia then, they might not get out for a long time. Thompson had accumulated a considerable inventory of film. Through trickery he obtained a letter signed by Kerensky giving him permission to leave the country without having his film examined. In mid-August he packed his precious cameras and his film record of the Russian Revolution onto a Trans-Siberian train and began the long trip home.

Harper stayed on into September, frustrated that she could not get out any truthful stories about the growing mood of extremism. A young man on a streetcar snarled at her that she and all the damned bourgeoisie would soon be killed. Foreigners in the city could see Kerensky getting weaker by the day and the power of the Bolsheviks growing. And yet foreign newspapers that arrived in Petrograd weeks late praised the Provisional Government and Kerensky as the one man who could restore order and keep Russia in the war.

Russia had one more curve ball to throw at Harper before she departed. On the day she was scheduled to leave, her train was suddenly cancelled. The commander in chief of the army, the Cossack general Lavr Kornilov, was marching on the city to take control of the government. Many had long ago concluded that only a strong man such as Kornilov at the head of the government could save the revolution from falling to the Bolsheviks.

Soldiers burst into Harper's hotel that night. No one knew if they were soldiers from the Provisional Government, the Bolsheviks, or Kornilov. They interrogated her and marched off all the Russian officers. She ran into Arno Dosch-Fleurot in the hotel lobby, from whom she learned that Kornilov had failed. They were both overcome with emotional frustration and used "not exactly polite" language. "We all knew it was the last chance. The Bolshevki were armed; the Red Guard was formed. The split was definite; Kerensky was doomed."

The Bolshevik Revolution

"We were a strange lot we Americans," Bessie Beatty noted late that summer, when correspondents, embassy officials, businessmen, and other Americans in the city formed a tight community with strong opinions about Russia. "Some of us were uncompromising idealists, and some pragmatists, and more were the usual complex mixture of both."

People often showed up in Beatty's hotel room for rousing late-night discussions. Someone would make a thoughtful observation about the sincerity of the Bolsheviks or predict a date for the restoration of the monarchy, and they would be off in excited debate. Every shade of political opinion was expressed. "Most often the

talk turned to the necessity of making the people at home understand the complex and difficult situation as it really [was]."

One night conversation turned to the Bolshevik movement, and
one person made the familiar claim that Bolshevism was a German plot to take Russia out of the war. A newcomer to the group,
Albert Rhys Williams of the *New York Post*, asked how many of
those present knew any Bolsheviks. No one did. A socialist and
advocate for social causes back in America, Williams had covered
the war from its beginning. He had just traveled in other parts
of Russia, he explained, meeting with workers and peasants and
thought it was shortsighted to dismiss the Bolsheviks without
knowledge of them and their ideas.

The following night Williams brought to the gathering a genu-
ine Bolshevik named Peters. He hailed from the Baltic States and
spoke English with a British accent. The young man impressed
Beatty. On that occasion and on other nights that followed, Peters
and Williams "opened up many windows on the Revolution to
[her] that would otherwise have been closed."

By late summer most of the American correspondents had taken
sides on Bolshevism. Dosch-Fleurot remained the most objective.
Listening to the fiery rhetoric of Leon Trotsky at a meeting of the
Petrograd Soviet convinced Dosch-Fleurot that a Bolshevik revolution was inevitable. He persuaded Trotsky to sit for an interview.
"Tell me what you will do when you get the power," the reporter
asked. Trotsky responded unequivocally that the Bolsheviks wanted
an immediate peace with Germany. Dosch-Fleurot managed to
wrangle the interview past government censors to send out that
nightmare scenario message to *World* readers in the days leading
up to the Bolshevik take-over.

Dorr, Harper, and Thompson, who supported the Provisional
Government, witnessed the aborted Bolshevik uprising in July but
departed Russia before the Bolsheviks came to power. They hurried home to share their views with the American public through
books. Harper titled her book *Runaway Russia*. For two of the three
books Thompson published in 1918, he chose titles that reflected
his disapproval of the Bolsheviks: *From Czar to Kaiser: The Betrayal of*

20. Journalist Louise Bryant's name is rarely mentioned without being associated with her more famous husband, the war correspondent John Reed, but Bryant established her own reputation with her coverage of Russia's Bolshevik Revolution. Source: Louise Bryant Papers (MS 1840), Manuscripts and Archives, Yale University Library.

Russia and *Blood Stained Russia*. In *Inside the Russian Revolution*, Dorr lamented that "the most striking parallel between the French and the Russian revolutions lies in the facility with which both were snatched away from the sane and intelligent men who began them and placed in the hands of fanatics."

Beatty fell in with Reed, Bryant, and Williams. When John Reed and his wife, Louise Bryant, arrived in September, Bryant made a chart of the various political parties—the Mensheviks, the Menshevik Internationalists, the Right and Left Socialist Revolutionists, the Bolsheviks—and of the array of governing bodies: the Duma, the Petrograd Soviet, the Council of the Russian Republic, the All-Russian Soviet, and so on. It was the only way for a newcomer to get her bearings.

The wild, raw democracy of the process impressed Bryant. Everywhere she went people engaged in spirited discussion over this or that political philosophy or strategy. A democratic congress in September drew sixteen hundred representatives from across Russia. Delegates filled the immense Alexandrinsky Theater. From their assigned seats in the orchestra pit, the foreign correspondents watched the drama of an endless succession of speakers. Often a peasant who had never made a speech in his life poured out his most heartfelt thoughts and kept the audience's rapt attention. Little was accomplished, but from sunset to dawn, speakers vented grievances and proposed solutions.

The same wild democracy that stalled legislative bodies did the same in the army. When they visited the Latvian front in October, Williams and Reed found military units virtually crippled. Units had lost up to 60 percent of their strength through casualties and desertions. Those soldiers who remained were poorly fed and equipped. Regular army command and soldiers' councils struggled with each other over military decisions, while an increasingly radical rank and file flexed its opposition to both.

The two reporters attended an extraordinary five-hour meeting conducted in the middle of a battle, at which thousands of soldiers voiced their grievances. While a German artillery barrage sounded an ominous backdrop, soldier after soldier stood up to denounce the war, the Provisional Government, and Russia's capitalist allies. Reed imagined that never before in history had a fighting army convened such a peace meeting during a battle. Certainly it did not bode well for Russia remaining in the war.

A similar scenario played out back in Petrograd. Kerensky and the Provisional Government improvised cabinets and coalitions. Great conferences and councils convened to discuss and plan. Meanwhile, ordinary Russians, the peasants, workers, and soldiers, were taking matters into their own hands. Peasants seized estates; soldiers deserted their units; and workers went on strike or took control of factories. In September Bolsheviks won a majority in the Petrograd Soviet.

A sense of doom haunted the city in October. From her hotel window Louise Bryant watched wagon caravans carrying art treasures from the Hermitage Museum, bound for safe storage in Moscow. Even factory machinery was carted away, and everyone assumed that the city would soon be evacuated. Meanwhile, loud speeches in the Council of the Russian Republic called more insistently for peace. "And through all the confusion moved Kerensky, far from serene, occasionally breaking down, crying out from the tribunal, to indifferent ears: 'I am a doomed man. I cannot last much longer!'"

Some scholars have since suggested that the female reporters covering the revolution often spoke from the margins of the action. They were less inclined to dwell on the causes of the revolution than on the impact of events on individuals. That theme played out in Bryant's reporting. Whether she was interviewing former Women's Battalion soldiers bitter because they were now derided by all sides or painting a picture of Katherine Breshkovsky, the "grandmother of the revolution" called back from exile in Siberia and now living in a modest room at the Winter Palace, Bryant gave the impression of pulling back a curtain to see characters behind the grand political drama.

Through Breshkovsky Bryant arranged a much-coveted interview with Alexander Kerensky. Along with another correspondent, she showed up at Kerensky's headquarters in the Winter Palace.

When they entered his office, "Kerensky lay on a couch with his face buried in his arms, as if he had been suddenly taken ill, or was completely exhausted." Bryant recalled, "We stood there for a minute or two and then went out. He did not notice us." Kerensky had stomach trouble, the secretary explained, plus a bad lung and kidney. He kept going only with brandy and morphine. With sad resignation she confessed, "We are going to wake up here one morning and find that there is no Provisional Government." Within two weeks her prediction came true.

When day dawned on November 7, 1917, nothing portended well for Alexander Kerensky, the Provisional Government, or Russia's continuing involvement in the war. In that chilling way history has of aligning enough small events to make a large event seem suddenly inevitable, so the pieces fell in place for the Bolsheviks. The Russian fleet had declared for the Bolsheviks; the Petrograd garrison likewise declared. Bolshevik supporters won majorities in the soviet councils. All reports from the front indicated that more and more of the troops wanted immediate action on the Bolshevik call to end the war.

Even the old baron staying in Bessie Beatty's hotel seemed pleased with the prospect of a Bolshevik take-over. He was a monarchist through and through. His title and estates depended on the return of the monarchy. A week earlier Beatty had dined with him in the home of an Englishman, where they toasted the czar and sang the now-forbidden old national anthem. But he despised Kerensky and felt confident that a few weeks of Bolshevik incompetence would bring the Russian people around to his way of thinking.

As Kerensky and the Provisional Government bobbed like a cork on a stormy sea, assailed by forces from inside and outside the country, from the right and the left, by the demands of fighting a war, and by a counterrevolutionary energy that grew stronger by the day, reporter John Reed roamed the city in great excitement. Knowing that he was an eyewitness to history, he took on the responsibility to capture it. He went everywhere and talked with everyone, from marathon conference sessions that often lasted

21. Reporters Bessie Beatty (left) and Louise Bryant pose with a Russian naval officer in 1917. Photo courtesy of Occidental College Special Collections and the Beatty Family.

until the early hours of morning, to private meetings and interviews, to factories, breadlines, and the smart cafés on Nevsky Prospect, always with his notebook in hand. His hotel room became an archive of proclamations, newspaper clippings, drafts of speeches, and pamphlets.

One year later, in a Greenwich Village flat, Reed would surround himself with this material, his notebooks, and his memories and give form to the revolutionary chaos in his classic book *Ten Days That Shook the World*. Using the techniques of literary journalism that he had helped to popularize with his earlier war reporting, he brought to life the main characters: Kerensky thundering nearly hysterical speeches; Trotsky condemning his opponents to the garbage heap of history; the short, stocky, bald figure of Lenin in shabby clothes, belying his overarching influence on events.

Reed gave dramatic structure to the swirl of events by setting them in two rival locations, the Winter Palace and the Smolny Institute. The Winter Palace was the opulent residence of the former czar, which now housed the Provisional Government and the Duma, the one scrambling desperately to salvage its revolutionary vision and the other being rendered increasingly irrelevant by fast-moving events. The Smolny Institute, a former school for girls of the privileged class, was now the base for the Petrograd Soviet, controlled by the Bolsheviks, and the meeting place for the All-Russian Congress of Soviets, the massive, unruly gathering of representatives from across Russia.

Although generations since have seen the Bolshevik Revolution primarily through the eyes of John Reed, other American journalist observers included Albert Rhys Williams, Louise Bryant, and Bessie Beatty. Granted access denied to other reporters, these four watched the final pieces fall into place. Reed's book focused on events of November 6–15, but the Bolshevik seizure of power came on November 7. A more momentous and dramatic day would be hard to imagine. "They were dreaming big dreams in Russia that night; scheming big schemes," as Beatty put it.

At nine o'clock that morning a servant informed Beatty that Bolshevik soldiers, the Red Guard, had just taken possession of the hotel. Soon they knocked on her door, and the familiar ritual began of interrogations, room inspections, and the marching away of Russian officers. The two local newspapers still being published gave spotty reports of events unfolding around the city. The Bolsheviks captured the Telephone Exchange, the Telegraph Agency, and the Baltic Train Station. Some government ministers had been arrested, the chief of the city militia shot, and skirmishes occurred between soldiers and the Red Guard.

Beatty found four armored cars lined up before the Winter Palace. It wasn't unusual in these chaotic times to have to ask soldiers which side they were on. But the car doors bore freshly painted Bolshevik red flags, and the word "Proletariat" adorned one of them. Beatty talked her way into the palace and found the ministers of the Provisional Government inside, fifteen of them seated around a mahogany table waiting grimly for events to unfold. Already impotent relics of the first revolution, they were guarded by a handful of military school cadets and another of the women's battalion that had formed after Bochkareva. The women had enlisted to fight German invaders and been reluctantly thrust into the role of guardians of the old order. Kerensky had gone to the front to round up loyal troops, they told Beatty.

Beatty made her way through several street skirmishes to Smolny Institute, where the Second All-Russian Congress of Soviets was under way. There she met up with Bryant, Reed, and Williams. They pushed through a seething crowd of workers, peasants, soldiers, and professionals. Sixteen hundred delegates from throughout Russia overflowed the available chairs, filled the aisles, sat on windowsills, and perched everywhere. Even as they awaited the start of the congress, the repeated boom of cannon fire filled the hall. When delegates learned that the cruiser *Aurora*, anchored in the Neva River, was shelling the Winter Palace, where ministers of the government still sheltered, they exploded with anger.

Why were the Bolsheviks seizing power now, speakers asked, only weeks before a constitutional assembly was planned to decide the form of government? Speaker after speaker rose to protest or to challenge those who protested; each met with heckles or cheers. Finally those delegates opposing the Bolsheviks declared that they would perish with their comrades at the Winter Palace and walked out of the meeting. Reed recorded the words of Trotsky as the delegates marched out, "Let them go. They are just so much refuse which will be swept away into the garbage heap of history!"

The promise of a confrontation at the Winter Palace was too tantalizing. The reporters hurried out. They paused first at a room in Smolny to get passes from the Bolshevik's Military Revolutionary Committee. The area outside Smolny was alive with cars and trucks arriving and departing on secret missions. Reed approached some soldiers loading bundles of papers into a truck. They were going "downtown—all over—everywhere," they told Reed. They would likely be shot at, but if the reporters wanted to go along, they could.

Off the truck raced at top speed, bumping and swaying from side to side, with the four correspondents lying on the bed of the truck next to rifles and bundles of papers. Reed was at his dramatic best when the action flew fast and the pulse ran high. Sentries and armed men challenged the truck with raised guns, but it sped past them. A soldier on the truck tore open one of the bundles and tossed papers into the air. The correspondents joined in, grabbing papers and throwing them from the truck. The papers snowed down in the dark streets, where passersby rushed to grab them to learn of the latest bewildering turn in the revolution.

In the fleeting glow of passing streetlights, the reporters read one of the papers.

TO THE CITIZENS OF RUSSIA!

The Provisional Government is deposed. The State Power has passed into the hands of the organ of the Petrograd Soviet of Workers' and Soldiers' Deputies, the Military Revolutionary Committee, which stands at the head of the Petrograd proletariat and garrison.

The cause for which the people were fighting: immediate proposal of a democratic peace, abolition of landlord property-rights over the land, labour control over production, creation of a Soviet Government—that cause is securely achieved.

LONG LIVE THE REVOLUTION OF WORKMEN, SOLDIERS, AND PEASANTS!

Military Revolutionary Committee
Petrograd Soviet of Workers' and Soldiers' Deputies.

"How far they had soared, these Bolsheviki," Reed was moved to observe, "from a despised and hunted sect less than four months ago, to this supreme place, the helm of great Russia in full tide of insurrection!"

On December 15 Russia signed an armistice with the Central Powers, followed on March 3, 1918, by a punishing peace treaty that ended Russia's participation in the war. For nearly a year, Allied leaders had been haunted by the prospect of Russia leaving the war. In that nightmare a wave of some forty divisions of battle-hardened German troops swept from the eastern front to the stalemated trenches of northern France. Now it came true.

CHAPTER NINE

Credentialed with the AEF

In this war, I consider a trained newspaperman worth a regiment of cavalry. If he is in a position to serve his country with the typewriter and does not, he is lacking in his duty.

—General JOHN PERSHING

Floyd Gibbons of the *Chicago Tribune* sailed for Europe in February 1917, during a curious wartime interlude for the United States. On February 1, when Germany resumed its policy of unrestricted submarine warfare, attacking any ship, of any kind, from any nation, without warning, the United States reacted immediately. It broke diplomatic relations with Germany and expelled its ambassador, but stopped short of declaring war, awaiting only some further provocation to force that final, fateful step.

The *Tribune* wanted a story on the United States' lack of preparation for a war that it seemed certain to enter. England had paid a bitter price in 1914 for its lack of preparedness. The *Tribune* chose Gibbons to go to England and write the story of its costly mistake, so that America could profit by that example. At considerable expense the *Tribune* arranged passage for Gibbons aboard the ship taking German ambassador Count Johann Heinrich von Bernstorff back home, because that ship had been granted safe passage by all the warring nations. However, Gibbons didn't think like management. Safe passage meant less to him than a good story. He wanted to face the same anxiety and danger as a regular traveler on the high seas. He promptly cancelled the reservation and booked instead on the armed merchant ship *Laconia*, reasoning that it was more likely to have a run-in with a German submarine, providing him with a dramatic story.

Gibbons had a reputation for staring danger in the face. During the Mexican border dispute in 1916, when revolutionary leader Pancho Villa warned that he would shoot on sight any "gringo" found in Mexico, Gibbons called his bluff. He traveled into the Mexican hills to report on the revolution. He eventually fitted out a private boxcar, attached it to Villa's train, and was in the thick of three of Villa's biggest battles. The words "The Chicago Tribune—Special Correspondent" painted on the side of the boxcar sent the message that this correspondent was a force to be reckoned with. Given the chance Gibbons would have similarly emblazoned the *Laconia*.

For eight days the *Laconia* took all precautions against lurking U-boats. It sailed a zigzag course, traveled in blackout at night, and kept its lifeboats swung over the railings for quick launch. Three times during the voyage, five sharp blasts of the ship's whistle signaled the order to abandon ship, alerting passengers to assemble for a lifeboat drill. For the entire voyage passenger conversation regularly turned to the subject of German submarines, as it did again the night of February 25 in the first-class lounge. Gibbons had just thrown out a question to his fellow travelers about the chance of being torpedoed when the ship gave a sudden sideways lurch. Had that been a torpedo, they wondered? Perhaps a dud torpedo, since the jolt felt so slight? But the warnings of the ship's whistle told the story.

The ship already listed to starboard as the passengers gathered on deck to climb into lifeboats. A signal rocket shot into the night sky and exploded high above, summoning help. Gibbons spent six hours on the dark and frigid Irish Sea before being rescued by a British ship. As the ship searched for other survivors, Gibbons began capturing the story. The chief steward told of the U-boat surfacing and a German officer asking him for the ship's identity and its weight. One of the ship's crew saw a lifeboat get smashed while being lowered and a woman and child swept overboard and lost.

The instant he reached land, Gibbons cabled the *Tribune*: "I'm here in Queenstown soaked, frozen; ice on my face, ice in my hair, dripping water on the floor, I can hardly move my fingers to write the story. I was torpedoed on the *Laconia*." He then banged out a four-thousand-word story that captured all the heart-wrenching drama of being torpedoed by a German submarine. "Is it the *casus belli*?" he asked at the end of the article, the final outrage that forces the United States to take the plunge into war? The article created a sensation in newspapers throughout the country and was read on the floors of both houses of Congress. Six weeks later, on April 6, 1917, the United States entered the war.

Paul Scott Mowrer, of the *Chicago Daily News* Paris office, thought long and hard about enlisting in the army but eventually decided against it. It would take many months to bring U.S. troops to France and train them for combat. If he enlisted, he would be held out of the action all that time. French officials he spoke with doubted whether the United States could get sufficient forces to the war zone in time to influence the outcome.

Mowrer chose instead to accept a French invitation to join the Anglo-American Press Mission, a new group of British and American reporters that reflected a shift in French attitude toward the press. From the start of the war, French censorship had been the strictest, suppressing almost all news about the fighting. It was a boneheaded practice that gave Germany the lion's share of news coverage in the world press.

The mission would be an exclusive group attached to French General Headquarters that would include only three French, four British, and four American correspondents. Correspondents were selected to give the widest possible news distribution. Mowrer, and Wythe Williams of the *New York Times*, brought the clout of two major urban newspapers. Robert Berry of the Associated Press and Henry Wood of United Press represented the two largest news associations, which between them distributed news to nearly two thousand newspapers. France had arrived late to the realization that news, like steel, manpower, or food, was also a resource of war that needed to be managed. It would take time for France to find the proper balance between controlling and enabling the press. The United States, just beginning the formation of its army, was starting the same process from square one.

Floyd Gibbons and the handful of other American correspondents who witnessed the historic arrival in England of General John "Black Jack" Pershing, the man chosen to lead the American Expeditionary Force (AEF), were not at liberty to say where it occurred. However, Gibbons did manage to sneak into his story that the general was warmly welcomed by the lord mayor of Liverpool.

"Lean, clean, and keen" were the words Gibbons chose to describe Pershing and the 190 officers accompanying him. As a brass band struck up "The Star-Spangled Banner" and Pershing and staff marched down the gangplank, expressions of approval whispered through the British observers on the pier. These Americans were tall, trim, and broad shouldered. They had the bearing of confident soldiers. None made a bigger impression than the commander himself. He might have been recruited by Hollywood. His carriage and poise, his stiff jaw and steady gaze marked him as a leader. "No man ever looked the more ordained leader of fighting men," claimed *New York Tribune* reporter Heywood Broun. Pershing's arrival on June 8, just two months after the United States entered the war, gave renewed hope to America's dispirited allies.

General Pershing would have been quite happy not to have any reporters at all with the AEF. In theory he accepted their usefulness to an army. "I consider a trained newspaperman worth a regiment of cavalry," he told UP reporter Wilbur Forrest back in Washington when Forrest asked if he should enlist. However, in practice they were an obvious threat to military secrecy, not to mention a damned nuisance. Only one month had passed since his appointment as commander of the U.S. Army in Europe had thrust him into the quagmire of conflicting personalities, policies, Allied expectations, and a monumental planning and organizational challenge. He had more pressing things to do than jabber with newsmen.

Like all the other great challenges that he now faced, this one too yielded to his thoroughness. Following the lead of the British and the French, he would control journalists by restricting their number. Initially, fifteen was thought sufficient. Journalists would wear military uniforms and be subject to military rules and strict censorship. To be his point man with these scribblers, Pershing selected one of their own, someone with vast experience covering the current conflict and many other wars: Frederick Palmer.

The forty-four-year-old Palmer had been newspapering half his life. He first met John Pershing when Pershing served as military observer in Manchuria during the Russo-Japanese War and Palmer was an embedded reporter with the Japanese army. Palmer had covered the European conflict since it began and been the only American correspondent accredited with the British early in the war. He knew the advantages and frustrations of being attached to an army. In fact Palmer knew more about this European war than anyone on Pershing's staff. Two weeks before the United States entered the war, Palmer lectured at the Army War College about his war experiences. On the topic of censorship, he recommended the appointment of a chief civilian censor with army officers as assistants.

He had not been seeking the position, having just received a lucrative offer of $40,000 a year from the *New York Herald* to cover the United States' role in the war. But other newsmen were joining the colors, entering officer-training programs, and Palmer felt the same call to duty. He decided to accept General Pershing's offer of a commission as an army major at $2,100 a year, working as censor for the AEF and the chief of its press division.

To him would fall the task of organizing and controlling the unruly group of new journalists come to Europe to cover the greatest war story yet, the entry of the sons of America into the conflict. Palmer would play a key part in defining the role of the AEF correspondents and the picture of the AEF reported to the American public. He did not initially appreciate just how difficult and thankless a job it would be.

The French outdid the British in welcoming General Pershing, which made for stirring news stories for readers back home. Immense crowds cheered his motorcade in Paris; children perched on lampposts for a view; old men wiped away tears of joy; from balconies and windows along the route women and children tossed flowers and bits of colored paper. A sea of American flags waved an exuberant welcome.

The following week the correspondents were conducted in secrecy to an unnamed French port to see the arrival of the first contingent of American troops. The United States' hastily assembled army looked raw and clueless. "Is this England or France?" one doughboy yelled as their ship pulled in. One asked Heywood Broun if the enlisted men could drink in the saloons. "Say, where the hell is all this trouble, anyhow?" one asked Floyd Gibbons. When Paul Scott Mowrer reported the arrival of another contingent, he described them as "rollicking off the transport cheering, laughing, and kidding like an excursion of schoolboys."

Unlike Broun and Gibbons, Mowrer had already reported on more years of fighting than any of these soldiers would ever see. It made him proud and homesick to move among the soldiers and talk with them. But he pitied them as well because they were absolutely clueless about what awaited them. "It was as if I and others had never written of Verdun or the Somme," he noted. "Eager, gay, self-assured, they were going to battle as to a picnic."

To veteran United Press reporter Wilbur Forrest, the American troops parading through Paris on July 4 looked exactly like what they were, civilians who had been thrown into uniforms and hurried to France to show the weary Allies that the United States really was in the war. Their uniforms didn't fit; they held their formations badly; their shoulders slumped; and their feet dragged. Such things didn't matter to the cheering French crowds, but Forrest overheard the conversation of two disappointed French officers: "If this is what we may expect from the Americans, the war is lost."

On the busy schedule of events that day, one stood out as potentially more newsworthy. Pershing paid his respects at the grave of

22. Army cars carrying the credentialed correspondents line up outside press headquarters in Neufchâteau for a trip to the front, April 25, 1918. Source: National Archive, 111-SC-11339.

the Marquis de Lafayette, the French nobleman who fought with America in its war of independence. A crowd of officers, dignitaries, and reporters crowded around the grave. Pershing stood at attention, fired a crisp salute at the tomb, and then he offered, "Lafayette, we are here." The simple but eloquent line perfectly captured the mood of the moment, the historical juncture in the war. The bond long ago forged between the two countries during the American Revolution was being formally acknowledged. Published and repeated innumerable times, the remark galvanized Europe and the United States and achieved immortality.

For this fame Pershing had correspondents to thank, because he never uttered that famous phrase. General Pershing was not an orator. Uncomfortable on any occasion that required public remarks, he would resort to brief and blunt comments. "Soldier language," correspondent Wilbur Forrest called it. Therefore, the job of articulating American thoughts on this occasion fell to a member of Pershing's staff, Colonel Charles E. Stanton. Although French airplanes swooping low over the proceedings drowned out much of his remarks, he finally placed a wreath on the grave and uttered the famous words, "Lafayette, we are here."

When the French crowd insisted on remarks from the general, he stumbled his way through a few comments, visibly embarrassed. Colonel Stanton had summed things up well, Pershing said, noting that it was an inspiration to stand before the tomb of Lafayette. He ended by repeating part of Stanton's phrase, "We are here." That last insistent statement best reflected his true feelings and precisely what France and the United States wanted to hear. So in the news stories, the entire, well-chosen phrase was attributed to Pershing.

The provincial town of Neufchâteau became headquarters for the AEF Press Office and the fifteen correspondents sent from newspapers and news services. This isolated location put them a two-hour journey from Pershing's headquarters at Chaumont, 150 miles from the distractions of Paris, and a one-hour train ride from the camp where the First Division, the first AEF troops in France, was in training.

Here Frederick Palmer would play nanny to this unruly group of "war correspondents," who had little or no experience with war. A few had covered the fighting in Mexico, but most had never traveled outside the United States. They had been city reporters, crime reporters, drama critics, or sports columnists, more experienced at covering city council meetings or writing human interest stories than at interpreting military strategy. Now they were dressed in the uniform of officers, without any designation of rank. Only a green armband with a red "C" for correspondent gave any indication of their unique status.

These new war reporters stood in marked contrast to the seasoned war correspondents who preceded them, men such as Palmer himself, Richard Harding Davis, and Granville Fortescue. But what this new group lacked in war experience, it made up for with curiosity and enthusiasm. Everything was new to these reporters: French culture, training camps, military procedure, the conduct of the Allies, hospitals, soldiers, battles, weapons, censorship. Given the long wait before Americans actually entered combat, this fresh perspective would serve them well.

"I went among villages thronged with bronzed young men in khaki, boys newly arrived from home, my own people from my own country," Paul Scott Mowrer rhapsodized during a July tour of the training camps. "To see them here in this foreign land on the edge of the all-consuming holocaust seemed wonderful and strange beyond expression." The troops seemed very much to be in the settling-in phase, lounging about villages, shaving, writing letters, mingling with the village children. But in a clearing on the edge of camp, grizzled French army instructors drilled these fresh-faced Americans in the fine art of digging trenches and the use of hand grenades and machine guns.

Heywood Broun, former drama critic for the *New York Tribune*, watched French soldiers exasperated with the trainees because they did not take their instructions seriously. The readers of *Everybody's Magazine* got a glimpse of their men in training in Herbert Corey's article "Just Boys." Americans had to be stirred up before they got into a fighting mood, he observed, or they felt inclined to give the enemy soldier a fair chance. "They must learn to look on man-killing as a job instead of a sporting transaction." Almost imperceptible on these practice fields, the far-off rumble of artillery could be heard, playing its war song, giving a hint of what lay in store for the Americans.

American "Firsts"

When the American troops first arrived in France, Herbert Corey called them a "happy army." "The Americans are living the Great Adventure," he declared. "They tell one they are having the time of their lives. The old world is magnificently new to them." By fall, after months of training and no fighting, the newness had worn off the experience. As the Allies slogged through the Battle of Passchendaele in Belgium and the Eleventh Battle of the Isonzo in Italy, Americans were still held in training.

The correspondents had thoroughly covered the troops-in-training stories. They had dutifully reported on all the British and French politicians and generals who stopped by the camps. They wrote about the vast buildup of infrastructure, the dock facilities, railroads, warehouses, ordinance factories, hospitals, equipment repair shops, horse and mule stables, and the YMCA huts that provided entertainment and cigarettes. In September the Press Office packed restless reporters into cars and drove them to Dijon to show off the giant bake ovens that would feed the troops. Only a few years earlier, the United States had completed the construction of the Panama Canal, cleaving a hemisphere with a waterway after the French had failed at the attempt. Coverage of the United States' massive infrastructure of war suggested that this war would also yield to American engineering and enterprise.

But packaged tours to ovens did not satisfy editors back home hungry for war news, nor did they placate the highly competitive correspondents eager to scoop their rivals with an exclusive story. Some reporters held out at isolated Neufchâteau awaiting developments. Others deserted for more pleasant surroundings in Paris or disappeared on private news-gathering excursions. Palmer counseled patience. He sent chiding telegrams to absent reporters to return to the fold. Only those correspondents resident at Neufchâteau, he warned, would get advance notice when American troops finally went into action.

On October 22, when that long-awaited event finally occurred and American troops moved onto the fighting line for the first time, the Press Office handling of coverage proved so inept that it nearly caused an open rebellion of correspondents. Reporters learned that the personal initiative that had served them well as hometown reporters did not always work under the army's system of press regulations. Others learned the disadvantages of playing by army rules.

Major Robert McCormick, publisher of the *Chicago Tribune*, happened to command a battery of artillery in the First Division. When he got wind that his unit had done so well in training that it would be the first American unit sent unto the line, he immediately sent word to *Tribune* reporter Floyd Gibbons to join him. Unbeknown to the AEF Press Office, Gibbons attached himself to Artillery Battery A, in the hopes it would be first on the field and first to use its weapon. Gibbons wanted to witness the firing of the first American shot of the war.

At 4:00 a.m. Gibbons traveled with the men by train to the town of Luneville, about thirty minutes behind the front. Everyone was in high spirits and jangling with nervous energy. To test these students of war, the French were moving them into a relatively quiet sector, where the opposing lines had remained stationary for almost three years. Midnight passed before the troops were fully installed on the front line, facing for the first time German troops some eight hundred yards away. They took up positions beside French soldiers who "gushed their congratulations and shook [them] by the hand. Some of [them] were hugged and kissed on both cheeks."

Another artillery unit beat out Battery A for the honor of firing the first American shot of the war. So auspicious was the occasion that Gibbons took care to include in his dispatch the name of each man in the gun crew and his exact role, who loaded the piece, who prepared the fuse and who set it, who gave the command and who fired the first shell, an honor that went to Sergeant Alex L. Arch. Gibbons had traveled with the troops as they went into action and witnessed the entire operation, one of only two American reporters to see the American baptism of fire.

Unfortunately, coverage of this major event did not work so well for the accredited journalists who followed Press Office rules and awaited the official announcement at Neufchâteau. Alerted late about unfolding events, they arrived outside Luneville to discover that the French command was intent on following its own censorship guidelines. The correspondents would not be permitted to enter the sector with the troops or even to circulate among them on the march. They had to be satisfied with watching the troops pass by and with a briefing on operations by the First Division chief of staff. During the briefing the officer mentioned in passing that the reporters were late to the game, since two of their number had been with the troops for a couple days and were with them now up on the line.

All the flaws in the American control of the news exploded to the forefront at Neufchâteau that night. Correspondents fumed indignantly that Gibbons had gotten advance notice of the American move, bypassing Press Office rules. He should be arrested and his story impounded, they suggested to Palmer. When Gibbons finally appeared at headquarters, he was not permitted to rush his story onto the cable, as he had planned. The other reporters would draw lots to determine the order in which their stories would be put on the cable. Gibbons would go last in line. In the highly competitive world of news scoops, where mere minutes could determine whether one newspaper beat the other with this biggest news story since the AEF reached Europe, it was an intolerable penalty. Gibbons flew into a rage, calling the other correspondents "lazy and contemptible fat cats who waited for the news to fall into their laps, while real reporters got out and dug." Gibbons finally got to draw lots with the others, but the full description of his dramatic entrance into the front with the First Division had to wait until he wrote a book about his war experience the following year.

When the Americans withdrew from their positions after a few weeks, Gibbons termed the whole affair "nothing more than a post-graduate course in training," under the careful direction of French instructors. However, that did not detract from its historical significance. It was there in the Luneville sector, Gibbons

23. These AEF "visiting" correspondents gathered at Neufchâteau, April 25, 1918. Left to right, back row: J. W. Grigg (*New York World*); Don Martin (*New York Herald*); Captain F. P. Adams (*Stars and Stripes*); Bert Ford (International News Service). Left to right, front row: C. Kenimore (*St. Louis Post Dispatch*); F. J. Taylor (United Press); Frank P. Sibley (*Boston Globe*); Henri Bazin (*Philadelphia Public Ledger*); John T. Parkerson (Associated Press). Source: National Archive, 111-SC-11337.

could report, "that the first American fighting men faced the Germans on the western front. It was there that the enemy captured its first American prisoners in a small midnight raid; it was there that we captured some prisoners of theirs, and inflicted our first German casualties; it was there that the first American fighting man laid down his life on the western front."

Visiting Correspondents

In January 1918, when Frederick Palmer turned over command of the Press Office to another former newsman, Gerald Morgan, the rigid control of the journalists became more liberal. The change gave hope to *Boston Globe* correspondent Frank Sibley, who had been tapping his foot impatiently in Paris for nearly three months awaiting approval of his novel request to attach himself to the army's Twenty-Sixth Division, made up of men from New England. He had traveled with the division in Mexico and followed it through training as it prepared for service in Europe. This put him in the unique position of knowing the officers and men and sending regular news stories so readers in New England could follow their hometown boys. The arrangement had worked well at keeping readers informed and interested in the division.

In October 1917, when the Twenty-Sixth sailed for France, the *Globe* sought approval for Sibley to go with it, to be permitted to report on nothing else in the war except what happened with the Twenty-Sixth. The army rejected the idea. AEF policy had already been established. Fifteen correspondents would be accredited with the army and operate out of the Press Office. Period.

Undeterred, Sibley sailed with the division anyway and then renewed his requests from Paris. His patience was finally rewarded in January, when he became the first "visiting correspondent." He was not an "accredited" correspondent, and he could not wear the green armband with the red "C." Nor could he cover any other facet of the war or any other operations of the AEF except what happened with the Twenty-Sixth Division.

Through press association news and its own network of correspondents, the *Globe* thoroughly covered the rest of the war. Sibley's role, on the other hand, was "to keep the families at home informed of the experiences of their boys in France." The arrangement would not work as well for all divisions, since many of them, such as the famous Rainbow Division, included soldiers from many parts of the country. But Sibley set the standard for what soon became commonplace as all divisions acquired their own visiting correspondents, who could send home personalized coverage well suited for those with relatives serving in those units. These reporters would follow their divisions through the training camps and into action.

The Twenty-Sixth got its "post-graduate course in training" on the line at Soissons in February 1918, under the careful supervision and support of the French. Traveling with them Sibley gave perhaps the fullest account to this point in the war of the experience of an individual army unit. In fact, because he was as green to fighting as the men he covered, Sibley's emotions often mirrored those of the soldiers. "There was something very impressive in the way the Yankees went into a sector," he reported. "They were so excited, so interested, so happy over it—and so utterly unconcerned about the danger. If a plane buzzed overhead, every man gazed as long as it could be seen. At each distant explosion of gun or shell, the whole column remarked 'Powie! There's one!' And they searched the horizon for the smoke puff."

Being continuously with this unit, Sibley brought a greater depth to his reports. The personalities of men, the idiosyncrasies of battle, the encounters with the enemy, were not merely summarized from a report but told by an observer who knew the men and everything they had been through. Sibley chronicled their first prisoners lost, first raid, first German prisoners taken, night patrols, and dramatic parachute jumps from exploding observation balloons. He could report all the details of the raid for which two men later won the Croix de Guerre and the death of the first division soldier and his emotional burial in a nearby village cemetery. A bottle was buried with him containing his name and date of death for future identification. Just beyond his resting place, two long rows of freshly dug graves awaited additional members of the Twenty-Sixth.

During this period the Twenty-Sixth began to copy the French practice of issuing daily intelligence reports, to provide additional information for journalists. The reports focused primarily on enemy activity—the number of shells they fired, their movements and other activities, and in less detail, reported the division's activities. The practice would eventually be adopted across the AEF.

One day, after all units of the Twenty-Sixth had moved into position, the division got a visit from the accredited correspondents from Neufchâteau. They arrived at the railroad station in their automobiles to hear a French general make a speech about the Twenty-Sixth. He welcomed these Americans as brothers, he said. They were eager to gallop into the fighting, whereas his own soldiers were content to trot and conserve their energies. But the French would teach them all the wiles of the wild beast before turning them loose to go it alone.

The accredited correspondents recorded the speech, then drove away. They were not on hand weeks later to see the men of the Twenty-Sixth leave the line. Sibley could report, "They had a new swing, lacking some of the buoyancy of a month before, but showing in place of that buoyance a canny conservation of energy. Perhaps the difference is best expressed by saying they went in highly trained green men and came out real soldiers. They no longer howled with ignorant enthusiasm for the chance to go against anything that might turn up. But they had a quiet confidence in their ability to handle anything the Boche might offer."

Since there wasn't any American fighting to write about in February 1918, when Irvin Cobb returned to Europe for his second stint of war reporting, he wrote about the restless soldiers and airmen gathering at training camps and airfields, itching to join the fight, and about the behind-the-scenes war preparations, building up infrastructure and matériel.

Cobb's brand of reporting for the *Saturday Evening Post* always filtered the conflict through his personal experience. He would venture into a situation, painting the scene, reporting conversations with those he met, drawing out a warm sketch of personalities and the regional character of the polyglot American fighting force.

Well known as a humorist and storyteller, Cobb often spent a spare night entertaining the men in the training camps. One of his favorite routines on such occasions was to perform skits on African American life, "dialect stories," he called them. They went over well with American and British troops.

African Americans were most conspicuous with the A E F in labor battalions, unloading ships, building depots and warehouses, chopping trees. Stories about them by Cobb or their occasional mention in dispatches from other correspondents milked the humor of racial prejudice, characterizing blacks as simple-minded and docile.

In March Cobb motored up to Noyon to see French and British troops in action, resisting a massive German offensive. It was there he began to sense a change in the Allied attitude toward Americans. The Allies had long expected—fervently awaited—the American martial juggernaut to turn the tide of the fighting. But nearly a year into American involvement, that grand army had still not materialized.

"Behind their hands and under their breaths, the Poilus called our soldiers 'Boy Scouts' and spoke of our efforts as 'The Second Children's Crusade,'" Cobb reported. The French people began to whisper that "the United States had failed to live up to its pledges." Cobb blamed the tongue-waggers who had led the French to expect so much in so short of period of time. He knew otherwise, that American convoys were delivering some two hundred thousand doughboys to France every month, that the great American war machine waited like a coiled spring to snap into action.

In mid-May Cobb got his chance to report on fighting Americans, though not those he expected. Someone informed him that American soldiers were on the battle line with the French, and they had seen action. They were African American soldiers, including one former National Guard unit from New York. Since there had been no official announcement to this effect, Cobb was skeptical.

Along with two New York correspondents, Lincoln Eyre (*New York World*) and Martin Green (*Evening World*), Cobb made the 180-mile, seven-hour journey to the trenches north of the town of Ménehould, west of Verdun, to check out the story.

There the reporters found two black regiments that had been attached to the French army. The reporters happened to arrive the day word came that the French were going to award the Croix de Guerre to two of the black soldiers, Henry Johnson and Needham Roberts of the 369th Infantry. Johnson's decoration would carry the golden palm, signifying extraordinary valor.

Serving as nighttime sentries, the two men had been attacked by a large German raiding party. Severely wounded, they fought off the Germans with rifles and grenades. When Johnson's ammunition ran out, he used his rifle as a club and then resorted to a bolo knife.

As far as scoops went, this was a good one. The two men were the first Americans to be awarded this prestigious decoration. The presence of blacks in the AEF had barely been noted by the press. No one had written about black fighting men. A story about these ignored warriors, honored for bravery while most of the AEF waited to see battle, deserved front-page headlines.

For the New York reporters, this was also a good local story. Eyre's article on the visit ran under the headline "Two N.Y. Negroes Whip 24 Germans; Win War Crosses." But it was left to Cobb to give the story national prominence in the two-million-circulation *Saturday Evening Post*.

A native southerner and a product of his times, Cobb carried his fair share of racial prejudice. But his article, "Young Black Joe," which ran in two issues of the magazine and appeared in his war book *The Glory of the Coming*, featured both the heroism of these two soldiers and the quality of the black fighting men. "They were soldiers who wore their uniforms with a smartened pride; who were jaunty and alert and prompt in their movements; and who expressed as some did vocally in my hearing, and all did by their attitude, a sincere heartfelt inclination to get a whack at the foe with the shortest possible delay." Cobb concluded: "If ever proof were needed, which it is not, that the color of a man's skin has nothing to do with the color of his soul these twain then and there offered it in abundance."

Cobb's article, which appeared in August 1918, was widely republished. It brought to national attention the role of black soldiers and, in particular, the 369th Infantry Regiment, which would gain fame on the battlefield as the "Harlem Hellfighters."

Fuller coverage of African American involvement in the AEF would wait until a black journalist—Ralph W. Tyler—was credentialed with the AEF on September 28, six weeks before the end of the war. Working for the government's Committee on Public Information, he was assigned to the black 92nd Division and reported on it during the Argonne fighting. As much as censors allowed, he drew attention to the prejudice faced by African Americans in the AEF.

Getting into the Fighting

Beginning in May 1918 the A E F followed the lead of the Twenty-Sixth by issuing daily news summaries. Typically they provided little fresh information. But such was not the case on May 28. On that date the A E F reported that American troops had successfully engaged in their first offensive operation, capturing the village of Cantigny, taking two hundred prisoners, and inflicting heavy losses on the enemy. Although Cantigny did not amount to much in terms of the great battles then raging along the western front, it demonstrated to the Allies that American soldiers had the mettle to press the attack. For correspondents it served as a model for future offensives. The reporters at press headquarters received a briefing the night before the attack. They then joined the troops that night to watch preparations and be on hand for the battle.

These rookie war reporters had no script for how to cover the fighting. When the troops climbed from their trenches, *Collier's* writer Jimmy Hopper suggested to Wilbur Forrest that they follow along. War correspondents were often under fire and in danger because they were so near the fighting, but they rarely charged into the action. Reasoning that a dead, wounded, or captured reporter was of no use to his newspaper, Forrest declined. However, as explosions from a rolling artillery barrage led the way, Hopper followed the doughboys toward Cantigny.

Forrest watched all the action from a safe distance, until the village was captured. Then he made his way to the rear, where a facility had been set up for correspondents. He wrote his story and put it in the hands of a motorcycle messenger who rushed it to the nearest telegraph station. It was a competent story, but nothing compared to Hopper's. In the confusion of battle, Hopper had gotten lost and wandered into the village alone. There a group of Germans, dazed by the artillery barrage and thinking Hopper an officer, surrendered to him. He herded them to the rear until he could pass them off to the troops. Then he helped carry out a wounded soldier and stopped with medics to examine another soldier shot through the stomach. Of the latter he wrote, "He was a walking dead man and didn't know it."

Being a magazine journalist, Hopper did not have the pressure of daily newspaper deadlines. He happily related his experience to the other correspondents. Forrest sent the story to United Press. Several weeks later Hopper's own account appeared in *Collier's*.

For the next few days, as A E F troops held off repeated German counterattacks, correspondents swarmed over the front to follow the United States' first offensive action of the war, the first time the A E F had actually captured territory from the Germans. The name Cantigny appeared in newspaper headlines all over the United States: "Americans Capture Cantigny," "Repulse Counterattacks," "War Department Pleased," "London Papers Praise Cantigny Victors."

Inspired perhaps by Hopper's experience, Forrest soon afterward convinced a nearby French unit to take him on a nighttime raid into no-man's-land. He was by now acknowledging that there was "something in the exhilaration of battle which distracts the mind from danger." It was a quiet night in the sector when he lined up with the patrol. Before crawling from the trench, they tested the darkness with a sweep of machine-gun fire, a grenade, and a parachute flare. Two officers, half a dozen soldiers, and Forrest worked their way through the first tangle of barbed wire. Forrest was disoriented in the darkness, where every slight sound seemed to threaten death. Here and there bones or body parts flashed horrific images. When they came near the German trench, the rat-tat-tat of a machine gun stitched the blackness, forcing them to lie motionless. They found no unusual activity in no-man's-land that night. The work of the patrol had ended. They crawled and wriggled their way back through wire to the safety of the trench. By risking his personal safety, Forrest too had earned a memorable story.

Saving Paris

At the end of May, the full force of the German spring offensive fell hard on beleaguered British and French troops, sweeping them from the strategic Chemin des Dames ridge. It pushed rapidly beyond and brought German troops to the Marne River for the first time since 1914. For the second time in the war, the German army threatened Paris.

On the morning of May 31 two American correspondents, Wilbur Forrest and Paul Scott Mowrer (*Chicago Daily News*), ventured out from Paris to gather "local color," which they would cable that night to supplement information in the official French communiqué. Forrest and Mowrer were assigned not to the AEF but to the French Anglo-American Press Mission. They were the only American reporters in the area that day. In fact there were no American troops within one hundred miles.

Leaving Paris that morning they gave their French soldier chauffer instructions to get as close to the action as possible without risking capture. He sped them to the town of Dormans on the Marne and had just started across its ancient bridge when he came to an abrupt stop. German machine guns guarded the far end of the bridge. Forrest thought it was his day to die. But the chauffer reversed gears and raced backward. Apparently the Germans were too surprised by the maneuver to spray them with lead. The reporters stopped with some French colonial troops from Senegal manning artillery on the crest of hills along the south bank of the river. They were positioned to blast the bridge the moment the Germans started across.

Armed now with enough color, the correspondents headed back to Paris, eager to write up their stories and rush them onto the cable. They had not traveled far when an auto raced past them in the opposite direction, and the reporters instantly recognized the uniforms. "Americans!" they both yelled and ordered their driver to give pursuit. When the reporters caught up with them and established who they were, the four lieutenants asked if they knew where Château-Thierry was. It was just up the road, the correspondents explained, but in the opposite direction.

They suggested to the young lieutenants that it was not a good idea to be kicking up a cloud of dust since the Germans were only a few hundred yards away, hidden by a tree line and also moving on that town. They pointed out the French troops concealed in the nearby brush, which the soldiers had not seen. "This confirmed our suspicions that these compatriots of ours were so green at the war game that they needed chaperoning," Forrest concluded. As the two reporters guided the soldiers to Château-Thierry, they met up with their entire unit, the Seventh Machine Gun Battalion. The battalion was tired and dusty from eighteen hours on the road but eager to get into the fight. Forrest and Mowrer led them into Château-Thierry.

The reporters hurried back to French headquarters with one fantastic story. The war had shifted away from its stalemated trench fighting to a war of mobility. Green American troops rushed gamely into their first real baptism of fire at the iconic Marne River to stop the German thrust toward Paris. And even better Forrest and Mowrer learned that no other reporters had gotten wind of the battle. They would have an exclusive. They wrote throughout the night and early next morning presented their stories to the censor before the articles went on to Paris and from there to the cable head at Brest. The American censor attached to this French unit killed the stories. The curious role played by these two journalists in the battle of Château-Thierry would not see publication until Forrest's 1934 war memoir.

Unbeknown to Forest and Mowrer, two other American reporters had also stumbled onto the Americans at Château-Thierry. Don Martin of the *New York Herald* and Edwin L. James, the new correspondent for the *New York Times*, green themselves to war and only accredited with the A E F for two weeks, were on a leisurely news hunt with their conducting officer when they picked up a disturbing report that the Germans had achieved a breakthrough and were advancing toward the Marne. Out on the highway trucks loaded with American soldiers forced the reporters' car off the road. The press car sped along in the dusty wake of the column until it got close enough to yell for an explanation. It was the Seventh Machine Gun Battalion. "There's a big fight," an excited soldier yelled, "and we're going to be in it."

Other correspondents in the field on news-gathering excursions also got wind of Americans moving into the action and converged on the sector. Once again those correspondents waiting at press headquarters were the last to know. They had gotten no advance notice of the biggest American story of the war. The Press Office had definitely dropped the ball on this one. By way of compromise, it announced that all news stories would be embargoed until noon the following day, giving all reporters just enough time to get to Château-Thierry and then race to Paris with their stories. Six reporters left Neufchâteau at midnight, pushed their way through traffic-clogged roads, read signposts with flashlights, and by daybreak pulled up to the American lines. They surveyed the scene, talked to some soldiers, and got back on the road to Paris. The official French communiqué had been issued announcing the battle, which was important in determining what could be written into the stories.

On the scene from the start, Edwin James gave some of the best eyewitness description. From various vantage points during the fighting, he painted the picture of the American men in action, arriving after forced marches from the distant training camps, repelling German advances over Marne bridges. He reported hearing French officers praise the Americans' sturdy defense. He ended his account of the battle by reassuring his readers that "American soldiers in large numbers [were] between the Germans and Paris, between the Kaiser and victory."

The French command, sensitive to the publicity value of the American action, permitted the correspondents to downplay the French role in the battle by saying that the Americans had stopped the German thrust on the Marne and saved Paris. It was an overstatement of the American role, especially since the German thrust had not yet been stopped, but it made for glorious copy. Floyd Gibbons's account rose to hyperbolic levels in heaping laurels on the American fighters: "In the eleventh hour, there at the peak of the German thrust, there at the climax of Germany's triumphant advances, there at the point where a military decision for the enemy seemed almost within grasp, there and then the American soldier stepped into the breach to save the democracy of the world."

24. *Chicago Tribune* reporter Floyd Gibbons was wounded at Belleau Wood while covering marines advancing into battle. Source: Harris & Ewing Collection, Prints and Photographs Division, Library of Congress, LC-DIG-hec-11352.

25. The helmet worn by reporter Floyd Gibbons when he lost an eye at Belleau Wood. Photo courtesy of Special Collections, Raymond H. Folger Library, University of Maine, Orono, Maine.

The fighting on the Marne spread out from Château-Thierry to nearby Belleau Wood. Additional American units summoned to what was still an emergency situation raced along the roads bordering the Marne. As so often was the case when the fighting became more fluid, refugees packed the roads fleeing for safety. They cheered the Americans flying by in their trucks. Clearly this was a new phase for the Americans, being fed into hot fighting, giving the impression that they were coming to the rescue.

Unlike the correspondents' panicky scramble to catch the action at Château-Thierry, the reporters received an advanced briefing of the marines being sent in to stop a German advance through Belleau Wood. Such pre-battle briefings allowed correspondents to write an advance story based on the objectives laid out in the briefing, which is precisely what Floyd Gibbons did. Before the battle commenced, Gibbons cabled a dramatic story to the *Chicago Tribune* describing the marines charging through the wood and routing the Germans. A risky strategy, for sure. He then hurried to the scene to gather local-color details that he would send out that night to fill in the blanks.

Gibbons landed at a hotly contested piece of the battle, where marines were exchanging machine-gun fire across a field of grain with Germans concealed in a tree line. When the orders came to advance and the men climbed from their trench, a marine gunnery sergeant was the first to climb out and exhort the troops with words Gibbons immortalized: "Come on, you sons-o-bitches! Do you want to live forever?" Gibbons did not name the sergeant, but the quotation is popularly attributed to First Sergeant Daniel Joseph "Dan" Daly, who had already won *two* Congressional Medals of Honor in previous wars.

The rousing command must have inspired Gibbons because he too set off at a crouch across a waist-high field of oats, following battalion commander Major Benjamin Berry. A burst of machine-gun fire made them hug the ground, and one bullet caught the major in the arm. Gibbons was crawling toward him to offer assistance when a bullet struck his arm as well. It registered as a sharp burning sensation, he would later write. He was examining the hole in his uniform when a second slug cut the top of his shoulder. Again only a burning sensation, no gush of blood. His arm still worked. So he continued crawling toward Berry, yelling encouragement as he went, until a third bullet took out Gibbons's left eye. It fractured his skull and exploded a three-inch hole in his helmet. Surprisingly, he did not lose consciousness but lay there for several hours until nightfall allowed him to crawl off the field.

For an enterprising correspondent, tragedy is opportunity. From a hospital in Paris, Gibbons was soon sharing with *Chicago Tribune* readers the excruciating details of "How It Feels to Be Shot," and "Good Morning, Nurse," about his time in the recovery ward. German planes bombing the city by night provided that all-important local color.

Gibbons recovered quickly and headed for home. The tall, handsome correspondent cut a dashing figure, with an eye patch and his arm in a sling. When he arrived in New York, a Marine Corps honor guard met him at the pier, bringing the news that France had awarded him the Croix de Guerre with Palm for his valor at Belleau Wood. The honor added to his celebrity on the lecture circuit that fall and bolstered the sales of his memoir, *And They Thought We Wouldn't Fight,* which he hurried out in October as the war rushed to a conclusion.

The Counteroffensive

Manning the United Press office in Paris, Webb Miller would have been the first to admit that congratulating the Americans for rescuing Paris after Château-Thierry and Belleau Wood was a bit premature. Standing in his open office window, he could almost set his watch by the regular fall of the artillery shells on the city. French aviators had located the Germans' "Paris Gun" seventy-five miles from the city. Seventy-five miles! It could fire a shell every twenty minutes. Miller sometimes waited at the window to see where it would hit. There was no sense being too curious, since he was not permitted to write anything about the bombardment other than what showed up in the official French communiqué. When the rumble of artillery drew closer to the city, terrorized Parisians crowded trains heading south.

No one in the Paris press corps knew what was happening. Miller and staff made plans for how they would cover the German entrance into the city. But on July 18, at the noon presentation of the official communiqué, it was announced that Marshall Foch, Allied supreme commander, had started a great counteroffensive. The Germans were fleeing. This time Paris really was saved.

Furious activity marked the following weeks. On the French front, two UP reporters worked in shifts seven days a week, one setting out each morning at 6:00 a.m. in a "flash car," so named because its driver was supposed to "go like the devil all the time." The other took the "noon ride" looking for stories at a more leisurely pace. After each wrote his story, it was handed over to a motorcycle courier. Couriers arrived at the UP office in Paris day and night, also carrying stories from the three UP correspondents on the American front. United Press reporters, in constant competition with their much-larger rival, the Associated Press, continually showed the enterprise needed to beat them by minutes or hours getting stories cabled home. Or when fortune smiled on them, getting an exclusive.

Fortune smiled on UP reporter Fred Ferguson when he decided to do some stories on how American troops lived in the trenches. One night, when the other correspondents returned to press headquarters, Ferguson remained behind to spend a night with the troops. However, his planned feature story turned into a headline-grabbing scoop in the middle of the night when the Germans launched their first gas attack against the American line. Those who took too long to don or properly adjust their gas masks paid the price, struggling like drowning men for breath, sucking like bellows to force air into their damaged lungs. Despite the desperate efforts of doctors, Ferguson watched the victims turn blue, stiffen, foam at the mouth, then die. He concluded that the horrific sight "would stir the fighting blood of every American to view the hospital where lay the victims of the first German gas attack." As the only reporter on the scene, Ferguson had the story to himself for one day. His next scoop would require more inventiveness.

During the series of summer successes, American troops fought under French command. Now that the emergency situation on the Marne had passed, the time had come to form the American units into an American army. It would no longer serve in a support role but have its first major objective and fight under American leadership.

The operation began mysteriously when Gerald Morgan of the AEF Press Office, asked Ferguson where he had been that day. He had been on a routine news-gathering trip, he said. He had traveled along the Vesle River, visiting a few hospitals, an airfield, and a YMCA hut. Follow that same route tomorrow, Morgan instructed, and every day until further notice. Stop at the same hospitals, the same airfield, and the same YMCA hut. All the other correspondents received similar instructions to repeat the exact routine they had followed that day. The reason Morgan gave was that they did not want to give any clues to German spies or aerial reconnaissance that an American offensive was in the works or where it might come.

For one week not much news was gathered from the American lines, as each day the reporters dutifully rode their cars along the exact same routes. That continued until September 11, when the twenty-four accredited correspondents set out predawn for a 150-mile journey to a hotel in the town of Nancy. That night General Dennis Nolan, chief of army intelligence, gathered the reporters in a room at the hotel. Behind him hung a map of a sector of the front named Saint-Mihiel. The American objective in the coming offensive was to eliminate the Saint-Mihiel salient that had remained in German hands since the start of the war. Nolan detailed every phase of the operation with an hour-by-hour timeline—how it would commence with an artillery barrage at midnight, how American tanks would be used for the first time, how air reconnaissance and artillery would work together, and how the infantry would advance on a well-timed schedule. The correspondents had never before been so fully taken into the army's confidence.

Although Nolan played down the significance of the operation as having limited objectives, it was hard to miss the importance being attached to it. It was the first all-American operation, under General Pershing's direct planning and leadership. Secretary of War Newton Baker would stand by Pershing's side to watch the battle. The Signal Corps laid a special telegraph wire between Nancy and Paris for the press to report the American offensive to the world.

A few hours later, when the artillery cut loose, many of the correspondents hurried to the hotel roof, where they could watch the heavy guns flashing on the horizon. The distant concussions made the hotel tremble. While his colleagues enjoyed the show, Fred Ferguson remained in his room pounding away on his typewriter, writing his account of the battle.

Although such things never were reported, the correspondents knew that the battle was something of a set-up. To avoid having the salient cut off, the Germans had already begun to retreat from the area. There might well be tough fighting, but given the symbolism of this first American offensive, every possible resource and effort had gone into ensuring that it would be a success. Therefore, Ferguson concluded that it would unfold pretty much the way General Nolan had outlined it. Ferguson wrote out an account of the battle in a series of fifty-word flashes—the charge out of the trenches, the taking of the first objective, the second objective, and so on. Each flash carried a time when it was to be transmitted.

When he finished, he roused from sleep Gerald Morgan, chief censor for the AEF, and explained his plan. He asked Morgan to censor the copy in advance and then cable the installments to United Press when circumstances of the battle indicated that they accurately reflected what had occurred. And he asked that multiple copies be sent out over multiple cable lines in case the army telegraph to Paris became jammed with traffic. Morgan agreed.

The correspondents arrived at the battle lines by midmorning and watched the well-orchestrated battle unfold. Tanks and the infantry moved forward on schedule; German prisoners came to the rear; the wounded shared with reporters details of the fighting. Everything progressed smoothly, and all objectives were met. While the diligent reporters gathered the news, Ferguson's news flashes were arriving in America throughout the day and being sent out to the hundreds of UP newspapers—the only accounts available of the critical battle. When the correspondents arrived back at press headquarters in Nancy, intent on rushing out their stories of the battle, a telegram awaited Ferguson from United Press, congratulating him on his biggest scoop of the war.

The Battle of the Argonne Forest

For the final battle of the war, the massive offensive known as the Battle of the Argonne Forest, or alternatively the Meuse-Argonne Offensive, press headquarters moved to the town of Bar-le-Duc. The dilapidated town, located some fifty miles south of the embattled fortress of Verdun, possessed the nearest telegraph facility to the battle area. On the night of September 25, 1918, some fifty correspondents crowded into an abandoned storefront on a Bar-le-Duc side street. They represented a mix of those who had been covering the war for years, those who had been with the AEF since its arrival in France in 1917, and newcomers just arrived on the scene.

A massive Allied offensive was about to kick off along the entire western front. As General Fox Conner explained to the correspondents, this time there was to be no limited objective; the battle was to the finish. American troops had been given the hardest assignment in the whole theater-wide offensive, Conner explained. He pointed out on a large wall map a spot between the river Meuse and the Argonne Forest. German resistance would be stiffest here because it was a "hinge" on the whole western front, closest to German territory and to the vital rail lines at Sedan. Also the terrain was difficult, and the Germans had fortified their positions well with trenches, machine-gun nests, tank traps, pillboxes, and barbed wire, the whole area being well supported with roads and rail lines to bring up ammunition. The explanation served as the general's tacit explanation in advance should American progress not match that of its Allies and for the expected high casualties.

Correspondents rode their cars to the front the next day. By noon, when the troops had made surprising advances, Edwin James of the *New York Times* moved through the captured German trenches and passed dugouts, gun positions, and villages blasted by American artillery. He wrote enthusiastically about the American tactic of "pinching out" the enemy rather than attacking frontally as the Allies had so often done unsuccessfully, and about how all of this was accomplished by American soldiers, many of whom had never before been in a battle.

The pinching movement soon devolved into an all-out frontal engagement that met with mixed results. On-the-scene coverage of the action quickly became an exercise in confusion and frustration. Fortunately, the new news-bulletin system of the Press Office worked to perfection. Motorcycle couriers and Signal Corps wires brought every development to press headquarters as quickly as it happened. Summary bulletins reported the action in sufficient details to allow reporters to cable out daily updates. Soon few reporters even bothered to visit the front lines.

It was through the news-bulletin system that reporters first learned of the most dramatic story of the campaign. One of the army's press officers in the field sent in a report on September 29 that part of the Seventy-Seventh Division in the Argonne Forest had advanced beyond other units and was in danger of being cut off. That possibility became reality on October 3, when German troops surrounded a unit commanded by Major Charles Whittlesey, and the name "Lost Battalion" came into existence to describe the doomed unit.

Division reports now came in twice a day, updating the situation with the battalion. Some six hundred men were trapped in a wooded ravine, holding out while attempts were made to break through and rescue them. A couple of couriers managed to sneak out and report the dire condition of the men, many dead and the rest running out of food, water, and ammunition. Airplanes tried to drop messages and food, but these fell out of reach. Reporters drove over to the Seventy-Seventh headquarters to follow the story, and their accounts soon gripped the nation.

The Seventy-Seventh Division was made up mostly of men from New York City, so the story of its heroic stand played well in that city's newspapers. Damon Runyon, famed columnist for the *New York American*, and Thomas Johnson of the *New York Sun* camped out at division headquarters for two days, going without much sleep as they followed each exciting development. By the time help finally reached the beleaguered survivors on October 7, all America was following the story.

Runyon, Johnson, and a few other reporters met the 194 survivors when they were brought out of the forest; 107 officers and men had been killed. The exhausted soldiers plunked down in a clearing to enjoy a smoke and some hot chocolate. Reporters located Major Whittlesey sitting on a stump, but he waved off their questions: "Don't write about me, just about these men."

Runyon had met many of the men of the Seventy-Seventh when they trained at Camp Upton, on Long Island. He marveled that these heroes were just ordinary guys, "brokers, clerks, gangsters, newsboys, truck drivers, collegians, peddlers." He found one young man who used to sell newspapers on Times Square. Now droopy-eyed with exhaustion and thoroughly caked with mud, the fellow beamed a wide smile of pride for his role in the unit's gallant stand.

Trucks scheduled to take the men behind the lines never appeared, so with weary determination Major Whittlesey assembled his men on the road to march out. It was hard to imagine a more pathetic and noble group of soldiers. "Worn out, dirty, hungry, thirsty, they would not give in," Johnson noted. They "walked heavily, numbed by utter exhaustion, clothes tattered and filthy, faces like drawn masks of putty, with the fixed stare of determination." Johnson noted that the other soldiers from the division who had gathered to welcome the survivors had tears in their eyes as the Lost Battalion marched out. This had all the makings of a great story.

To top off their accounts, reporters tracked down Major General Robert Alexander, commander of the Seventy-Seventh Division. The general was in an expansive mood and compared the men of the Lost Battalion to the defenders of the Alamo. Every man had fought bravely. Every man had refused to surrender. Alexander pulled out a piece of paper with a typewritten message. It was the call for surrender sent from a German officer to Major Whittlesey. He passed it around to the correspondents to read—"Americans, you are surrounded on all sides. Surrender in the name of humanity. You will be well treated."

"And what did Whittlesey tell them?" one reporter asked.

"What *should* he tell them?" Alexander boomed. "He told them to go to hell!"

This story just kept getting better. A ravaged battalion, cold, hungry, thirsty, sleepless, down to its last few rounds of ammunition, face-to-face with annihilation, had thumbed its nose at the Germans. What more perfect illustration of the American fighting spirit? In mid-October, as the war raced to its now-inevitable conclusion, the story landed on every front page in the United States.

Pins marked the front lines on the large wall map at press headquarters. They played a game of hopscotch throughout October, as the Germans threw reinforcements at each American advance, and key locations changed hands repeatedly. But the pins told the story of the steady cumulative movement forward by American troops.

With the final fighting of the war at hand, reporters worked at a fevered pitch seven days a week to keep their readers informed. Meeting that responsibility in the driving rain, fog, brutal cold, and deep mud of the American sector challenged reporters to their limits. It filled each long day to get to the front, quickly gather the news, and race back to the Press Office to send it out. Much of that time was spent on traffic-snarled roads of liquid mud.

By this stage of the war, news gathering on the American front had settled into a routine. Reporters seldom visited the frontline trenches where the fighting actually occurred. For one thing it took too long, involving a several-mile hike through the communication trenches; and second, scenes from the trenches had become old stuff. To UP correspondent Webb Miller his duty was clear: "find out what was happening and get the news back to the telegraph wires. This left little opportunity for sight-seeing."

On October 29 Edwin James could tell readers of the *New York Times* that American troops had brought up their largest artillery to shell the key German rail line at Sedan. That same day, even as new enemy divisions rushed in and heavy fighting continued, Austria-Hungary surrendered, followed the next day by Turkey. The dominoes were falling quickly.

While Webb Miller remained at Bar-le-Duc to watch things play out at the front, his United Press colleagues dispersed to be in place for the expected armistice. Fred Ferguson stood ready to cover postwar diplomatic developments in Paris, while Frank Taylor waited in Switzerland, poised to rush into Germany the moment the armistice was signed. All the American correspondents waited on a heightened edge of anticipation for the greatest story of the war: the end to the fighting.

26. United Press correspondent Webb Miller flew over the ceasefire line on the western front the day after the armistice went into effect. Photo courtesy of the Dowagiac Area History Museum.

CHAPTER TEN

After the Fighting

There had been a mutiny of sailors. . . . It was said the revolt had spread to Berlin. . . . There was a crucial struggle going on inside the beaten land. The shape of the peace—if, indeed, peace there was to be—depended on its outcome. And that had to be a story!

—LOWELL THOMAS, *Good Evening Everybody*

In those days of early November 1918, when the whole world waited breathlessly for the armistice, "the biggest news in the history of newspapers, perhaps in the history of humanity," the AEF correspondents worried how best to cover so grand and historic an event.

As the sole representative of the United Press syndicate at the front, Webb Miller felt the weight of responsibility. His account of how this horrific war ended would run under front-page, banner headlines in hundreds of newspapers. He needed a bold plan to be on the front the precise moment the armistice went into effect, to witness the cease-fire, and then beat his competitors back to press headquarters to send out his story.

He hit on the idea of being an aerial observer to history. He visited the nearby airfield where America's greatest flying ace, Eddie Rickenbacker, commanded a squadron. If he could get someone to take him up on the day of the cease-fire, he explained to Rickenbacker, he could witness the effects of the armistice along the entire front in this sector, then fly back to Bar-le-Duc and beat the competition with the biggest scoop of the war. Rickenbacker liked the idea. He hooked Miller up with ace pilot Jimmy Meissner, and the two made plans to fly over the front lines on the day the war ended.

In the final days press headquarters in Bar-le-Duc stood forty miles behind the front lines. To remain closer to the fighting, Miller spent one memorable night at the great citadel at Verdun. The monumental battle for Verdun in 1916 had cost some half a million casualties. A labyrinth of subterranean corridors had sheltered French soldiers during the battle. Miller spent the night on one of the five-tiered bunk beds lining the dank concrete catacombs that still housed some ten thousand French soldiers. At night they became "a side show of Dante's Inferno. . . . Many suffered from light shell shock and made the night hideous with their screams, mutters, and hysterical laughs. . . . Others coughed their lungs out with touches of gas."

At nine o'clock on the morning of November 11, Miller was at army headquarters at Souilly, when the commanding general rushed from his office waving a slip of paper. "Boys, it's over. Armistice at eleven o'clock." Miller phoned Meissner and asked if he was ready to fly. Heavy fog covered the entire area, Meissner reported. They could fly, but Miller wouldn't be able to see a thing.

Miller's backup plan was to be standing on the front line when the clock counted down to the end of the war. Fortunately, he had his own car, with a former race-car driver who wove like a madman through a dense fog on roads clogged with war traffic. As they neared the front, incoming artillery rounds exploded uncomfortably close by and cut the air with shrapnel. You could still die in the last minutes of a war.

At the edge of the battle zone, Miller hurried through the ankle-deep mud in the communication trenches that ran to the battle line. At the forward command bunker, he had the pleasure of informing the captain commanding this section of the line about the armistice. The time was 10:45, and the captain had not yet been notified. The men clustered around Miller for details, and word quickly swept along the trench.

Five minutes later the field telephone jangled. As the captain jotted down the text of the official armistice order, Miller read over his shoulder and copied it: "Fighting to cease at eleven . . . hold lines where they are . . . do not fire unless attacked . . . no crossing of armistice line or communication with the enemy." The captain immediately telephoned his outposts to read to each the text of the order. As the hour approached, all the men kept their eyes fixed on their wristwatches. Far in the distance, the fog-muffled cannonading diminished and then stopped. A few rat-a-tat-tats from nearby machine guns put final punctuation on the fighting. And then it was eleven o'clock. The greatest war in the history of mankind was over. Miller reported,

> It would make a better story if I could tell of men cheering, yelling, laughing, and weeping with joy, throwing their tin hats in the air, embracing one another, dancing with delight. But they didn't. Nothing happened. The war just ended. . . .
>
> The men stood talking in groups. The captain let me talk on the telephone to the outposts. No drama there, either. They said they couldn't see anything in the fog or hear anything. Further up the line it was the same. The army's reason for existence had suddenly ceased. The men didn't know what to do next.

Miller ran back to his car and told the driver to go as fast as he could back to Bar-le-Duc. Their speed hit fifty, sixty, seventy as they flew past long lines of troops marching to the front. These men were only a few miles from the front lines, and they didn't know the war was over. As he passed the head of each column, Miller leaned from the car and yelled, "'War's over. The Armistice. The Armistice.' Heads came up, shoulders went back, the news flashed down the columns like an electric current. You could see it travel. Columns halted and cheered."

Miller was the first correspondent back to press headquarters. His fingers never flew so fast over the typewriter. He wrote the story in fifty-word sections and rushed each through the censor and to the army telegraph, sending them at the "urgent rate" of $0.75 a word. Twenty-three minutes later his closest competitor appeared, and then others dribbled in. Miller finished up and headed back to the front.

The end unfolded differently in the Twenty-Sixth Division, which had gotten official word of the armistice at 7:00 a.m. The Twenty-Sixth had been fighting in the Verdun sector for twenty-five days, longer than any other American unit. Some of the artillery batteries kept firing up to the bitter end. As the clock wound down, Frank Sibley reported men gathering around the guns, all eager to fire the last shot in the war. In one battery each man took his turn firing the gun. In another five officers pulled the lanyard together to fire the gun for the last time. The grandest gesture unfolded at another battery that attached long ropes to the lanyards on four artillery pieces. Some two hundred men grabbed hold of each rope, while one man counted off the seconds. At 10:59 he signaled, and the men gave a tug. The four guns fired simultaneously, and eight hundred men sent a yell reverberating across no-man's-land toward the German trenches.

Later that day Sibley reported the celebration in nearby Verdun. Four of the Twenty-Sixth's regimental bands paraded through the streets, American doughboys marching together with French soldiers and black Senegalese fighters. The U.S. flag was hoisted on a tower of the cathedral. A French general gave a speech that lavishly praised the Americans. Of course the men of the Twenty-Sixth didn't understand a word of it, but they grasped the gist and cheered heartily.

Early in the cold, clear light of November 12, Webb Miller stuffed himself into a fur-lined flying suit, mittens, and cap and climbed into the machine gunner's seat of Lieutenant Meissner's airplane for his postponed flight over the front. At a height of fifty feet, they skimmed along the armistice line for ten miles. Where it ran through a valley, not a soul was visible. A small American flag had been stuck in the ground to indicate the front line. Miller saw some doughboys playing ball, while two hundred yards away a cluster of Germans watched. Elsewhere Americans stood in open fields around bonfires; others laid laundered clothing on the ground to dry. One soldier bathed in a brook. A burial party dug graves on a knoll. A short distance away another unit prepared for an inspection, all its equipment arranged neatly on the ground. In less than twenty-four hours the front had been transformed from a slaughterhouse to a picture of calm.

Only the scars of the fighting remained to tell the story. Newly dug trenches crisscrossed the landscape. Water filled the moonscape of shell holes. Miller and Meissner passed over three villages that had been reduced to rubble and a forest with its trees stripped of limbs. It was a "scene of unutterable, sickening desolation. Debris of war lay scattered everywhere, trench helmets, bits of clothing, broken rifles, machine guns, tangles of barbed wire, blankets, stretchers."

Despite it being a violation of the armistice order against crossing the line, Meissner banked the plane and headed toward Germany. Within minutes they sighted retreating German troops. They swooped low over one column, and the men laughed and waved. Then suddenly in their path, a great column of fire and smoke erupted high into the air. The concussion of the blast rocked the plane. In quick succession seven more such blasts blew into the sky, violently tossing the aircraft. The Germans were blowing up ammunition dumps. When Meissner climbed to a safe eight thousand feet, the vast panorama of the front presented itself. German troops jammed every road in every direction, going home from war.

Back at the airfield, Meissner made a bad landing. He hit a mud hole, tearing off the wheels and bouncing high in the air before slamming on the nose and shattering the propeller. Among the men who rushed to the scene was one livid French aviator. He had been on a mission to deliver important dispatches to a French general. Those dispatches were in the flying suit that Miller had grabbed for his flight. He made Miller strip out of the suit right there beside the broken plane and then rushed off on his assignment.

"Hell of a good story," said the chief censor, Gerald Morgan, when Miller submitted his write-up at press headquarters. No other correspondent had seen the spectacle of the German retreat. Miller could report, "I had seen the last drama of the front."

Inside a Defeated Germany

The urge, of course, for Webb Miller was to talk with those retreating soldiers and follow them right back to Germany to find out how that proud nation was handling defeat. So many dire stories and rumors had found their way out of Germany in the waning days of the conflict: open rebellion seized the military; the kaiser abdicated; the country became a republic with a new constitution; a Russian-style revolution threatened to engulf the entire nation; the population was starving. Every editor of every newspaper in the United States ached for an eyewitness report from inside Germany. But the armistice order was clear in forbidding anyone from crossing the lines. However, those journalists not accredited with the A E F were not bound by armistice restrictions.

Days after the armistice, Arno Dosch-Fleurot sat in a German hotel staring at his breakfast—a cup of inky liquid and two saccharin tablets. He had entered Germany without problem from Copenhagen. Dosch-Fleurot dropped the artificial sweetener into the artificial coffee, took one sip, and could go no further. Also set before him was a slab of black "war bread" and a gelatinous substance they were calling jam. Shortages inflicted by the Allied naval blockade had forced the inventive Germans to create substitutes for foods, drinks, fuel, and many materials of war. They used the word *ersatz* as a generic term for such substitutes. Acorns or beans replaced coffee beans in *ersatzkaffee*. One taste of the foul liquid and Dosch-Fleurot no longer thought of Germans as the enemy but instead considered them a population that had suffered under the punishment of living on *ersatz*.

He discovered that the German capital lived an *ersatz* political existence. Dosch-Fleurot had a knack for penetrating to the heart of a political situation, no matter how ill-defined or dangerous it might be. Only two months earlier he had escaped from revolutionary Russia when his reporting got him in trouble with the Bolsheviks. For twenty-two months he had watched that revolution unfold and coined the term "Red Terror" in his dispatches to describe the killings, torture, and systematic oppression employed by the Bolsheviks. Now the red revolution had transplanted a curious version of socialism to Berlin, and Dosch-Fleurot found himself in the heart of developments.

A Workers' and Soldiers' Council ruled Berlin but functioned under the control of the long-established Socialist Party. He interviewed socialist leaders. Because Dosch-Fleurot had witnessed events in Russia, he became popular with the younger liberals and radicals in the city. He sat up late with them in cafés for their intellectual debates about revolution.

If he worried how the former enemy capital would welcome an outside spectator to its postwar unrest, he got his answer early in his stay. The manager of his hotel woke him one morning, holding a copy of a Berlin newspaper. It held an article about Dosch-Fleurot, identifying him as an American correspondent who had "invented the stories of German atrocities in Belgium" and now had the "impertinence to come to Berlin to gloat over Germany's defeat." It also identified his hotel.

The manager was incensed that one of his guests would be so menaced. Even as he helped the journalist compose a letter in response to the article, the telephone began to ring with well wishes from influential citizens. Ignore the article, they told him. The writer does not understand that Germany needs to make friends. The article actually served as a most effective advertisement of Dosch-Fleurot's presence in the city. Within a week he had met nearly everyone of importance in Berlin and gotten a sense of the fragile political situation.

Dosch-Fleurot sat in on debates of the Workers' and Soldiers' Council between the socialist and Communist elements. Russian-trained Communists were in Berlin to lend their support for a Communist takeover. Violence erupted on Christmas Day and spilled into the new year. When "proletarian shock troops" captured parts of the city, a volunteer force of ex-soldiers came to the defense of the government, and Dosch-Fleurot interviewed their commander. Germany was as efficient at countering revolution as it had been at conducting war. Dosch-Fleurot continued

27. Lowell Thomas in the uniform of an AEF correspondent. Thomas made an unauthorized trip into Germany immediately after the armistice to report on the social upheaval in the defeated country. Source: James A. Cannavino Library, Archives & Special Collections, Marist College, Poughkeepsie, New York.

to travel in Germany, Austria, and Poland for another year, chronicling the unrest.

In the weeks after the armistice, AEF headquarters hopped from Bar-le-Doc to Verdun to Luxembourg as the army worked its way to the German city of Coblenz, where it would administer its assigned zone of occupation. Those reporters who remained with the AEF chafed at the continuing military control and censorship and the armistice restriction preventing entry into Germany.

On November 21 five of the accredited correspondents defied military orders and set out for the German border, believing that their mandate to report the news superseded military rules. Entering Germany in two army cars with army drivers, Herbert Corey (Associated Newspapers), Lincoln Eyre (*New York World*), Cal Lyon (Newspaper Enterprise Association), George Seldes (Marshall Syndicate), and Fred A. Smith (*Chicago Tribune*) quickly encountered a column of retreating German soldiers and began to learn something about the German state of mind. The soldiers were happy the war was over. Some had decked their trucks and cannons with greenery. Some units sang marching songs. Most readily conceded that the German army could not have continued fighting: "*Kaput. We could do no more.*" But some officers had already taken up the "one tenet of that dangerous cult which [was] gaining ground in Germany, a cult that would have the promise of future wars if the autocracy were to remain . . . that 'the German armies have never been defeated.'"

What also became strikingly clear was how firmly the revolutionists controlled things. Whereas one officer threatened to arrest the reporters, a soldier from a local Workers' and Soldiers' Council provided them with credentials that earned them warm receptions in the cities they visited. Because they had explained that they wished to report to the American people the truth about conditions in Germany, including the desperate food shortages, the group was labeled the "American Food Mission," which warmed their welcome.

At this point the journalists sent their nervous army chauffeurs and cars back out of Germany, along with a note to the Press Office explaining their absence: "Opportunity has been afforded us to visit the interior of Germany and we are availing ourselves of it, considering this of the greatest importance at the present time."

In Frankfurt the newly formed government gave a banquet in their honor. They landed their biggest scoop with an interview of General Hindenburg, chief of the General Staff, who was presiding over demobilization. In a frosty conversation they managed to get the general to answer the question, "What was chiefly responsible for Germany's defeat?"

The Americans, he responded, the numerical strength of the American army and their fighting spirit. Having Germany's celebrated general credit the Americans for his defeat vindicated their entire trip. The interview would eventually make the front pages in thousands of American newspapers.

Meanwhile, the A E F command had worked itself into a frenzy over the runaway journalists. It was outrageous that accredited correspondents should go into Germany ahead of the army of occupation. The military equivalent of an "all-points bulletin" went out to all Allied units of occupation to apprehend the miscreants. Cable offices received instructions not to transmit any stories from them. Belgium and the Netherlands were asked to watch for the newsmen, and Allied authorities at Channel ports were ordered to arrest them if they attempted to cross to England.

George Seldes returned on his own, and the other four were apprehended and faced a judge advocate general. The military wanted to imprison them for six months, but through the intercession of presidential advisor Colonel Edward House they avoided that fate. Instead, as punishment their stories were impounded until late December, when the news value had considerably diminished. Smith's account of their adventure received wide distribution and highlighted the critical food shortages and how the German people had been kept in the dark about the deteriorating military and economic situation. He had attended a rally in Frankfurt, at which one revolutionary leader said that German hopes rested with President Wilson, for whom the audience gave three rousing cheers.

Two other newsmen also found the temptation to sneak into Germany irresistible. In early December Lowell Thomas and Webb Waldron (*Collier's Weekly*) sneaked across the Swiss-German border. Thomas had recently returned to Paris after a long stint with the U.S. government's Committee on Public Information. Working with motion-picture cameraman Harry Chase, Thomas shot films to support the war effort, first on the Italian front and then with the British in the Middle East. It was in Palestine that Thomas became acquainted with Thomas Edward Lawrence, an Oxford-educated archaeologist who had become a leader of the Arab Bedouin revolt against the Turks. Through films and lectures that Thomas presented around the world and through his 1924 book *With Lawrence in Arabia*, Thomas immortalized the British officer as Lawrence of Arabia.

Traveling as uniformed correspondents, Thomas and Waldron arrived in Berlin at the very moment when the newly created German republic was moving rapidly to a climactic confrontation with a Communist uprising. The first face they could put on the revolt belonged to a German sailor who stopped them on the street to check their papers. He just happened to be a good-natured fellow from New Jersey. He had been visiting relatives in Germany at the start of the war and been drafted into the German navy. He participated in the naval mutiny and was now with the rebellious sailors occupying the Imperial Palace. Plied with cigarettes and brandy, he talked with the journalists through the night about his role in the revolution.

Amid the strikes, street violence, and the threat of civil war, everyone in Berlin was eager to tell his or her story to the American journalists. When Friedrich Ebert, the current chancellor, met with them, he looked like "a man on the ragged edge of breakdown." Ebert couldn't predict what would happen in Germany but conceded, "There is only one thing I know and it is this: if my government falls, Germany will turn to a dictator, and then you Americans will have to come back."

The following day they met with Karl Liebknecht and Rosa Luxemburg, the two leaders of the Communist Party plotting to overturn the government. Since Luxemburg opposed the use of force and Liebknecht thought it a necessary expedient, the two leaders ignored the reporters and argued hotly with each other about revolutionary philosophy and tactics. Days later their revolt exploded with strikes and bloody street fighting.

Thomas bragged in his autobiography that he and Waldron were the first foreign correspondents to reach Germany and stay long enough to get shot at. A German journalist who formerly worked for the Associated Press befriended the two reporters and began to release stories about them via Copenhagen. Even as they dodged riots, sniper fire, and machine-gun bursts on the street and spoke with everyone of note in Berlin, their exploits were reported outside Germany. By the time the reporters departed in late January 1919, Liebknecht and Luxemburg were dead, their revolution was defeated, and an election had endorsed Ebert.

Without credentials or travel passes, the pair had to sneak back into France. Again it was Colonel House who prevented them from getting into trouble for their unauthorized adventure. Their experience and interviews were of such substance that House arranged for them to brief some members of the American delegation to the peace conference, which had just gotten under way.

Those correspondents remaining with the AEF finally found their way into Germany on December 11. They had been sent in advance to the city of Coblenz so they could capture the official entry of the U.S. army into Germany with the crossing of the Rhine River. This long-anticipated event would be the biggest news story since the armistice.

Correspondents Webb Miller (UP) and former sports writer Damon Runyon (Universal Service) found a room together at the poshest hotel in town and luxuriated in the first clean room, bath, and soft bed they had enjoyed in many weeks. The luxury was so intoxicating that they overslept on the big day. Fortunately, their room overlooked the bridge over which U.S. troops would make their triumphal entry into the city. Miller watched it from the window. Runyon refused to even stir from his comfortable bed, so Miller narrated the spectacle for him: "General Parker has walked out to the middle of the bridge. . . . The troops are starting to cross the Rhine." Runyon reported the event exactly as it had transpired, with him lying in bed while Webb Miller described the scene.

This blasé attitude gave a fair reflection of the mood among the correspondents in Coblenz. All Europe seethed with political unrest and violence as empires died and new nations were born, but in Coblenz the correspondents "dwelt on an island surrounded by a sea of misery." The reporters in Coblenz had lost their sense of purpose. They drank and gambled far too much. They covered petty events and wrote stories about unimportant issues. The history-making events occurring all around him meant nothing to Miller. "I had spent months in the midst of the greatest events in recorded history," he explained. "The reaction of those last weeks of strain set in; I couldn't interest myself in the aftermath." He could not bear the idea of covering the upcoming peace conference to watch politicians haggle over the ruins of Europe. The United Press granted Miller's request for transfer to its London office.

The haggling over the ruins of Europe did not wait for the peace conference. Editors could scarcely sort out the topsy-turvy twists that history and politics took in the months after the war. Empires that had stood for hundreds of years collapsed of their own inflated weight. The weapons of war that still littered the continent found new purpose to settle old scores and carve new national borders. The Baltic States declared their independence. Poland was forging its frontiers. The nations of Yugoslavia and Czechoslovakia came into existence. Revolution simmered in Germany and degenerated into a "chaos of terror" in Russia. "Every old, festering sore in Europe had broken out," as nations squabbled for territory.

Every few days Harold Williams in the *New York Times* office in Bern cabled a summary of reports and rumors. National borders were in flux. Agreements were made one day and broken the next. Italian prisoners were fighting with the Poles against the Ukrainians; German forces in Russia sold or gave arms to the Ukrainians and fought with them and the Bolsheviks one day and opposed them the next. Williams encountered former residents of the Austro-Hungarian Empire who no longer knew to which country they belonged, which country should stamp their passports, or how to address the letters they wrote to family back home. A trainload of American and British citizens arrived from Vienna, fleeing political unrest, although they reported that most of the population was too desperately cold and hungry to care about politics.

By the end of December, Williams noted with alarm:

> I have no hesitation in saying that the spectacle of European ruin is simply appalling. Nineteenth century civilization is broken down. I do not mean merely that dilapidated trains crawl dismally; that postal and telegraphic communication is hardly better than in Napoleonic times; that famine and pestilence are creeping over Europe, but that there is a collapse of human, moral energy, a revival of primitive, barbaric instincts, and the fierce endeavor to have one's little private will by force. . . . I don't wish to appear to be preaching, but only the imagery of the Apocalypse can do justice to the present state of Europe.

History and Heroes

One month after the armistice, standing on the battlefield at Passchendaele (also known as the Third Battle of Ypres), Lieutenant Colonel Frederick Palmer was startled by the distinct report of a howitzer. But it was only an echo in his imagination. Palmer had seen the fighting at Ypres in 1915 as an accredited correspondent with the British army. He returned now, while writing another book on the war, to savor its history. The war had to be captured while memories were still fresh and individuals available.

No area of Europe had been more contested in the war than this corner of Belgium, the scene of five massive battles with hundreds of thousands of casualties. But already those events were fading. Now on that battlefield a misty rain "made the scattered wrecks of tanks look spectral in the midst of weed-covered shell craters, some shivering, drenched Belgians had sat down by the road after having tried in vain to find the remains of their homes. A British sentry sat in the drizzle on a box while he watched some German prisoners methodically salvaging out of the earth, mixed with human bones, any iron worth saving. This generation has seen enough of war to realize its foolishness."

With censorship restrictions now lifted, correspondents could begin telling the story of the United States' role in the war. Webb Miller, who couldn't interest himself in the peace conference or the turmoil in former enemy lands, busied himself writing the histories of several AEF divisions. Palmer, as former correspondent, former AEF chief press officer, and former confidant to General Pershing, already had four war books to his credit and was working on the fifth.

When Palmer left his position in the AEF Press Office in January 1918, he became a top advisor to General Pershing and was put in charge of the AEF War Diary. His new role gave him the freedom to visit all locations of the U.S. army and those of the Allies. His book *America in France* (1918) chronicled the United States' role through September 1918. What impressed him most at that point was the building, equipping, and supporting of the huge U.S. Army in France, what he called "Our Great Project." He traced the steps of that buildup from the earliest "blue print," when Secretary of War Newton Baker described France as "a sheet of white paper on which we had to write our undertaking," through the successive levels of training and engagement, stopping just before the final battle in the Argonne Forest. Now he worked on a new book to capture that final campaign.

As the war diarist for the AEF and Pershing's trusted confidant, Palmer had probably seen more of the fighting during the Argonne Offensive than anyone else. He frequently visited the front lines to collect information on fact-finding assignments for Pershing. On one single day early in the offensive, he found himself at army, corps, and division headquarters and then traveled "three miles beyond the trenches with [the American force's] advance against machine-gun nests."

Not surprisingly, when he hurried out *Our Greatest Battle (The Meuse-Argonne)* in 1919, it captured both the voice of a tactician and the dramatic, firsthand narrative of a seasoned war correspondent. Here is Palmer's description of how the front had to be adjusted after a day of fighting:

> Platoons and companies which had become mixed with their neighbors, and individual men who had strayed from their units, must be sorted out and returned. Gaps in the line must be filled; groups that had become "bunched" must be deployed; groups whose initiative had carried them forward to exposed points might have to be temporarily withdrawn—all by feeling their way in the darkness. The sound of machine-gun fire broke the silence at intervals as the watchful enemy detected our movements. A shadowy approaching figure, who the men hoped was the welcome bearer of that warm meal from the rolling kitchens, might turn out to be an officer who directed that they stumble about in the woods and ravines to some other point, or creep forward in the clammy, dew-moist grass with a view to improving our "tactical dispositions," which does not always improve the human dispositions of those who have to carry out the orders.

What differentiated this book from Palmer's previous work was that the end of the war brought freedom from censorship. He could now write with candor about the experience of the soldiers and mistakes in command. By mid-October 1918 "as the processes of the Argonne battle became more systematic, they became more horrible. They would have been unendurable if emotion had not exhausted itself, death become familiar, and suffering a commonplace. . . . The capacity to retain vitality and will-power in the face of cold and fatigue, and not to become sodden flesh indifferent to what happened, was even more important than courage, which was never wanting." He commented on the deficiencies of commanders: "Some of our leaders had not yet learned to apply in the stress of action and the conflict of reports the principle that when committed to one plan it is better to go through with it than to create confusion by inaugurating another which may seem better."

Palmer made a conscious decision not to mention the name of any individual soldier below the rank of division commander or to single out any recipient of the Medal of Honor or the Distinguished Service Cross. "I like to think that our men didn't fight for Crosses; that they fought for their cause and their manhood," he explained. That was the sentiment of a war diarist rather than a correspondent. There were other reporters, in the wake of the fighting, intent on just the opposite: giving American readers the individual heroes that they rarely had during the war.

One day in early 1919, with public focus now shifted to the Paris Peace Conference, *Saturday Evening Post* writer George Pattullo was bouncing around in the back of an army truck in the north of France with the artist Joseph Cummings Chase. The *Post* had sent Pattullo to post-armistice Europe in search of stirring war stories. Chase had been commissioned by the army to create a record of American valor by painting the men who had been the most courageous during the war, those who received the Distinguished Service Medal, Distinguished Service Cross, and the Medal of Honor. Because wartime censorship restrictions had rarely allowed the mention of the names of individual soldiers, except for airmen, the United States had been largely bereft of heroes during the war. Now with the fighting concluded, the nation needed to find justification for the cost and sacrifice. It was time to tell how heroically many ordinary Americans had fought.

Just the previous month, Chase told Pattullo, he had painted a second portrait of General Pershing in Paris and was struck by the change in the general's appearance. The painting completed just a few months ago during the fighting in the Argonne had revealed a man dark, tired, and grim, even melancholy. War had aged the general, grayed his hair, and accentuated the lines on his face. By contrast the painting Chase completed in January showed a man more light-hearted and at ease who had just shrugged off the weight of the world.

Chase was full of such stories. Perhaps the most inspiring one had been told to him by General George Duncan, commander of the Eighty-Second Division. Apparently, during fighting in the Argonne, a Tennessee corporal in that division had killed a couple dozen Germans, wiped out a bunch of machine-gun nests, and captured over a hundred of the enemy—all single-handed. If true it just might be the single most remarkable display of valor by any soldier in the war. Pattullo instantly recognized the story's potential.

Pattullo was, in fact, heading to the Argonne. When he arrived he checked in at the Eighty-Second, where Chase's story was confirmed. Pattullo just happened to arrive on the scene while an investigation was under way to substantiate the details prior to recommending Sergeant Alvin York for the Congressional Medal of Honor. Pattullo accompanied York and the army investigators to the scene of the battle. He followed along taking notes as York walked over the same ground and recounted his story.

On October 8, 1918, German machine guns had been taking a terrible toll on his battalion. York was part of a sixteen-man unit ordered to get behind German lines and take out the machine guns. York led the investigators through the heavy brush and tree cover that had allowed his unit to get close enough to capture a group of Germans. That's when heavy machine-gun fire opened up, killing six Americans and wounding three others. York took command of the remaining six men. While they guarded the prisoners, York worked his way into position to take on the machine guns. He recalled the harrowing experience:

> Those machine guns were spitting fire and cutting down the under-growth all around me something awful. And the Germans were yelling orders. You never heard such a racket in all of your life. . . . As soon as the machine guns opened fire on me, I began to exchange shots with them. There were over thirty of them in continuous action, and all I could do was touch the Germans off just as fast as I could. I was sharp shooting. . . . All the time I kept yelling at them to come down. I didn't want to kill any more than I had to. But it was they or I. And I was giving them the best I had.

York could see the German machine guns in their "fox holes"

and the tops of the heads of the gunners. It reminded him of the turkey matches back home in the Tennessee hills, where he had to shoot the heads off turkeys, a feat at which he excelled. He fired off several clips from his rifle. He pointed out to Pattullo a scar on a tree where he thought he might have missed one of his shots. But that was York's gift: he almost never missed. At this point in the fight, six German soldiers charged him with fixed bayonets. York had fired most of his rifle ammunition, so drew his automatic pistol and shot them before they reached him.

"You killed the whole bunch?" one of the investigators asked.

"I teched off the sixth man first, then the fifth, then the fourth, then the third, and so on. That's the way we shoot wild turkeys at home. You see you don't want the front ones to know that we're getting the back ones, and then they keep coming until we get them all."

After that stunning display, one of the German officers captured earlier offered to convince the German soldiers still on the ridge to surrender, if York would only stop shooting. At the end of the engagement, York and his six men marched their prisoners back to the American lines. At battalion headquarters a lieutenant counted 132 prisoners. "York, have you captured the whole German army?" the officer asked. "I got a tolerable few of them," York replied.

The investigators, York, and Pattullo paused at the foot of a hill where much of this action had occurred. There six wooden crosses marked the graves of the fallen from York's platoon. Pattullo offered, "I cannot understand, even now, how any of you came out alive."

"We know there were miracles, don't we?" York responded. "Well, this was one. I was taken care of—it's the only way I can figure it."

For three days Pattullo conducted his own investigation, until finally persuaded that he had all the makings of a remarkable story. And, the best part: four months after it occurred nothing about York had appeared in the press.

Pattullo's story in the April 26, 1919, issue of the *Saturday Eve-*

ning Post enshrined York as the most famous soldier of the war. It laid out for readers the events of that October 8 fight in the Argonne Forest in which York distinguished himself. But heroic deeds aside, what truly resonated with *Post* readers—and all of America—was York's homespun American background. He was born in a log cabin in 1887 and left school after the third grade to work on the family farm. He became a crack shot with pistol and rifle to put food on the table and earn money competing in shooting competitions.

A heavy drinker, gambler, and all-around hell-raiser in his youth, he found religion and became an elder in his fundamentalist church. Because his religion opposed the taking of human life, he would have qualified for conscientious objector status, but he responded to the draft. When he confessed his continuing misgivings to his captain, the officer held long sessions with York in which he quoted Scripture to justify war. Once convinced York became the exemplary soldier who would distinguish himself in the Argonne fighting.

The Thrill of Hope

Three days out from New York, with December seas turning heavy and the earnest YMCA workers below deck offering French lessons and music concerts, Simeon Strunsky, literary editor of the *New York Evening Post*, took stock of the historic moment. The main body of newsmen—over one hundred—heading to the peace conference had sailed on the *Orizaba* a day ahead of him. One day behind him sailed the president of the United States and his peace delegation, making what Strunsky thought to be the most momentous transatlantic voyage since Columbus. "We are on our way to the last act of the biggest show in history," he wrote. "We are one of the last waves which the suck of the war has sent lapping from the west against the east."

The literary editor's mind thought in such grandiloquent terms. Woodrow Wilson and his entourage were the concentrated counterflow of more than four hundred years of westward migration, Strunsky imagined—all those pioneers, fugitives, adventurers, and buccaneers who went to the New World, all those fleeing famine, plague, pogroms, church disputes, and wars, out of whom America had built its strength and its vision. Strunsky himself had been born a Jew in the Russian Empire.

The mood was just as elevated among the more than one hundred correspondents, editors, and publisher sailing on the *Orizaba*. They were the best reporters their publication had to offer—the likes of Ralph Pulitzer, Lincoln Eyre, and Herbert Bayard Swope—being sent on the choicest and most challenging journalistic assignment imaginable. The peace conference would gather world political leaders, the best experts and most experienced diplomats, representatives of every nation and would-be nation, combining their expertise and wisdom to solve the intractable problems of ending the war and ensuring the peace.

During the voyage a few reporters instructed their colleagues in topics that might prove useful at the conference. French lessons were popular. W. E. B. Du Bois lectured about the African colonies, publisher S. S. McClure on French politics. The journalists onboard organized a group they named the United States Press Delegation to support and advocate for proper recognition of their members at the conference. This level of professional interaction and support was unprecedented. Journalism historian Joseph R. Hayden has suggested that the interaction of the journalists on the *Orizaba* and at the peace conference, with the opportunity to meet colleagues from other publications who were of varying experience and professional standing, amounted to journalism's first convention, where it took a step toward a more professional status.

Their transatlantic crossing had been timed to take them to Europe in advance of the president so that they could chronicle his arrival. The start of the peace conference still lay a month in the future, but the president's schedule would take him first to Paris and then to the other Allied capitals. Pundits in America and Europe speculated about how he would be received.

"Everybody feels that something very big happened in Paris yesterday." *New York Times* reporter Charles Grasty struggled to explain the significance of the triumphant reception accorded President Woodrow Wilson in the French capital on December 15. Some 150 American journalists had already gathered in Paris in anticipation of the peace conference.

What they saw in Paris left them all grasping for superlatives. Fifty thousand French soldiers lined Wilson's five-mile carriage route, holding back hundreds of thousands of jubilant Frenchmen. Captured guns and other battlefield trophies lined the way. Nothing in living memory matched the exuberance of the French welcome. They cheered, "Welcome Wilson," "Long live Wilson," or in great choruses, simply resounded with "Wilson, Wilson, Wilson."

Europe had a complicated relationship with the American president. Throughout the war he had "hovered in the distance, a gigantic but mystic figure holding the balance of the world in his hands," one British journalist observed before Wilson's departure for Europe. Even while he kept the United States on the sidelines of the fighting, American aid in the form of finances, food, and war supplies kept the Allied ship afloat. When he brought America into the war, he became a saint to millions in Europe.

Wilson always seemed the most deliberate, the most fair-minded of world leaders. He became the standard-bearer for peace in January 1918, when he outlined a fourteen-point blueprint for peace negotiations. These points embraced such concepts as open agreements, free trade, democracy, self-determination, and the proposed creation of a "general association of nations," a league of nations that would put an end to future wars. Texts of the speech were widely distributed during the final year of the war and even dropped behind German lines to encourage Germany's surrender on the expectation of a just settlement—which it did. A Paris newspaper labeled him the "Apostle of International Justice."

Amid the tumult Grasty ran into Britain's press magnate Lord Northcliffe. What were his impressions of Wilson's reception in Paris, Grasty asked? From what Northcliffe had read about the League of Nations, it seemed a somewhat abstract and academic subject, but he confessed, "The nearer you get to the battlefields where the dead are buried, the stronger the desire becomes for it." Novelist Gertrude Atherton, reporting for the *New York Times*, did not think the French believed in anything so illusory as eternal peace. Rather they held Wilson in high regard because they thought his combination of vision, justice, and love of peace could best tackle the current troubles of Europe, particularly the threat from Bolshevism.

Grasty finally concluded that something had indeed changed in Paris. Yesterday despair and cynicism surrounded all the fine theories about disarmament and the League of Nations. Yesterday expectations for the peace conference were that it would punish Germany but do little to change the toxic political dynamic on the continent. Today a new optimism reigned. Wilson roused that same warm glow of hope in London, Manchester, Milan, and Rome.

Covering the Peace Conference

For the six hundred journalists, editors, publishers, and writers from many countries, the conference did not start well. In their first meeting the major powers (Britain, France, the United States, and Italy) ruled to exclude correspondents from conference sessions and forbade delegation staffs from discussing anything substantive with reporters, other than what was divulged in the official communiqués.

A howl went up from the correspondents. At home headlines growled about "gag orders" and the suppression of conference news. Wilson's idealistic plans for "open covenants of peace, openly arrived at" had taken aim at the secret, backroom agreements that had contributed to the war in the first place. "Open" agreements required that the citizens of the world be privy to discussions that would affect their future. Connect the dots, and it became obvious that the process required well-informed correspondents who could explain and interpret each development emerging from the conference. They needed access to conference proceedings, to the leaders formulating the treaty, and to the legion of experts accompanying each national delegation.

The volatile Herbert Bayard Swope headed the correspondents' grievance committee that submitted an insistent petition to the president, stating that unless the press was given reasonable access to information, the reporters would pack their bags and go home, and of course, inform their readers why. The Big Four gave ground but only slightly. A few representative correspondents would be allowed to attend some plenary sessions, and the sharing of information between staff people and correspondents would be tolerated to some degree. Correspondents chalked it up as a win, and it strengthened their sense that they were not merely observers but participants in the historic conference. This was the greatest peace conference in history, the greatest deliberative body in the world, the best statesmen deciding issues of momentous importance. Journalists were the eyes of the world. What they reported and how they reported it shaped public opinion. It revealed motives and agendas. It lent weight to arguments.

Paul Scott Mowrer quickly learned that the press department of the American delegation had little to offer. Two former newsmen staffed the department, Ray Stannard Baker and Arthur Sweetser. They had little information to share and also idolized Wilson. "In their eyes, anything he did was right, and anyone who differed with him was an enemy of mankind."

Baker, on the other hand, marveled at the newsmen's sense of entitlement to conference news. He complained, "These ambassadors of public opinion, at least those from America—had come, not begging, but demanding. They sat at every doorway, they looked over every shoulder, they wanted every resolution and report and wanted it immediately."

What the American press office did have were charts that showed the relationships of all the various experts and staff people to one another and to the commissioners. Mowrer began to cultivate acquaintances among the American experts, mostly university professors, and among experts serving with other delegations. He found that once they learned that he knew about Europe, they were eager to talk. Deciphering their expertise for the American reader became a daunting challenge. Conference negotiations ranged over highly complex political, economic, geographic, and social problems of peacemaking. The experts with each national delegation had compiled exhaustive studies of such arcane topics as demilitarization, mandates, self-determination, war guilt, and reparations. Some were specialists in political and diplomatic history, international law, geography, cartography, education, or agriculture.

For the five-month duration of the conference, journalists worked a grueling six or seven days a week, attending multiple briefings, conducting interviews, exchanging news with other correspondents, and distilling tidbits from French newspapers. A plush international press club meeting room, set up by the French, became a second home for many correspondents, where they could write their stories or mingle with colleagues. American reporters had a similar room in the Hôtel de Coislin, where "they came to get official statements, to read notices posted for upcoming events, to receive passes for official gatherings, to use typewriters in an emergency, and, if they wished, to file their copy."

All the major powers had sophisticated public relations operations that attempted to ingratiate and influence journalists. Will Irwin charged that the "larger nations had transformed their departments of war propaganda into departments of peace propaganda. Before the delegates ran a line of skirmishers—agents of superpublicity, eminent directing journalists who showered flattering attention on representatives of the foreign press, humbler figures with engaging personalities. These expounders of national aims took the reporters ostentatiously into their confidence in both daily conferences and private meetings, and they put forth a deluge of mimeographed matter."

Correspondents also suffered the assault of those who represented one cause or another. They showed up daily at Mowrer's desk with a pamphlet or an appeal, seeking his help to reach the American president. Nations and would-be nations, special committees and appointed representatives, the aggrieved and disenfranchised swarmed to Paris with but one mission: to talk with Wilson and enlist his aid with their cause. "From Africa, Asia, the

Near East they came, and from all over Europe—Koreans, Syrians, Zionists, Ethiopians, Burmese, Ukrainians, Aaland Islanders, Macedonians, Georgians, Hindoos, and a host of others."

"Whatever Americans might think of Woodrow Wilson," Mowrer noted, "to the lost tribes and oppressed peoples of the earth, as well as its cranks, schemers, and dreamers, he was a new messiah, the man half human, half divine, who alone could help them realize their frustrated ambitions." Having exhausted every other option for reaching Wilson, they now appealed to an American newsman to arrange for them even a few minutes with the president so they could plead their case.

One distinguished-looking and determined Polish professor of mathematics came back day after day. He had spoken before all the learned societies of Europe, he told Mowrer, and had clippings in a scrapbook to confirm it. His equations proved that, contrary to the commonly held view, the Earth was really flat. But that was not why he wanted to reach President Wilson. He had a plan to assure world peace. It was a very simple plan, and that was the beauty of it. A celestial railroad would be constructed, reaching out from the North and South Poles. Should any country start a war, trains would instantly be dispatched to their location to devastate them with bombs.

Woodrow Wilson would be the last person with whom Mowrer could share plans for world peace, since he never saw him. Whereas the French and British leaders, Georges Clemenceau and David Lloyd George, met on a fairly regular basis with correspondents from their nations, Wilson met only once with American reporters. Will Irwin was surprised to see how haggard and exhausted Wilson looked on that occasion. Gone was that glow of triumphant confidence from his exuberant welcome to Paris, replaced now with the weariness from battling European politicians grasping for the plunder of war. France was the principal opponent of the League of Nations plan, Wilson told the reporters. It was demanding that league members bind themselves to defend France from Germany for fifty years, which were unacceptable terms for other nations. As disagreements deepened between the major powers, they relied more on the press to publicize their positions and rationales.

The German delegation arrived at the conference on April 29. Its diplomats were sequestered in the old Hôtel des Réservoirs in Versailles and the fifteen accompanying German correspondents in an adjacent hotel, with both hotels surrounded by a high stockade guarded by sentries. Every correspondent wanted to know their reaction to the treaty, but contact with them was forbidden. Burnett Hershey (*New York Sun*) solved the problem by buying a set of clothing that allowed him to masquerade as a German diplomat—striped trousers, frock coat, Tyrolean hat, heavy spectacles, and a worn attaché case. In this disguise he bluffed his way into the stockade compound and introduced himself to the first correspondent he met. With his assistance Hershey got into the private session in which the German representatives railed to their correspondents about the humiliating terms of the treaty. The head of the German delegation, Count Ulrich von Brockdorff-Rantzau, called Georges Clemenceau a "senile old man, hurling insults at our people."

By accident Hershey actually sat beside the count while he addressed the reporters. "The Fatherland has been dealt a heavy blow," the count said grimly. "There is work to be done. We are Germans. We will not forget. We will rise from this shame." Hershey hurried back to his hotel room and, remaining in frock coat and Tyrolean hat to "keep the mood," wrote the only real scoop of the conference.

A month later, on June 28, the signing ceremony of the peace treaty with Germany played out in the Hall of Mirrors in the Versailles Palace. It came five years to the day from the assassination of the archduke in Sarajevo that precipitated the Great War. From a gallery at the far end of the hall, the press watched two sullen German representatives, Dr. Hermann Mueller and Dr. Johannes Bell, walk stiffly forward and affix their signatures to the treaty.

Each one of the conference delegates did the same. Then suddenly from outside came the thunderclap of guns firing a salute and the cheering of a distant crowd.

The guns pealed more joyous salutes when Clemenceau, Lloyd George, and Wilson appeared on a terrace. Photographers captured the moment as the three stood together, "three men well content; three men who had just remade the world."

To Paul Scott Mowrer, the guns did not sound like celebration. They brought back a flash of vivid memories from the war, the anguish of 1914, all the brutal sacrifice and inspiring campaigns that led to so costly a victory. They also spoke of the current chaos of Europe, "the famine, pestilence, hatred, and misery war had bequeathed." Mowrer strained to end his experience on an optimistic note:

> Excited by the sudden swirl of my thoughts, I sank on a bench and with paper and pencil wrote as fast as I could the words that came into my head. "Will this war be indeed the last of all wars?" I scribbled. "Shall our sons know peace, and their sons, and mankind forever?" There is none who dares even to prophecy such a blessing. . . . Let us henceforth, every man, keep watch, not alone over other classes, other nations, but over his own class, his own nation. . . . Let him who sees a danger declare it. Let him who seeks to avoid it be resolute. Let him who truly loves peace be ready to sacrifice for peace, as so many have sacrificed for war.

Appendix

Journalists Mentioned in *American Journalists in the Great War*

The dramatis personae of journalists reporting the Great War changed and evolved throughout the conflict. War correspondents gave way to well-known writers and beat reporters who wanted to take a crack at reporting war, grab a piece of the excitement. Some covered all four years of the fighting, others just American involvement.

American Journalists in the Great War offers only a sampling of the hundreds of men and women who reported World War I and but a small collection of the adventures they experienced.

The following is a list of those journalists mentioned in this book and their primary affiliation(s). A mini-bio provides background on those correspondents featured in the book.

Charles Inman Barnard: *New York Tribune.*

John Bass: *Chicago Daily News.*

Bessie Beatty (1886–1947): *San Francisco Bulletin.* Beatty interrupted her round-the-world news-gathering trip in 1917 to cover revolutionary Russia. Following the war she was editor of *McCall's Magazine* from 1918 to 1921. From 1940 until her death, she hosted a popular radio show on WOR in New York.

James O'Donnell Bennett: *Chicago Tribune.*

Heywood Broun (1888–1939): *New York Tribune.* Broun left his position as drama critic to accompany the AEF to Europe in 1917. He frequently got into trouble with military rules and reporting restrictions. His AEF credentials were revoked over his articles critical of Pershing and the army. He published two books on his war experiences.

Louise Bryant (1885–1936): Bell Syndicate. Along with her husband, John Reed, Bryant covered Russia's Bolshevik Revolution. She remained active in socialist and feminist causes and supported the Bolshevik Revolution through lectures and testimony before a congressional committee. After Reed died in 1920, she continued to write about European affairs. The 1981 movie *Reds* is about her time with Reed.

Harry Chase: Committee on Public Information.

Irvin Cobb (1876–1944): *Saturday Evening Post*. Cobb made two visits to the war and lectured about them back home. He traveled behind German lines in 1914 and, on his second trip, reported on the battle of Chateau-Thierry. When few journalists took note of African American soldiers, Cobb wrote about them for the *Post*. After the war he wrote many books, worked for *Cosmopolitan* magazine, and wrote for vaudeville and silent films.

Herbert Corey: Associated Newspapers, *Everybody's Magazine*.

Daniel Thomas Curtin: *Times* (London), *Daily Mail* (London).

Richard Harding Davis (1864–1916): Wheeler Syndicate, *Scribner's Magazine, Metropolitan Magazine*. Davis was a well-known writer and cultural icon before the war. Famous for his coverage of the drama and pageantry of earlier wars, he never quite adjusted to World War I. The brutal tactics of the German army in 1914 and the barriers to news coverage drove him home in anger and frustration. He became a strong advocate for U.S. entry into the war. His final war story, "The Man Who Had Everything," is a gritty rendering of war through the character of an American volunteer who loses his commitment to the war but still soldiers on.

Rheta Childe Dorr (1866–1948): *New York Evening Mail*. Dorr was a popular muckraking journalist and political activist, supporting the causes of women and the working class. She had several journalistic assignments in Europe prior to the war, including one to Russia after its 1905 revolution. She returned there to report on Russia between its two 1917 revolutions.

Arno Dosch-Fleurot (1879–1951): *New York World*. Dosch-Fleurot reported throughout the war, from the first days in Belgium, to the Russian Revolution, and post-armistice Germany. He continued to work for the *World* as its Berlin correspondent until 1931, when the paper was sold. He then became a diplomatic correspondent for the Associated Press and later for the International News Service and Universal Service. He reported from Europe during World War II.

Madeleine Zabriskie Doty (1877–1963): *New York Tribune, Chicago Tribune*. A lawyer, social reformer, and peace activist, Doty made three trips to report on the war. During her 1916 travels in Germany, she reported on the severe food shortage. Her final war excursion came as part of a round-the-world trip to assess the uneven social and economic development in different countries, particularly as they concerned women.

Robert Dunn (1877–1955): *New York Evening Post*. An enterprising reporter, Dunn landed a scoop on the Battle of Mons, and later reported from Germany, the Balkans, and Russia. In 1918 Dunn was commissioned as an officer in the U.S. Navy and served as an intelligence officer in Constantinople and London. His autobiography, *World Alive*, which includes some of his war stories, was published in 1956, after his death.

Lincoln Eyre: *New York World*.

Fred Ferguson: United Press.

Wilbur Forrest: United Press.

Granville Fortescue (1875–1952): *Daily Telegraph* (London), *New York American*. One of the most active and knowledgeable correspondents covering the war, Fortescue reported extensively on the western front in 1914. He later took a German army tour for journalists, traveled with the Russian army, and reported on the British landing at Gallipoli. His writings and recriminations in the British press about Gallipoli helped put an end to that disaster and bring down the man who had championed it, Winston Churchill.

Edward Lyell Fox: *New York American.*

Floyd Gibbons (1887–1939): *Chicago Tribune.* Gibbons cut his teeth on war reporting while covering the Pancho Villa expedition of 1916–17. Sailing to Europe just prior to U.S. entry into the war, he traveled on a ship that was sunk by a U-boat. His dramatic account of that experience galvanized American opinion about entering the war. He chronicled the early phases of the AEF in France, up through the Battle of Belleau Wood, at which he lost an eye while charging into action with the marines. From 1919 to 1926 Gibbons edited the Paris edition of the *Chicago Tribune* and headed the paper's foreign service. He later worked as a radio commentator for NBC.

Charles Grasty: *New York Times.*

Horace Green: *New York Evening Post.*

Martin Green: *New York Evening World.*

Walter Hale: *New York Times.*

Harry Hansen: *Chicago Daily News.*

James Hare (1856–1946): *Leslie's Illustrated Weekly.* Hare, a photographer, covered the Spanish-American and the Russo-Japanese Wars. During the first two years of World War I, he captured images of the conflict on many fronts. On May 7, 1915, he rushed to Ireland to photograph survivors of the *Lusitania.* He returned home in 1917 to capture the United States' preparation for war, but in 1918 he went back to Europe and traveled with the Italian army until the armistice.

Florence MacLeod Harper: *Leslie's Illustrated Weekly.*

Burnett Hershey: *New York Sun.*

Jimmy Hopper: *Collier's.*

Will Irwin (1873–1948): *New York Tribune, Times* (London), *Saturday Evening Post.* A working journalist since 1900, Irwin vaulted to fame in World War I for his coverage of the Battle of Ypres, for which he was given access to confidential British government sources. He was subsequently blacklisted by both the

British and the French. After a two-year period back in the United States, he returned to the war zone and was injured in a shell explosion, which cost him the hearing in one ear. After the war he championed the causes of international peace and the League of Nations. During World War II he wrote some war coverage for the North American Newspaper Alliance.

Edwin James: *New York Times*.

Owen Johnson: *New York Times*.

Thomas Johnson: *New York Sun*.

Roger Lewis: Associated Press.

Cal Lyon: Newspaper Enterprise Association.

Don Martin: *New York Herald*.

Robert McCormick: *Chicago Tribune*.

John McCutcheon (1870–1949): *Chicago Tribune*. Reporter-artist McCutcheon gained experience covering conflicts in the Spanish-American and Boer Wars. He rushed to Europe at the outset of World War I and chronicled the initial sweep of the German army through Belgium and later covered fighting in the Balkans.

Webb Miller (1891–1940): United Press. After his reporting on the Pancho Villa expedition, United Press sent Miller to Europe. As bureau chief of UP's Paris office, he covered American involvement, dramatically captured the final hours of the war, and then reported from occupied Germany. One highlight of his postwar career involved his coverage of Mohandas Gandhi's "salt march." Because he was the only journalist reporting the march, his reports of the beating of Gandhi's followers became a worldwide sensation and some fifty years later served as the basis for the salt march sequence in the 1982 movie *Gandhi*.

Gerald Morgan: *Metropolitan Magazine*.

Paul Scott Mowrer (1887–1971): *Chicago Daily News*. After covering the First Balkan War (1912–13), he worked as a war correspondent out of the *Daily News* Paris office. In 1917 he was accredited with the French army's newly created Anglo-American Press Mission. He and reporter Wilbur Forrest got a potential scoop on the emergency introduction of American troops at Château-Thierry, but censors killed their stories. Mowrer stayed in Europe to the cover the Paris Peace Conference in 1919.

Mary Boyle O'Reilly (1873–1939): News Enterprise Association. An NEA staff reporter stationed in Europe, O'Reilly was in place to report on the opening of the war. She grabbed headlines with her reports on the destruction of the Belgian city of Louvain and life in German-occupied Brussels. She reported from Belgium, France, and England and was in London in 1915 during the zeppelin attacks. Back in the United States in 1917, she lectured about her war experience.

Frederick Palmer (1873–1958): *Everybody's Magazine,* Associated Press, United Press, International News Service. Palmer had reported on six previous wars before rushing off to Europe at the start of World War I. He was named as the solitary American journalist to be accredited with the British Expeditionary Force. In 1917 General Pershing recruited Palmer to serve with the AEF as censor and liaison with the war correspondents who would report on American involvement. Postwar he wrote prolifically on war history and covered his last conflict—a rebellion against the Cuban government—in 1930. His career covering and writing about war spanned five decades.

Joseph Medill Patterson (1879–1946): *New York Tribune.* The son of the publisher of the *Chicago Tribune,* Patterson got a taste of war reporting during the 1900 Boxer Rebellion. Along with filmmaker Edwin Weigle, Patterson covered the German army early in World War I. He joined the U.S. Army in 1917 as a private and rose to the rank of captain. He was gassed and wounded while serving in five campaigns. After the war he founded the tabloid newspaper the *Illustrated Daily News,* which later became the *New York Daily News.*

George Pattullo: *Saturday Evening Post*. Immediately after the armistice, Pattullo wrote an article about Medal of Honor recipient Alvin York that enshrined York as one of the most famous American soldiers of the war.

E. Alexander Powell (1879–1957): *New York World*. During the period of American neutrality, Powell reported from more fronts than almost any other journalist. After U.S. entry he joined the army as an intelligence officer and was wounded in September 1918. After the war he had a long, successful career as an adventure and travel writer, publishing some twenty books between 1920 and 1954.

Ralph Pulitzer (1879–1939): *New York World*. President of the Press Publishing Company, which published the *New York World* and the *Evening World*, Pulitzer visited Europe early in the war and scored a scoop by being the first journalist to report on the war from an airplane. He published a book on that experience.

John Reed (1887–1920): *The Masses, Metropolitan Magazine*. Reed soared to fame as a war correspondent for his coverage of the Mexican Revolution. His vivid, literary style earned him the title of "America's Kipling." In two tours in World War I Europe, Reed wrote of trench fighting on the western front and about fighting and life behind the lines in Turkey, the Balkans, and Russia. In 1917 he and his wife, Louise Bryant, covered the Bolshevik Revolution, which strengthened his already strong socialist sympathies. His famous book on the revolution, *Ten Days That Shook the World*, appeared in 1919. He fled the United States to evade charges of subversion and lived out the rest of his short life in Moscow, where he is buried in the Kremlin.

Elmer Roberts: Associated Press.

Boardman Robinson: *The Masses*.

Arthur Ruhl (1876–1935): *Collier's*. Originally a music critic for the *New York World*, Ruhl became a war correspondent for the popular magazine *Collier's*. He continued reporting for the entire war, on every front, with many of the belligerent armies. After the war he reported from the Balkans and eventually returned to work for the *World*.

Damon Runyon (1884–1946): *New York American*. Runyon arrived in Europe in October 1918 to be accredited with the A E F. He reported on the fighting in the Argonne Forest and American occupation of Germany.

George Schreiner: Associated Press.

George Seldes (1890–1995): Marshall Syndicate. Seldes was accredited with the A E F in May 1918. Along with several other journalists, he sneaked into Germany immediately after the armistice and landed an interview with German field marshal Paul von Hindenburg. He worked as an international correspondent in the 1920s and 1930s, reporting on Bolshevik purges in Russia and Mussolini's rise to power.

William G. Shepherd (1878–1933): United Press. Shepherd established his national reputation by providing a grisly eyewitness account of the horrendous Triangle Shirtwaist fire in Manhattan in 1911. His war reporting got off to an impressive start when he interviewed Britain's First Lord of the Admiralty, Winston Churchill. Shepherd continued to earn scoops by being the first reporter to gain access to the British front. In October 1914 he was accredited with the Austrian army. He wrote exclusives on Germany's first use of gas and its zeppelin raids on London. He also covered the Russian Revolution.

Frank Sibley: *Boston Globe*. Sibley was the first journalist given the status of "visiting correspondent" with the A E F. As such he reported solely on the Twenty-Sixth Division, composed of men from New England.

Fred A. Smith: *Chicago Tribune*.

Simeon Strunsky: *New York Evening Post*.

Henry W. Suydam: *Brooklyn Eagle*.

Raymond Swing (1887–1968): *Chicago Daily News*. When the war began, Swing was the Berlin bureau chief for the *Daily News*. He covered early battles, traveling with the German army, and reported on the fighting at Gallipoli. Following the war he had a twenty-seven-year career covering European affairs for Voice of America. His was a strong voice against the rise of Adolf Hitler and Fascism.

Herbert Bayard Swope (1882–1958): *New York World*. A former crime reporter, Swope made two trips to Germany during the war. His 1916 trip resulted in a series of articles about conditions in Germany that won the 1917 Pulitzer Prize for reporting. After the United States entered the war, he received a commission in the navy and worked for the U.S. War Industries Board. He covered the Paris Peace Conference and continued to work for the *World* until his retirement in 1929. He won two additional Pulitzer Prizes.

Frank J. Taylor: United Press.

Lowell Thomas (1892–1981): Committee on Public Information, *New York Tribune*. During 1917–18 Thomas worked for the U.S. Committee on Public Information, preparing films and lectures to support the war effort. Along with cameraman Harry Chase, he covered the Italian front, Egypt, and the Middle East. He met British colonel T. E. Lawrence in Palestine and eventually popularized Lawrence's wartime exploits as "Lawrence of Arabia" through lectures and a 1924 book. In Paris when the war ended, he and Webb Waldron made an unauthorized trip into Germany and reported on the unrest. His postwar career as a radio and television broadcaster with CBS extended for fifty years.

Donald Thompson (b. 1884): *Leslie's Illustrated Weekly*. Thompson was in Canada when the war broke out, but he quickly signed with a newspaper and sailed to Europe on a troop ship. Defying danger, military restrictions, and censorship, he soon established a reputation as the most intrepid photographer of the war, reporting from many fronts. He received several injuries. He worked primarily as a freelancer, selling photos and film to the highest bidder. *Leslie's* hired him to capture the Russian Revolution. His war movies, often shown in American theaters or on the lecture circuit, gave the public its first glimpse of the war.

Ralph W. Tyler: Committee on Public Information. The only black journalist credentialed with the AEF.

Webb Waldron: *Collier's*.

Stanley Washburn (1878–1950): *Times* (London). After a three-year stint as a reporter in Minneapolis, Washburn became a correspondent for the *Chicago Daily News* and covered the Russo-Japanese War. In the opening days of the World War I, he was recruited by Lord Northcliffe, owner of the *Times* of London, to cover events in Russia. Thus began the most extraordinary reporting career of the war. While covering fighting on the eastern front, Washburn rose to a position of unparalleled influence in Russian wartime affairs.

Edwin Weigle: *New York Tribune*.

Karl von Wiegand (1874–1961): *New York World*, United Press. As a Berlin correspondent for several years prior to the war, Wiegand was well placed for some of the first big stories to come out of Germany. He landed several noteworthy interviews and battlefield scoops. Wiegand returned to Germany after the war and was the first American reporter to interview Adolf Hitler and to warn of the rise of German Fascism.

Albert Rhys Williams: *New York Post*.

Harold Williams: *New York Times*.

Wythe Williams (1881–1956): *New York Times, Collier's*. Williams was working for the *New York Times'* London bureau when the war began. After moving to Paris, he struggled with the severe limitations placed on journalists but eventually provided coverage of the battlefields. In 1917 he began working for *Collier's* and was accredited with the AEF, an accreditation he lost in February 1918 for violating censorship regulations.

A Word about Sources

The convenience of writing about war correspondents is that they are writers. Their job was to tell about the war and, for some of them, to tell about their experience in war. Some managed to do both at the same time.

The war journalists themselves provided the principal sources of material for this book, primarily Irvin Cobb, Richard Harding Davis, Robert Dunn, Arno Dosch-Fleurot, Wilbur Forrest, Granville Fortescue, Floyd Gibbons, Will Irwin, John T. McCutcheon, Paul Scott Mowrer, Frederick Palmer, E. Alexander Powell, John Reed, Arthur Ruhl, William Shepherd, Raymond Swing, Stanley Washburn, and Wythe Williams.

Collectively, they covered the entire four years of the conflict. They wrote for the large-circulation newspapers, press syndicates, popular magazines, and profligately chronicled their experience in books written during and after the war. Davis, Irwin, and Ruhl each wrote three books about their war experience; Powell wrote four; Fortescue, Palmer, and Washburn, five.

Female journalists left an especially rich load of work from their coverage of revolutionary Russia. Bessie Beatty, Louise Bryant, Rheta Childe Dorr, and Florence MacLeod Harper made the phenomenon of a revolution in the midst of a world war come alive for me. Their stories animate that chapter of the book.

Richard Harding Davis and John Reed have continued to draw the attention of scholars, and to a lesser extent, so too have Cobb, Irwin, and Palmer. I benefitted from the insights of this research and also from scholarship on the Russian Revolution and on the work of wartime news photographers and filmmakers.

There is no better single source of information about American correspondents on the western front than Emmet Crozier's 1959 book, *American Reporters on the Western Front, 1914–1918*. It was my go-to reference for the early chapters and those about American involvement.

As much as possible, I let these journalists tell their own stories.

Bibliography

Bassow, Whitman. *The Moscow Correspondents*. New York: Paragon House, 1988.

Beatty, Bessie. *The Red Heart of Russia*. New York: Century, 1918.

"Berlin Accused of Stirring Up Discord in U.S." *New York Tribune*, August 15, 1915, 1.

Bernstorff, Johann Heinrich. *My Three Years in America*. New York: Charles Scribner's Sons, 1920.

Brooks, Sydney. "The Press in War-Time." *North American Review* 200, no. 709 (December 1914): 858–69.

Broun, Heywood. *The A.E.F.: With General Pershing and the American Forces*. New York: D. Appleton, 1918.

———. *Our Army at the Front*. New York: Charles Scribner's Sons, 1922.

Bryant, Louise. *Six Red Months in Russia: An Observer's Account of Russia before and during the Proletarian Dictatorship*. New York: George H. Doran, 1918.

Chatterjee, Choi. "'Odds and Ends of the Russian Revolution,' 1917–1920: Gender and American Travel Narratives." *Journal of American Women's History* 20, no. 4 (Winter 2008): 10–33.

Cobb, Irvin S. *Exit Laughing*. New York: Bobbs-Merrill, 1941.

———. *The Glory of the Coming*. New York: George H. Doran, 1918.

———. "Hopeless for Any Man to Attempt to Describe the War, Says Cobb." *Tensas Gazette* (St. Joseph LA), December 25, 1914, 2.

———. "A Little Town Called Montignies St. Christopher." *Saturday Evening Post*, October 10, 1914, 3–4.

———. *Myself to Date*. New York: George H. Doran, 1923.

———. *Paths of Glory: Impressions of War Written at and near the Front*. New York: George H. Doran, 1915.

Cole, Jaci, and John Maxwell Hamilton, eds. *Journalism of the Highest Realm*. Baton Rouge: Louisiana State University Press, 2007.

Corey, Herbert. "Just Boys." *Everybody's Magazine*, August 1918, 36–39.

———. "Visited Germany since War Closed." *Washington (DC) Evening Star*, January 24, 1919, 12.

Crozier, Emmet. *American Reporters on the Western Front, 1914–1918*. New York: Oxford University Press, 1959.

Curtin, Daniel Thomas. *The Land of Deepening Shadow: Germany at War*. New York: George H. Doran, 1917.

Davis, Belinda J. *Home Fires Burning: Food, Politics, and Everyday Life in World War I Berlin*. Chapel Hill: University of North Carolina Press, 2000.

Davis, Charles Belmont, ed. *Adventures and Letters of Richard Harding Davis*. New York: Charles Scribner's Sons, 1918.

Davis, Richard Harding. *The Deserter*. New York: Charles Scribner's Sons, 1917.

———. "The Germans in Brussels." *Scribner's Magazine*, November 1914, 565–70.

———. "Horror of Louvain Told by Eyewitness; Circled Burning City." *New York Tribune*, August 31, 1914, 1, 4.

———. *Notes of a War Correspondent*. New York: Harper & Brothers, 1897.

———. "Rheims during the Bombardment." *Scribner's Magazine*, January 1915, 70–76.

———. "Slipping into Mexico City Full of Bumps for Davis." *Spokane Spokesman-Review*, May 15, 1914, 4.

———. "Tells Experience as War Prisoner." *New York Tribune*, September 2, 1914, 1, 3.

———. *With the Allies*. New York: Charles Scribner's Sons, 1919.

———. "With the Allies in Salonika." *Scribner's Magazine*, April 1916, 405–12.

———. *With the French in France and Salonika*. New York: Charles Scribner's Sons, 1916.

Dell'Orto, Giovanna. *American Journalism and International Relations*. New York: Cambridge University Press, 2011.

Desmond, Robert W. *Windows on the World: World News Reporting, 1900–1920*. Iowa City: University of Iowa Press, 1980.

Dorr, Rheta Childe. *Inside the Russian Revolution*. New York: Macmillan, 1917.

Dosch-Fleurot, Arno. *Through War to Revolution*. London: Bodley Head, 1931.

Doty, Madeleine Zabriskie. *Behind the Battle Line, Around the World 1918*. New York: Macmillan, 1918.

———. *Short Rations: An American Woman in Germany, 1915 . . . 1916*. New York: Century, 1917.

———. "War's Burden Thrown on Poor of Germany as Food Supply Dwindles." *New York Tribune*, November 19, 1916, 1.

Dunn, Robert. *Five Fronts*. New York: Dodd, Mead, 1915.

———. *World Alive*. New York: Crown, 1956.

Eyre, Lincoln. "Two N.Y. Negroes Whip 24 Germans; Win War Crosses." *New York Tribune*, May 20, 1918, 2.

Ferguson, Fred S. "Deadly Fumes of Poisonous Gas Sprayed over American Troops." *Daily Gate City and Constitution Democrat* (Keokuk IA), February 27, 1918, 1.

Forrest, Wilbur. *Behind the Front Page*. New York: D. Appleton-Century, 1934.

Fortescue, Granville. *At the Front with Three Armies*. London: Andrew Melrose, 1915.

———. *France Bears the Burden*. New York: Macmillan, 1917.

———. *Front Line and Deadline: The Experiences of a War Correspondent*. New York: G. P. Putnam's Sons, 1937.

———. *Russia, the Balkans and the Dardanelles*. London: Andrew Melrose, 1915.

———. *What of the Dardanelles? An Analysis*. London: Hodder & Stoughton, 1915.

Foster, H. Schuyler, Jr. "A Quantitative Study of War News, 1914–1917." *American Journal of Sociology* 40, no. 4 (January 1935): 464–75.

Fox, Edward Lyell. *Behind the Scenes in Warring Germany*. New York: McBride, Nast, 1915.

Gaff, Alan D. *Blood in the Argonne: The "Lost Battalion" of World War I*. Norman: University of Oklahoma Press, 2005.

Gibbons, Floyd. *And They Thought We Wouldn't Fight*. New York: George H. Doran, 1918.

Gibbs, Philip. *The Soul of War*. London: Heinemann, 1915.

Gramling, Oliver. *AP: The Story of News*. New York: Farrar & Rinehart, 1940.

Grasty, Charles. *Flashes from the Front*. New York: Century, 1918.

———. "Greeted by High Officials." *New York Times*, December 14, 1918, 1.

Green, Horace. *The Log of a Noncombatant*. New York: Houghton Mifflin, 1915.

Guard, William J. *The Soul of Paris; Two Months in the French Capital during the War of 1914; Random Notes of an American Newspaper Man*. New York: H. Rogowski, 1914.

Hale, Walter. *By Motor to the Firing Line: An Artist's Notes and Sketches with the Armies of Northern France, June–July 1915*. New York: Century, 1916.

Hansen, Harry. "Find No 'Atrocity.'" *High Point* (NC) *Review*, October 1, 1914, 6.

Harper, Florence MacLeod. *Runaway Russia*. New York: Century, 1918.

Harries, Meirion, and Susie Harries. *The Last Days of Innocence*. New York: Random House, 1997.

"Hating Germany." *Northwest Worker* (Everett WA), April 26, 1917, 3.

Haverstock, Nathan A. *Fifty Years at the Front*. Washington DC: Brassey's, 1996.

Hayden, Joseph R. *Negotiating in the Press: American Journalism and Diplomacy, 1918–1919*. Baton Rouge: Louisiana State University Press, 2010.

Hohenberg, John. *Foreign Correspondence: The Great Reporters and Their Times*. 2nd ed. New York: Columbia University Press, 1965.

Hudson, Robert V. *The Writing Game: A Biography of Will Irwin*. Ames: Iowa State University Press, 1982.

"A Human View of the War in Europe." *New York Times Book Review*, May 7, 1916, 192.

Irwin, Will. "Detained by the Germans." *Collier's*, October 3, 1914, 5+.

———. "England Faces the Music." *Collier's*, September 19, 1914, 9+.

———. "England: The Puzzle." *American Magazine*, February 1915, 78–83.

———. "Flashes from the War Zone." *Saturday Evening Post*, July 15, 1916, 12–13, 70.

———. *The Making of a Reporter*. New York: G. P. Putnam's Sons, 1942.

————. *Men, Women and War*. London: Constable, 1915.

————. *Propaganda and the News, or, What Makes You Think So?* New York: McGraw-Hill, 1936.

————. *A Reporter at Armageddon*. New York: D. Appleton, 1918.

James, Edwin L. "Americans' Brilliant Feat." *New York Times*, June 6, 1918, 1.

"Joffre Reveals France at War." *New York Times*, March 8, 1915, 1.

Johnson, Owen. "France Sobered, Consecrated to War to the End." *New York Times*, October 31, 1915, S M 4.

Kahn, E. J., Jr. *The World of Swope: A Biography of Herbert Bayard Swope*. New York: Simon & Schuster, 1965.

Kauffman, Reginald Wright. "The News Embargo." *North American Review* 208, no. 757 (December 1918): 831–41.

Kitchen, Karl K. *After Dark in the War Capitals*. New York: Broadway, 1916.

Klekowski, Ed, and Libby Klekowski. *Americans in Occupied Belgium, 1914–1918*. Jefferson N C: McFarland, 2014.

Knightley, Phillip. *The First Casualty: The War Correspondent as Hero and Myth Maker from the Crimea to Iraq*. New York: Harcourt, Brace, Jovanovich, 1976.

Lasswell, Harold D. *Propaganda Technique in World War I*. Cambridge M A: M I T Press, 1971. Originally published as *Propaganda Technique in the World War* (London: Kegan Paul, Trench, Trubner, 1927).

Laurie, Clayton D. "'The Chanting of Crusaders': Captain Heber Blankenhorn and A E F Combat Propaganda in World War I." *Journal of Military History* 59, no. 3 (July 1995): 457–81.

Lawson, Anita. *Irvin Cobb*. Bowling Green O H: Bowling Green State University Popular Press, 1984.

Lehman, Daniel W. *John Reed and the Writing of Revolution*. Athens: Ohio University Press, 2002.

Lorenz, Alfred Lawrence, "Ralph W. Tyler: The Unknown Correspondent of World War I." *Journalism History* (Spring 2005): 2–12.

Lubow, Arthur. *The Reporter Who Would Be King*. New York: Charles Scribner's Sons, 1992.

Mathews, Joseph J. "Heralds of the Imperialistic Wars." *Military Affairs* 19, no. 3 (Autumn 1955): 145–55.

————. *Reporting the Wars*. Minneapolis: University of Minnesota Press, 1957.

McCormick, Robert Rutherford. *With the Russian Army*. New York: Macmillan, 1915.

McCormick, Robert R., and James O'Donnell Bennett. "War Reporters Compare Notes." *New York Times*, July 9, 1915, 4.

McCutcheon, John T. *Drawn from Memory*. New York: Bobbs-Merrill, 1950.

————. "With Davis in Vera Cruz, Brussels, and Salonika." *Scribner's Magazine*, July 1916, 91–97.

"Mexico, Mr. Reed's Account of the Insurgent Republic." *New York Times Book Review*, September 6, 1914, 373.

Miller, Webb. *I Found No Peace*. Garden City NY: Garden City, 1938.

Mohrenschildt, M. Dimitri von. "The Early American Observers of the Russian Revolution." *Russian Review* 3, no. 1 (Autumn 1943): 64–74.

Morgan, Gwen, and Arthur Veysey. *Poor Little Rich Boy: The Life and Times of Col. Robert McCormick*. Carpentersville IL: Crossroads Communications, 1985.

Morris, Joe Alex. *Deadline Every Minute: The Story of the United Press*. New York: Doubleday, 1957.

Mould, David. "Donald Thompson: Photographer at War." *Kansas History: A Journal of the Central Plains* (Autumn 1982): 154–67.

Mould, David H. *American Newsfilm, 1914–1919*. New York: Garland, 1983.

Mowrer, Paul Scott. *The House of Europe*. Boston: Houghton Mifflin, 1945.

———. "U.S. Soldiers Now in France Quick to Learn from Poilus." *Washington (DC) Evening Star*, July 30, 1917, 7.

O'Connor, Richard. *Heywood Broun: A Biography*. New York: G. P. Putnam's Sons, 1975.

O'Reilly, Mary Boyle. "Mary Boyle O'Reilly Sees Town of Louvain Burned; People Taken Out of Homes and Slain, She Says." *Seattle Star*, September 21, 1914, 1, 4.

———. "No Milk for Babies in Brussels; They Die Because They 'Are Enemies When the Fatherland Is at War.'" *Seattle Star*, September 18, 1914, 1.

———. "Where Are the Lost Women of Louvain?" *Seattle Star*, September 19, 1914, 3.

Osborn, Scott C. "Richard Harding Davis: Critical Battleground." *American Quarterly* 12, no. 1 (Spring 1960): 84–92.

Palmer, Frederick. *America in France*. New York: Dodd, Mead, 1918.

———. *The Last Shot*. New York: Charles Scribner's Sons, 1914.

———. *My Second Year of the War*. New York: Dodd, Mead, 1917.

———. *My Year of the Great War*. New York: A. L. Burt, 1915.

———. *Our Greatest Battle (the Meuse-Argonne)*. New York: Dodd, Mead, 1919.

———. "War Story of Pershing's Observer." *New York Times Magazine*, March 23, 1919, 72.

———. *With My Own Eyes*. Indianapolis: Bobbs-Merrill, 1932.

Patterson, Joseph Medill. "Antwerp Film Saves Cathedral." *New York Tribune*, October 22, 1914, 3.

Pattullo, George. "The Second Elder Gives Battle." *Saturday Evening Post*, April 26, 1919, 3+.

Peterson, H. C. "British Influence on the American Press, 1914–17." *American Political Science Review* 31, no. 1 (February 1937): 79–88.

Phillips, Percival. "Out in the Cold: The Tragedy of the War Correspondent." *Saturday Evening Post*, February 1, 1913, 14+.

Powell, E. Alexander. *Fighting in Flanders*. Toronto: McClelland, Goodchild & Stewart, 1915.

———. "In the Field with the Armies of France." *Scribner's Magazine*, September 1915, 261–79.

———. *Italy at War and the Allies in the West*. New York: Charles Scribner's Sons, 1917.

———. *The New Frontiers of Freedom from the Alps to the Aegean*. New York: Charles Scribner's Sons, 1920.

———. "On the British Battle Line." *Scribner's Magazine*, October 1915, 456–69.

———. *Vive la France!* New York: Charles Scribner's Sons, 1915.

Pulitzer, Ralph. *Over the Front in an Aeroplane, and Scenes inside the French and Flemish Trenches*. New York: Harper & Brothers, 1915.

Reed, John. "In the German Trenches." *Metropolitan Magazine*, April 1915, 7–10, 70–71.

———. *Ten Days That Shook the World*. New York: Boni & Liveright, 1919.

———. *The War in Eastern Europe*. New York: Charles Scribner's Sons, 1916.

Rinehart, Mary Roberts. *Kings, Queens, and Pawns: An American Woman at the Front*. New York: George H. Doran, 1915.

Rosenstone, Robert A. *Romantic Revolutionary: A Biography of John Reed*. Cambridge MA: Harvard University Press, 1990.

Ruhl, Arthur. *Antwerp to Gallipoli: A Year of the War on Many Fronts—and behind Them*. New York: Charles Scribner's Sons, 1916.

———. "The War Correspondent." In *The Story of the Great War*, vol. 1, edited by Francis J. Reynolds, 113–23. New York: P. F. Collier & Son, 1916.

———. *White Nights and Other Russian Impressions*. New York: Charles Scribner's Sons, 1917.

"Says Politicians Muddle War Policy." *New York Times*, July 7, 1915, 5.

Schreiner, George Abel. *Cables and Wireless, and Their Role in the Foreign Relations of the United States*. Boston: Stratford, 1924.

Shepherd, William G. *Confessions of a War Correspondent*. New York: Harper & Brothers, 1917.

Sibley, Frank P. *With the Yankee Division in France*. Boston: Little Brown, 1919.

Smith, John T. "Russian Military Censorship during the First World War." *Revolutionary Russia* 14, no. 1 (2001): 71–95.

Smith, Richard Norton. *The Colonel: The Life and Legend of Robert R. McCormick*. Boston: Houghton Mifflin, 1997.

Stephens, Rodney. "Shattered Windows, German Spies, Zigzag Trenches: World War I through the Eyes of Richard Harding Davis." *Historian* 65, no. 1 (Fall 2002): 43–73.

Strunsky, Simeon. "Voyage Sentimentale." *Atlantic Monthly*, March 1919, 322–28.

Sweeney, Michael S. "Reporters and 'Willing Propagandists': AEF Correspondents Define Their Role." *American Journalism* 29, no. 1 (2012): 7–31.

Swetland, H. M. *American Journalists in Europe*. New York: United Publishers, 1919.

Swing, Raymond. *Good Evening*. New York: Harcourt, Brace, & World, 1964.

Swinton, E. D. *Eye-Witness's Narrative of the War from March 30th to July 18th, 1915*. London: Edward Arnold, 1916.

Swope, Herbert Bayard. *Inside the German Empire*. New York: Century, 1917.

Teel, Leonard Ray. *The Public Press, 1900–1945*. Westport CT: Praeger, 2006.

Thomas, Lowell. *Good Evening Everybody*. New York: Avon, 1976.

Thompson, Donald. *Donald Thompson in Russia*. New York Harper & Brothers, 1918.

United States Army in the World War, 1917–1919: Reports of the Commander-in-Chief, Staff Sections and Services. Washington DC: Center of Military History, 1991.

Van Dopperen, Ron. "Shooting the Great War: Albert Dawson and the American Correspondent Film Company, 1914–1918." *Film History* 4, no. 2 (1990): 123–29.

Van Dopperen, Ron, and Cooper C. Graham. "Film Flashes of the European Front: The War Diary of Albert K. Dawson, 1915–1916." *Film History* 23 (2011): 20–37.

"War as It Is To-Day." *New York Times Book Review*, April 26, 1914, 1.

"War Correspondents Talk." *New York Times*, December 17, 1915, 11.

Washburn, Stanley. *The Cable Game*. Boston: Sherman, French, 1912.

———. *Field Notes From the Russian Front*. London: Andrew Melrose, 1915.

———. *The Russian Advance*. New York: Doubleday, Page, 1917.

———. "Teuton Reserves Used Up." *New York Times*, August 6, 1916, 3.

———. *Victory in Defeat—The Agony of Warsaw and the Russian Retreat*. Garden City NY: Doubleday, Page, 1916.

"When Przemysl Was Destroyed." *Arizona Republican*, September 6, 1915, 2.

Wiegand, Karl H. von. "Eye-Witness Tells How Living Sea Dashed into Breakers of Death As Germans Hurled Back Russian Lines." *Washington Times*, October 10, 1914, 1.

Williams, Albert Rhys. *In the Claws of the German Eagle*. New York, E. P. Dutton, 1917.

———. *Through the Revolution*. New York: Boni & Liveright, 1921.

Williams, Harold. "Central Europe Fears Big Spread of Bolshevism." *New York Times*, December 22, 1918, 1.

Williams, Wythe. *Passed by the Censor*. New York: E. P. Dutton, 1916.

York, Alvin Cullum, and Tom Skeyhill. *Sergeant York: His Own Life Story and War Diary*. Garden City NY: Doubleday, Doran, 1928.

Zacher, Dale E. *The Scripps Newspapers Go to War*. Urbana: University of Illinois Press, 2008.

Index

Page numbers in italics refer to illustrations.

Battle of Tannenberg, 63–64

Battle of the Isonzo, 212

Battle of the Marne, 57, 99, 109, 120, 165, 173, 223–27

Battle of Wirballen, 64–66

Battle of Ypres, 91–95, 98–101, 165, 252, 270

Battles of a Nation, 116

Bazin, Henri, *215*

Beatty, Bessie, *189, 198*; "Around the World in Wartime," 181–83; background of, 267; and Russian Revolution, 181–83, 186–90, 192–93, 195, 197–200

BEF. *See* British Expeditionary Force (BEF)

Behind the Scenes in Warring Germany (Fox), 83

Belgium: after the armistice, 252–53; and Battle of Haelen, 24; and Battle of Liège, 14–15, 18, 22, 24–25, 38–39, 43, 51–53; and Battle of Mons, 48, 52, 55–56, 99, 134, 165, 269; and Battle of Namur, 48, 52; and Battle of Passchendaele, 212, 252; and Battle of Ypres, 91–95, 98–101, 165, 252, 270; German invasion and occupation of, 22–34, 91–93, 92, 96–97; and prelude to war, 13–15; war atrocities in, 38–52, 58, 70–71, 76, 79, 84, 166, 245. *See also* Brussels

Bell, Johannes, 265

Bennett, James O'Donnell, 38, 45–46, 51, 53, 57, 267

Beringer, Guy, 172

Berlin: and German charm offensive, 50–52; Horace Green reporting from, 77; Karl von Wiegand reporting from, 63–66; postwar socialism and Communism in, 245, 249–50; social unrest in, 48; war correspondents in, 78, 82, 84–85, 89; William Shepherd reporting from, 68; wireless transmission from, 45, 156

Bernstorff, Johann Heinrich von, 37, 77, 86–87, 203

Berry, Benjamin, 228

Berry, Robert, 205

Bethmann-Hollweg, Chancellor, 89

Blood Stained Russia (Thompson), 193, 195

bluffing, 57

Bly, Nellie, 181

Bochkareva, Maria, 186–88, 200

Bolshevik Revolution, 192–202

Bolsheviks and Bolshevism, 184–85, 189–90, 244–45, 252, 261

Breshkovsky, Katherine, 196

British Expeditionary Force (BEF), 22, 25, 31, 56, 98–99, 106–9, 272

Brockdorff-Rantzau, Ulrich von, 265

Broun, Heywood, 206, 208, 211, 267

Brusilov, Aleksey, 142, 145

Brusilov Offensive, 175

Brussels: German invasion of, 29–31; refugees in, 23, 28, 39; war atrocities in, 41–42, 51; war correspondents in, 13–15, 18, 22–23, 27, 31–32, 38, 53

Bryant, Louise, 180–81, *194*, 195–200, *198*, 268, 273

Bulgaria, 135, 157–58, 162–64

The Cable Game (Washburn), 129

cable men, 1, 129–30

cable transmission of news, 1–3, 19, 31, 36, 45, 48, 65–66, 92–93, 96, 101–3, 232–33

campaign of frightfulness (*Schrecklichkeit*), 47

Cantigny, 221–22

censorship: and African American soldiers, 220; American, 45, 54–55, 89, 106, 108, 126–27, 207–8, 224, 232, 243, 247, 253; after the armistice, 253–55; Austrian, 126–27; British, 21, 25, 45, 54–56, 65–66, 93–101, 106–8, 157, 191; downside of, 19, 45, 157; end of, 253–55; and fall of Antwerp, 93–94; French, 26, 54, 106, 205–7, 214; German, 45, 84, 87; during Mexican civil war, 6, 11; Philip Gibbs on, 107; Russian, 146, 177, 188, 191, 193; during Russian Revolution, 177, 188, 191, 193; in Salonika, 159; and siege of Przemyśl, 74–75; Turkish, 148–52; of war correspondents, 19, 38, 54–55, 70; on the western front, 94. *See also* news management

Central Office for Public Mood, 77

Chase, Harry, 249, 268, 275

Hindenburg, Paul von, 63–64, 126, 248, 274
Hoover, Herbert, 96, 98–99
Hopper, Jimmy, 221–22, 270
House, Edward, 248, 250
Huerta, Victoriano, 6, 10

Imperial War Press Bureau of Austria. *See* Kriegspressequartier (KPQ)
Inside the Russian Revolution (Dorr), 194
Insurgent Mexico (Reed), 11–12
intelligence reports, daily, 217, 221
Irwin, Will, 95; background of, 270–71; on British army at western front, 98–101, 103; and British censorship, 93–97; and invasion of Belgium, 27–30, 181; at New York Society of Illustrators dinner, 115; at Paris Peace Conference, 263–64; routine of, as war correspondent, 60; on *St. Paul*, 21; and war atrocities, 39

James, Edwin, 224–25, 233, 236, 271
Jarotsky, Thaddeus von, 31
Johnson, Henry, 219
Johnson, Owen, 108, 114, 271
Johnson, Thomas, 234–35, 271

Kenimore, C., 215
Kennan, George, 172
Kerensky, Alexander, 188–89, 191–92, 196–97, 199–200
Kerensky Offensive, 188–89
Kitchener, Lord, 100–101, 114, 157
Kriegspressequartier (KPQ), 66–77, 84, 126

Laconia, 203–5
Lafayette, Marquise de, 209–10
Lafayette Escadrille, 74
The Last Shot (Palmer), 7–8, 11
Lawrence, Thomas Edward, 249
League of Nations, 260–61, 264, 271
Lewis, Roger, 45–46, 271
Liebknecht, Karl, 78, 250
Lloyd George, David, 264, 266
London, Jack, 2, 5
"Lost Battalion," 234–35

Louvain, 23, 27–32, 38–42, 45–47, 52–53, 59, 71, 93, 181, 272
Lowell, Thomas, 275
Lusitania, 18–19, 116, 156, 270
Luxemburg, Rosa, 250
Lyon, Cal, 247, 271

Majestic, 150, 153, 156
March Revolution. *See* Russian Revolution of 1917
Marie, Queen of Romania, 144
Martin, Don, 215, 224, 271
Marye, George, 120, 137
McClure, S. S., 259
McCormick, Medill, 5, 10
McCormick, Robert, 38, 50, 57, 175, 213, 271
McCutcheon, John: background of, 271; *Drawn from Memory*, 47, 147; at Gallipoli, 147; and German invasion of Belgium, 21, 27; at Salonika, 158–62, 166, 168–69; and Tampico Affair, 5, 12; and war atrocities, 45–47, 51, 53
Meissner, Jimmy, 239–40
Meuse-Argonne Offensive. *See* Battle of Argonne Forest
Mexican civil war, 5–12
Miller, Webb, 229, 236, 237, 239–44, 250–51, 253, 271
Mitchel, John, 89
Moore, George Gordon, 98
morale, 25, 85, 99, 121–23, 125–26, 129, 138–41, 144, 165
Morgan, Gerald, 31, 39, 58, 181, 215, 230, 232, 243, 271
Morgenthau, Henry, 152
Morris, Gouvreneur, 116
Mowrer, Paul Scott: with Anglo-American Press Mission, 205, 208, 211, 223–24; background of, 271–72; on British army at Mons, 54–56; and enlisting in army, 205; at Paris Peace Conference, 262–64, 266; reporting of, on American soldiers in France, 205, 208, 211, 223–24; on Woodrow Wilson, 264
Mueller, Hermann, 265
Mumm von Schwarzenstein, Baron, 50

Nagara, 154–55
Naudeau, Ludovic, 172
naval warfare, 148–49
neutrality: of European countries, 13–15, 34, 38, 41, 65–66, 126, 145, 158–59; Theodore Roosevelt on, 116; of United States, 18, 22, 34, 89, 145; of war correspondents, 2, 18, 22, 34, 38, 42–43, 50, 66–68, 67, 70, 76–77, 84, 101–2, 109
news management: by Central Powers, 63–90; and daily intelligence reports, 217; by French army, 57–60; by Germany, 48–53, 76–84; by Kriegspressequartier, 66–76; and news-bulletin system, 233–34; and wartime conditions in Germany, 84–90. See also censorship
Nicholas, Grand Duke of Russia, 120, 125
Nicolas, Czar of Russia, 137–45, 173, 186, 189, 197–99
no-atrocities letter, 43–47
Nolan, Dennis, 231–32
Northcliffe, Lord, 99–101, 117, 119–20, 122, 142, 157, 175, 260, 276

observation balloons, 59–60
Official Press Bureau, 107
Olympus Palace Hotel, 164–70
O'Reilly, Mary Boyle, 39–41, 40, 181, 272
Orizaba, 258
Our Greatest Battle (Palmer), 254
Over the Front in an Airplane (Pulitzer), 113

Page, Walter Hines, 98
Palmer, Frederick, 17; as advisor to General Pershing, 253; as AEF chief press officer, 207–8, 210–12, 214–15; and AEF War Diary, 253–55; America in France, 253; after the armistice, 252–55; background of, 272; books by, 7–8, 11, 253, 254; as censor for AEF, 207, 210–12, 214–15; and German invasion of Belgium, 22–25; The Last Shot, 7–8, 11; on the Lusitania, 18–19; on monotony of war, 213; as novelist and playwright, 7; Our Greatest Battle, 254; and Tampico Affair, 5–6, 10–12; and war atrocities, 53, 57; at western front, 104, 106–9, 113
Paris: American troops in, 208; defense of, by AEF, 222–29; evacuation of, 54–55; German advance on, 34, 48, 53–62; German bombing of, 51, 54; refugees in, 55; saving of, 120, 173, 222–29; and war atrocities, 53–62; war correspondents in, 53–58, 60, 93–94, 96, 101–3, 108–11, 158, 215–16
Paris Peace Conference, 250–55, 258–66, 272, 285
Parkerson, John T., 215
Pasha, Enver, 147, 150
Patterson, Joseph Medill, 49, 50, 52, 272
Pattullo, George, 255–58, 273
Pershing, John, 203, 206–10, 231, 253, 255, 267, 272
Phillips, Percival, 13
Ploeşti oil fields, 145
poison gas, 101, 115, 138, 165, 230, 240, 274
Poland, 72, 123, 139, 144, 247, 251; and Battle of Masurian Lakes, 63–64; and Battle of Wirballen, 64–66
Polk, Frank, 89
Powell, E. Alexander: background of, 273; on destruction of Rheims Cathedral, 110–11; on Donald Thompson, 190; Fighting in Flanders, 103; and invasion of Belgium, 91–93, 97; on lecture circuit, 115; at New York Society of Illustrators dinner, 115; reporting of, from western front, 103–6, 114–15; Vive la France!, 115; on war reporting, 37
propaganda, 34, 46, 66, 68, 86, 108–9, 111, 125, 142, 146, 263
Przemyśl, 72–75, 79, 83, 124–26, 134, 138
Pulitzer, Ralph, 111–14, 112, 259, 273; Over the Front in an Airplane, 113
Pulitzer Prize, 90, 275

racial prejudice, 218–20
Rasputin, Grigory, 173
"Red Terror," 244–45
Reed, John, 132; background of, 273; on German war tour, 78–82; Insurgent Mexico, 11–12; and Lincoln Steffens, 136; and Louise Bryant, 180–81, 194–95, 268; realistic reporting style of, 138, 169; reporting of, from eastern front, 134–39; and

Studies in War, Society, and the Military

To order or obtain more information on these or other University of Nebraska Press titles, visit nebraskapress.unl.edu.

CPSIA information can be obtained
at www.ICGtesting.com
Printed in the USA
LVOW10*1701230117

521880LV00004B/43/P

9 780803 285743